ASIAN STOCKMARKETS

THE INSIDE STORY

ANTHONY ROWLEY

FAR EASTERN ECONOMIC REVIEW

Published in Hong Kong by Far Eastern Economic Review
G.P.O. Box 160, Hong Kong

First published 1987

ISBN 962-7010-29-4

Printed in Hong Kong by Yee Tin Tong Printing Press Ltd.,
G.P.O. Box 47, Hong Kong.

For "Beetle" And Bear

Contents

Magic and myth of the Asian market-place

The stockmarkets of Asia, and especially those in the Pacific-Rim countries of East Asia, have become a focus of international investment attention during the past few years. Many Asian countries — again those authoritarian or "Confucian" nations of East Asia in particular — have shown that economic potential is something which can be converted into realised financial wealth, given the right conditions.

Annual economic growth rates may no longer be in the spectacular range of 10% or more seen during the 1970s but they are still extraordinarily high by world standards. Outsiders see the stockmarkets of the region as an obvious means to tap into this prosperity, other than through trade. There is, after all, virtually no country of any significance in Asia (saving those of communist Indo-China) which does not have a functioning stockmarket nowadays. Even the Himalayan Kingdom of Nepal has established one and Papua New Guinea, which came into contact with the modern world only 50 years ago, is thinking about it.

Beyond Japan, however, whose stockmarket is now the second biggest the world after New York (and home to billions of dollars of European and US portfolio investment) the Asian stockmarkets fall off rapidly in size and become terra-incognito for most foreign investors. Hongkong's is the biggest of the Asian stockmarkets after Japan, yet its US$35 billion capitalisation (as of mid-1986) was less than 3% of Tokyo's. The value put by the Japanese market on the shares of Dai-Ichi Kangyo Bank alone around this time roughly equalled the combined capitalisation of the Singapore and Kuala Lumpur stockmarkets.

What this says, of course, is that the Japanese market is very big, both in absolute and relative terms. At the end of 1985 the total capitalisation of the Japanese stock exchanges (around US$1.2 trillion or US$1,200 billion) was equal to the country's total Gross National Product (GNP). The United States' exchanges, on the other hand, were capitalised at around 50% of GNP. Since then, the

Japanese yen has strengthened dramatically, thus increasing the US dollar value of GNP. But Japan's stockmarket capitalisation has also risen sharply and is still equivalent to nearly 90% of Japan's GNP. Japan is not exceptional in this respect, however. Britain's stockmarket is capitalised at around 80% of GNP.

What stands out apart from the sheer size of Japan's stockmarket is the relative insignificance of other markets in Asia. With the notable exception of the city-states of Hongkong and Singapore (whose stockmarkets, like their external trade, are bigger than total GNP) Asian markets are often tiny in relation to the size of the economies they operate within. South Korea's market, for instance, is capitalised at less than 10% of the country's GNP, Taiwan's at a somewhat larger (though still modest) 21%, the Philippines at 17%, India's at 8%, Thailand at 5% and Indonesia's at a minute 0.1%. The other sub-Continental stockmarkets beyond India's — Pakistan, Sri Lanka and Bangladesh — are also tiny in this respect.

Looking at this in another way, the total GNP of the countries whose stockmarkets are covered in this book (excluding Japan's) amounted to around US$575 billion at the end of 1985 (for perspective, less than half the size of the Japanese economy). These countries are (apart from Japan): South Korea, Taiwan, Hongkong, Singapore, Malaysia, Thailand, the Philippines, Indonesia, India, Pakistan, Sri Lanka, Bangladesh and Nepal.

Yet, the total capitalisation of all their stockmarkets amounted to only around US$125 billion in 1985. If these markets were to grow so that they equalled only 50% of GNP — a by no means unreasonably large ratio — they would have to more than double in size, and absorb another US$160 billion of investment. If, in turn, only 10% of this were to come from foreign investors, that is still roughly equivalent to the total amount which US financial institutions have invested in stockmarkets around the world. If the Asian markets as a whole grew to the GNP-relative size of Japan's market, they would be capable of absorbing US$400 billion or so of new investment.

The obvious question which arises is why the markets outside of Japan are so small — and how is that Asian countries have been able to finance such dramatic growth over the past two decades with apparently little help from their stockmarkets. (Stockmarket capitalisations have admittedly been growing as rapidly, if not more so, than overall economies in countries such as South Korea

Table A

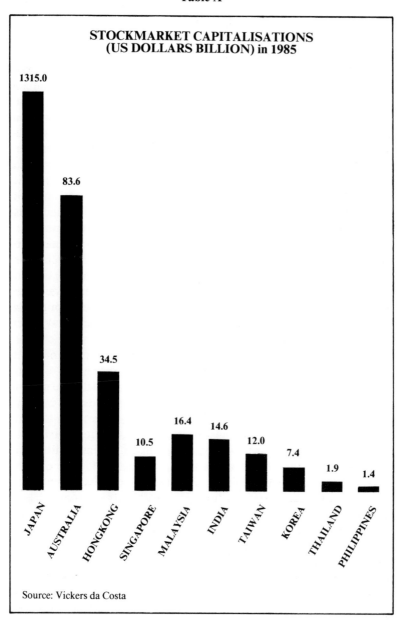

STOCKMARKET CAPITALISATIONS
(US DOLLARS BILLION) in 1985

1315.0
83.6
34.5
10.5
16.4
14.6
12.0
7.4
1.9
1.4

JAPAN
AUSTRALIA
HONGKONG
SINGAPORE
MALAYSIA
INDIA
TAIWAN
KOREA
THAILAND
PHILIPPINES

Source: Vickers da Costa

and Taiwan. But they start from a very low base and the argument about their smallness in relation to GNP remains valid). The primary determining factor in just about all the countries concerned is the dominance of banks (both government-owned and private) and of debt financing.

The power of Japan's banks was legendary until a few years ago when the huge export surpluses enjoyed by Japanese trading houses and manufacturing groups weaned the biggest corporations away from over dependence upon overdraft finance. Some of them now have treasury departments which are richer than the commercial banks. But in South Korea and Taiwan, whose financial systems are in many ways similar to Japan's (only ten years behind), the power of the banks is still enormous. So it is in other Asian countries. An Asian Development Bank study of capital market development in six Asian countries — Indonesia, South Korea, Pakistan, the Philippines, Sri Lanka and Thailand — showed that commercial banks controlled at least 40% of all financial institutions' assets in these countries. In Pakistan and Sri Lanka, the ratio was over 60%.

The dominance of the banks has meant the subjugation of capital-market development in general and of stockmarket development in particular. Financial institutions such as pension funds, insurance companies and mutual funds, which in many. Western countries absorb a large proportion of national savings and channel them into stockmarkets, either do not exist or are severely restricted in Asia. The massive pre-emption of national savings in Singapore and in Malaysia by state-run provident funds has cut deeply both into the market of private provident funds and into the amount of disposable income available for securities investment. Generally in Asia, neither pensions nor insurance (especially life assurance) are yet regarded as essential forms of financial provision. Tax laws have been, and still are, biased in favour of debt financing and against equity funding in most Asian countries.

On top of this, there is an underlying distrust of stockmarkets among many bureaucrats. Stockmarkets are often seen as little better than casinos, and the government's role is confined to heavy-handed intervention aimed at controlling speculation. The irony is that the absence of capital-market institutions in itself increases the relative influence of individual investors and thus the volatility of stockmarkets. In both South Korea and Taiwan, for instance governments put much more effort into (often unsuccessful) attempts to control stockmarkets than they do into promoting capital-market institutions which have longer term perspectives then individual investors and which would help to stabilise markets.

Fortunately, this is changing nowadays and the idea that capital markets do have a useful role to play is slowly taking hold across Asia. But South Korea, commonly supposed to be a "second Japan" in the making (in stockmarket as well as industrial terms) remains ambivalent in its attitude towards market development, as does neighbouring Taiwan. In both countries too, a strong suspicion of foreign influence continues to operate against the acceptance of foreign portfolio investment. In South Korea this translates into an acceptance of huge foreign debt rather than foreign portfolio investment. In Taiwan's case it manifests itself in a fortress-like mentality toward national reserve building.

In the countries of ASEAN in South-East Asia rather different factors have impeded the growth of stockmarkets. Several of these countries have markets whose history goes back a long time. Indonesia, for instance, has had a stockmarket of sorts since 1912, the Philippines since 1927 — and Singapore knew share trading before the turn of the century. But these markets were legacies of the colonial system under which all three countries (plus Malaysia) operated. The development of their economies in recent times has been financed largely outside of the stockmarket.

Singapore, though it has a very substantial stockmarket in relation to the size of the economy, has financed much of its infrastructure and industrial development through the medium of state-savings systems while the local stockmarket has served largely as a theatre of operations for Malaysian companies. In Malaysia itself, a major programme of industrialisation on the East Coast and elsewhere is currently underway but is being financed largely through borrowing from foreign banks and through supplier credits. Likewise Thailand, whose stockmarket for long grew at a snail's pace, both in terms of size and share prices, has a US$1.2 billion Eastern Seaboard development programme to finance, equal to more than half the size of its stockmarket capitalisation. The Philippines' stockmarket, until 1973 one of the biggest in Asia and well ahead of Hongkong's in turnover terms, has declined sadly, more so if anything than the national economy. In Indonesia, the stockmarket has become a virtual irrelevance in terms of total

Table B

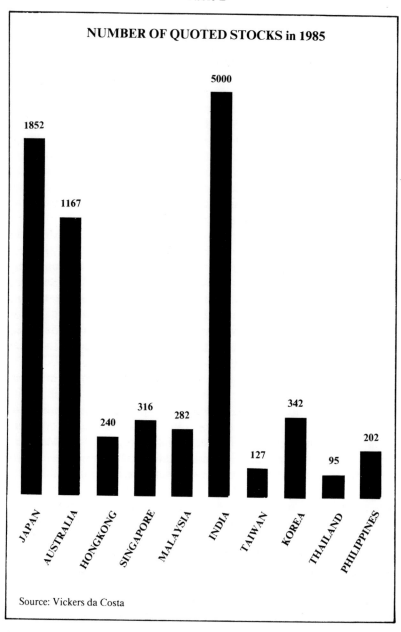

NUMBER OF QUOTED STOCKS in 1985

Source: Vickers da Costa

financing.

In most Asian countries (except Indonesia) the numbers of corporate listings on the stockmarket are quite large, both in relation to GNP and compared with other "emerging" stockmarkets of the world — Mexico and Argentina for example. India has nearly 5,000 companies listed, which dwarfs even the number on both Wall Street and Japan. But there is a preponderance of financial and property companies among the listings in many countries, especially in ASEAN markets. Manufacturing is not represented in proportion to its contribution to GNP. The valuation put by the market on companies is often modest too, especially in the case of South Korea (though not in Japan's).

All this adds up to official indifference toward stockmarket development in many Asian countries. Yet, such development is becoming an economic imperative. Quite apart from mounting volumes of foreign debt in South Korea, the Philippines, Malaysia and Indonesia, as well as in India, rising deficits on national budgets are encouraging Asian governments to consider privatising some of their (frequently loss-making) state enterprises. Short of selling such concerns back into the hands of the families from whom they were nationalised (in Pakistan for instance), or of choosing the politically unpalatable option of selling direct to foreigners, this implies a need to promote stockmarkets. The Philippines, India, Pakistan and Sri Lanka in particular need more developed stockmarkets to facilitate the divestment of state enterprises.

Apart from these structural deficiencies, other shortcomings — euphemistically termed "cultural" factors — set aside various Asian stockmarkets from those which Western investors are familiar with. The facade of internationalism which even the Tokyo stockmarket has acquired in recent years is deceptive in some ways. Beneath this facade lies a fundamental difference of approach, of culture and of market structure. The Japanese market is less "inscrutable" now than it was when foreign investors began arriving in force at the beginning of the current decade. But it would be dangerous to assume that Tokyo's Kabutocho is simply a Wall Street in the making, separated only by distance and by differences of form and not of substance.

In comparing Asian markets and market practices with those in the West it is easy to pass judgement and perhaps to lose

Table C

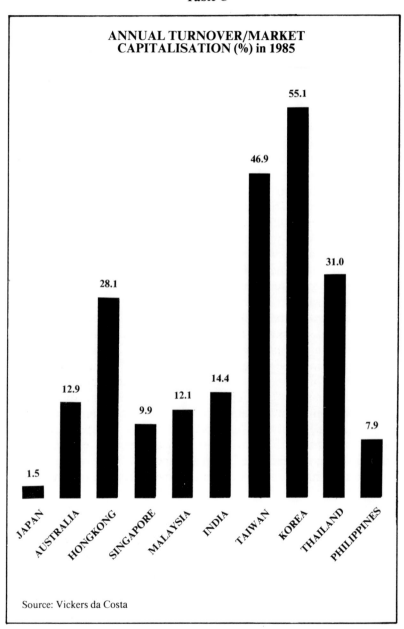

ANNUAL TURNOVER/MARKET
CAPITALISATION (%) in 1985

Source: Vickers da Costa

objectivity. One fund manager with a major US investment group bluntly declared during an investment seminar in Manila during 1986 that "in many Asian stockmarkets, fiscal fraud is almost a national pastime." This remark can hardly have endeared him to his (mainly Asian audience) and it is questionable whether it was altogether justified in relation to Western markets, let alone those of Latin America, the Middle-East and Africa. Asia's stockmarkets are by no means entirely clean but it is as well to bear in mind that neither New York nor the city of London are strangers to insider-dealing scandals or to various other forms of financial manipulation.

Securities-market officials in various East Asian centres argue that insider dealing is less common in their markets than in Western markets. They would find it hard to produce evidence to prove this assertion, however, because in the East insiderism tends to be more covert than that in the West. Very few offenders are prosecuted. East Asia may have its Ivan Boeskys — the so-called "Kwanghwamun Bear" of Seoul for instance — but any investigation of their activities does not become a cause-celebre; it simply gets hushed up.

In some countries of Asia, insider dealing is accepted as part of the culture — the culture of making money. Small investors do not mind too much whether company directors are making money from dealing on the inside, provided those on the outside can make something. This is not to condone insider dealing but (especially in Chinese societies) the "cultural" aspects cannot be disregarded. Some Western stockmarkets no doubt have, or certainly have had, their equivalent of the Seibi share-ramping groups which still operate in Tokyo. But again, such practices are less rigorously prosecuted in Eastern than Western markets.

For so long as the Seoul and Taipei stockmarkets remained completely closed to outside investment it could be argued that "cultural" differences in market practice were the business of the South Koreans and the Taiwan people, not of foreigners. If even the leading securities houses in Seoul regularly "fixed" the market (with official blessing) and if certain practices in Taipei's market verged upon the criminal, that was their affair. Not any longer. If South Korea is serious about attracting foreign equity investors and if Taiwan wishes to rid its stockmarket of the reputation of being one of the last places in the world into which the proverbial widows

Table D

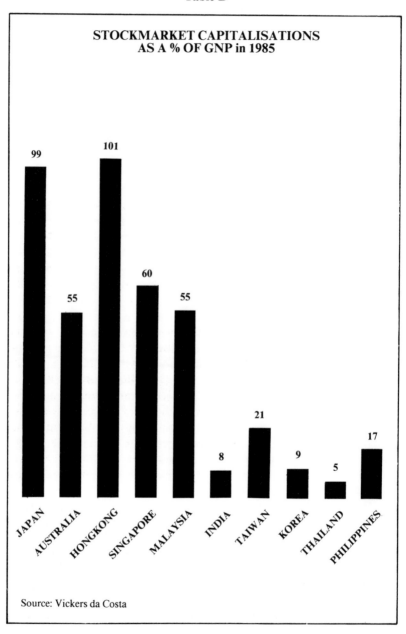

STOCKMARKET CAPITALISATIONS
AS A % OF GNP in 1985

Source: Vickers da Costa

and orphans should venture, then reforms must be made.

This book examines the prospects for such reform, and how the markets in Asia really work. It looks, for instance, at Singapore and how it was that the stockmarket there, along with neighbouring Malaysia's, was brought to its knees in 1985 by financial manipulation on a grand scale when so few investors, least of all foreigners, had any inkling of what was going on until it was too late. A lingering perception (outside Asia at least) of the Hongkong stockmarket as the plaything of a few local millionaires who decide its fate from a Chinese teashop every day, is also examined, as is the future of the Hongkong market after 1997 when the British colony reverts to China.

Bangkok and Manila both have markets that are open to outside investment. Yet, few people beyond the small coterie of London brokers and investment houses who have traditionally ventured into these markets know much about how they work. Wall Street is admittedly more familiar with Manila, both through America's colonial links with the Philippines, and because a handful of Philippine stocks are listed in New York. But the Manila market has to be assessed nowadays against a changing background of political and economic turmoil.

India's stockmarket has seized investors' imagination since Prime Minister Rajiv Gandhi came to power and appeared to nudge the nation's economy away from socialism and in the direction of capitalism. The great stockmarket boom in Bombay during 1985/86 fueled this belief, while the launching of an India Fund for overseas investors during 1986 offered a means for outsiders to capitalise on the situation. India's stockmarket is, however, very much a hostage still to political fortune and India's market mechanisms are frankly primitive. This is all the more (very much more) true of China where rudimentary forms of share dealing are reappearing nowadays.

There is little doubt that a great deal more money is going to become available to Asia's stockmarkets over the next decade, much of it from the United States and Europe, though probably a good deal more from Japan too than has been the case in the past. There are compelling reasons why international funds should gravitate toward the world's "emerging" stockmarkets in general and Asia's in particular.

The size of the Third World economies as a whole is roughly

equal to one third of the aggregate size of the OECD economies. Yet, according to the International Finance Corp. (an arm of the World Bank), the aggregate capitalisation of stockmarkets in the developing countries is equivalent to only 2% or so of the total for all world markets. The IFC argues that "high rates of national economic growth tend to coincide with high rates of return from equities" and that the higher annual rates of growth in many of the semi-industrialised Third World economies should continue to produce higher rates of return on equities than can be expected from the OECD countries.

The world's emerging stockmarkets have performed well too, vis-à-vis major markets, despite substantial currency devaluations and severe economic crises in some developing countires. During the period from 1976-88, the Capital International (CI) index measuring the world's (developed) stockmarkets as a whole rose by 11.4% and the CI index for US stocks by 12.2%. In comparable (US dollar) terms, South Korea's stockmarket rose by 19.3% over this period and India's by 19.1%. Only Chile among other emerging markets did better with a 20.9% rise. These returns are somewhat modified after withholding taxes but such imposts bite really deeply only in Thailand among the Asian markets.

The performance of just about every Asian stockmarket of any significant size was even more remarkable during 1986. Tokyo's market experienced one of its most remarkable bull runs in history, while among the more open markets of the region, Hongkong and Singapore also experienced dramatic rises. The Seoul and Taipei markets, likewise, performed very strongly, as did Bangkok's. Manila experienced a remarkable recovery from the bear market which had persisted for several years and the Indian market shot up to record highs (only to reatreat quite sharply again). In US dollar terms, the Tokyo market had risen 62.5% by the end of November 1986 compared with its level a year earlier while Singapore was 38.6% ahead on a similar basis and Hongkong had risen 28.4%. Wall Street, by contrast, rose only 17.5% and London by an even more modest 10.7% over the same period.

If price performance were all, then the stockmarkets of Asia would indeed be the place for the world's investors to head. But quite apart from the difficulty (and in some cases, such as Indonesia's, impossibility) of entering such markets, there are many factors which limit the scope for foreign investment. The markets

Table E

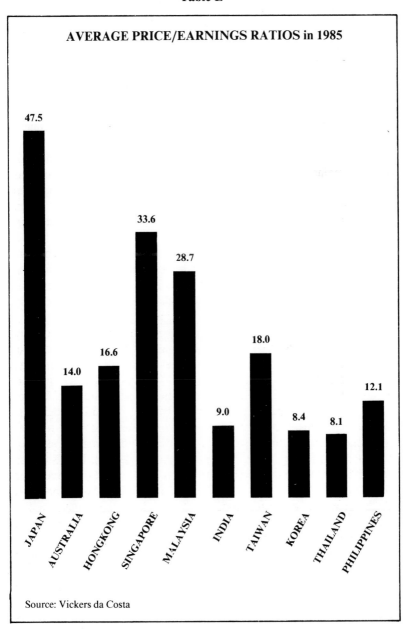

AVERAGE PRICE/EARNINGS RATIOS in 1985

Source: Vickers da Costa

are in many cases thin both in terms of liquidity and the amount of stock which is available to be traded. To a much greater extent than in the West, this is because of the prevelance of cross-shareholdings among Asian companies — surprisingly perhaps, not least in Japan. Markets in South Korea, Taiwan and Hongkong also suffer from this defect.

Asia does not have unlimited time to foster the further development of its stockmarkets. If they are unable to absorb foreign investment as fast as it becomes available then its seems reasonable to assume that international capital flows will be directed elsewhere. Certain Latin American stockmarkets — notably Brazil's which was capitalised at US$43 billion at the end of 1985 — and those of Chile, Venezuela and Argentina are considerably bigger in terms of capitalisation than the smaller Asian markets. Latin American markets have also performed well on the whole in financial (exchange-rate adjusted) terms.

Foreigners have been encouraged to think of Asian economies as being "open" and flexible. This is because many Asian nations,

Table F

Quality of the Market: Access to Market Information and Investor Protection

Country	Regular Publication of P/E, Yield	Market Commentaries in English by Brokerage Houses		Company Stock Reports		Disclosure Requirements Accounting Standards	Investor Protection	
India	P			LA		G	G	S
Indonesia	—	LA,	AR			A	P	S
Korea	C	IR				G	G	S
Malaysia	C	IR		SR		G	G	—
Pakistan	P	AR		AR		A	A	S
Philippines	P	LR		LR	AR	G	A	S
Thailand	C	LR,	AR	LA,	AR	A	A	S

KEY
LR   =   Prepared by local brokers or international manager
IR   =   Prepared by international manager/broker
AR   =   Annual Report of Securities Exchange
G   =   Good, of internationally acceptable quality: A = Adequate; P = Poor, requires reform.
S   =   Functioning Securities Commission or similar government agency concentrating on regulating market activity.

especially those in East Asia, have demonstrated a willingness to keep their economies open to trade and to external (direct) investment. If they had shown half the flexibility in allowing foreigners to invest in their stockmarkets that they have, for instance, over the question of exchange-rate adjustment and tariff reform, they would have received much bigger inflows of foreign equity by now than in fact is the case.

One of the biggest potential sources of such investment is the US pension-fund industry. Total assets of these funds in 1985 were around US$950 billion of which an estimated US$21 billion was invested in foreign securities. By 1990, it is calculated that the respective figures will be US$2,000 billion and US$80 billion, according to InterSec Research Corp. in the US. More detailed projections have been made by the US investment house Prudential-Bache. These suggest that the total assets held by US tax-exempt institutions (retirement plans, savings plans, endowments and foundations) at the end of 1984 were in excess of US$1.2 trillion or US$1,200 billion.

Assuming that these funds continue to grow at around 10% a year, they will be in excess of US$2 trillion by 1990 and US$5 trillion by the year 2,000. The common-stock portion of tax-exempt assets in 1984 stood at around US$600 billion (nearly one third of the total capitalisation of Wall Street). Historically, such institutions have held very little of their portfolio in the form of common stocks and bonds in overseas markets — perhaps only 3% or US$18 billion being committed to markets outside the US and Canada.

But attitudes toward foreign investment among tax-exempt US institutions are changing. By 1990, Pru-Bache expects the proportion of assets invested outside the US to grow to 5% of the total, or US$50 billion. By the end of the century it could exceed 15%. The newly-industrialised countries of Asia and elsewhere could — given the right circumstances — attract a disproportionately large percentage of these new commitments. And, since every 1% of the US tax-exempt stock assets invested outside the US represents US$6 billion (in 1985 dollars) the impact on smaller markets could be very substantial.

Hitherto, the bulk of US portfolio investment outside of North America has gone to Tokyo and London. In 1985 alone, US purchases of Japanese stocks totalled Yen 1.2 trillion or US$7.4 billion (having been running in excess of Yen 1 trillion a year since

1984). European purchases in the Tokyo market in 1985 were much bigger still — Yen 4.95 trillion, which again appears to be a sustainable annual figure nowadays. One obvious reason why so much US and European money heads for Japan is because the market there is fully open and free from exchange controls.

If neighbouring Asian markets, such as South Korea and Taiwan, were to hasten the liberalisation of their markets there is no doubt that a good deal more of this money would flow to them, especially given the very high ratings (in Price/Earnings ratio terms) of Japanese stocks nowadays. The impact of any outflow of foreign funds from the Tokyo market into neighbouring markets can be dramatic, as was seen late in 1986 when the Tokyo market was perceived to be over-bought and some funds shifted from there to Hongkong. The Hongkong market rose some 400 points, or around

Table G

		Indonesia	Pakistan	Sri Lanka
SECONDARY SECURITIES MARKET STATISTICS OF SELECTED COUNTRIES **(As at December, 1984)**				
Number of listed companies		24	347	266
No. of shares listed ('000 shares)		57,650	11,496	—
Total market capitalisation (US$ million)		$105.1	$1,250.4	—
Annual volume turnover of shares (million)		1,218	354	2,778
Annual turnover value of shares (US$ million)		$2.4	$7.7	$1,259.2
Turnover/market capitalisation		2.3%	0.6%	—
Average price-earnings ratio		5.4	—	—
Average dividend yield		—	—	—
New issues (US$ million)		$1.0	$19.7	—
Rights issues (US$ million)		—	$35.9	—
Special issues (US$ million)		—	--	—
Total corporate funds raised from equities (US$ million)		$1.0	$55.6	—
Stock market capitalisation as a % of GNP		0.1%	3.8%	—

Sources: ABD Study
         KLSE Investors' Digest & SES Journal
         Lyall & Evatt (Pte)

25%, in a matter of weeks, mainly as a result of the Tokyo exodus. There is also the question of Japan's role as an investor in other Asian stockmarkets. For a long time Japanese institutional investors (insurance companies and trust banks in particular) concentrated almost exclusively on the New York and London equity markets. They all but ignored the markets in neighbouring Asian countries. This is changing slowly. They are beginning to take positions in the Hongkong market and in Singapore/Malaysia. They have been modest buyers, too, of various special funds issued by South Korea and Taiwan. A senior executive of Nomura, the biggest of Japan's big-four securities houses, suggested to the author in 1986 that Japanese institutions would be turning their attention increasingly to other Asian markets in the next few years, including India's.

Whether international investment funds will flow directly into Asian stockmarkets, or whether New York, London and Tokyo investment houses will prefer to make a market in Asian stocks on their own exchanges, depends very much upon the pace of modernisation in the Asian markets. The collapse of the stockmarkets in Singapore and Malaysia following the so-called Pan-Electric crisis at the end of 1985 led to a good deal more offshore market making being done in Singapore shares by investment banks such as Morgan Stanley in New York.

At the same time, some of the biggest of the New York

Table H

Withholding Taxes For US-based Investors (Rates in Effect at Beginning of 1985)			
Country	Interest	Dividends	Capital Gains
Malaysia	none	none	none
Korea	16.125%	16.125%	none
Thailand	10%	20%	25%
Indonesia	20%	20%	none
India	47.3%	22.5%	22.5% (If held 3 yrs or more)
Pakistan	55%	15%	none
Philippines	15%	25%	0.25%

Source: IFC

investment banks — notably Goldman Sachs — are actively seeking to persuade companies in India, South Korea and Malaysia to issue stocks which can then be placed with Wall Street institutions and given a quote on a European stock exchange where listing rules are not quite so stringent as those in the United States. This is to be applauded in the sense that it could result in a dozen or more new Asian corporate names becoming known to Wall Street investors over the next few years. But in the long-term it is up to Asian countries to develop their own domestic markets if they want to attract the sums of local and foreign equity capital which they need.

The global unit trust and mutual fund industry, estimated to be something between US$500-600 billion in size nowdays, is a major player in offshore-investment flows. Of this insignificant the US accounts for around US$350 billion. Other centres pale alongside

Table I

Economic Indicators (as at end — 1985)		
	5 Yr. Growth GNP %	Per Capita Income US$
Australia	3.0	9177
China	8.3	361
Hong Kong	6.7	5993
India	5.1	196
Indonesia	6.1	556
Japan	4.2	10659
S. Korea	4.7	2009
Malaysia	6.9	1955
New Zealand	2.9	5879
Philippines	1.3	603
Singapore	8.1	6992
Taiwan	6.8	3161
Thailand	5.1	772

Source: Indonesia Asia.

this figure. Nevertheless the US$20 billion or so of such money managed in Hongkong — the principal offshore fund-management centre in Asia — is by no means insignificant in regional terms. Its potential to influence some of the smaller Asian stockmarkets is not inconsiderable.

Managed funds of one kind or another, unit trusts and mutual funds almost certainly will play an increasingly large part in helping to open up Asian stockmarkets to outside investment. This is due as much to the efforts agencies like the International Finance Corp. (IFC) as to those of British merchant banks and US investment banks who have been active in promoting such vehicles, starting (in Asia) with the Korea Fund.

At the end of 1986, the IFC was in the process of putting together various special funds for various Asian markets. The significance of these is that IFC will almost certainly use its political clout (as an arm of the World Bank) to secure tax and other concessions from the governments concerned, as a quid-pro-quo for directing money into their markets. This could mark a valuable first step on the road to reducing tax barriers to foreign investment. There are of course other barriers (such as exchange control and various foreigner-excluding pieces of legislation) in various Asian markets. But any pressure brought to bear in removing hindrances to foreign participation is welcome.

Japan: Not so Inscrutable

The Tokyo Stock Exchange (TSE) is so big in relation to other Asian stock exchanges that it is necessary to step back in order get it in perspective. Like Fuji, Japan's most sacred mountain, it is difficult to appreciate close up. Distance reveals the TSE to be indeed a Fuji-like edifice surrounded by a series of relative anthills which are the other Asian exchanges. Only the New York Stock Exchange (NYSE) on the other side of the Pacific rises higher on the stockmarket horizon but, like the physical terrain of Japan itself, the TSE is rising inexorably and the gap between it and the NYSE is steadily diminishing.

Stock market capitalisations (total value of listed securities at current market valuations) are, of course, notoriously volatile according to whether any particular market is experiencing a bull or bear phase. But, for perspective, the Tokyo Stock Exchange was capitalised at around US$1.2 trillion (US$1,200,000,000,000) at the end of 1985 while the total value of stocks on the NYSE was nearer US$2 trillion. Considering the fact that the US economy (in GNP terms) is nearly three times the size of Japan's, it can be seen that the Tokyo market is very big in relative as well as absolute terms.

The Tokyo market puts London (by far the biggest stockmarket in Europe) in the shade too. It is more than twice as big in terms of capitalisation. But it is against the other stock markets of Asia that Tokyo's size is seen to be so enormous. Hongkong is (or was as of mid-1986) the biggest of the Asian markets outside Japan, yet its US$35 billion capitalisation was less than 3% of Tokyo's. The combined capitalisation of Singapore and Malaysia's markets was around US$25 billion or nearer 2% of Tokyo's. In fact the value put by the Japanese market on the shares of Dai-Ichi Kangyo Bank alone at the end of 1985 roughly equalled the total capitalisation of the Singapore/Malaysia stock market as a whole. The other Asian markets pale even more alongside Tokyo's. Even South Korea, which is often described as a "second Japan" has a stock market capitalised at less than 1% of Japan's.

Yet for all its New York-challenging size, the Tokyo market is very different from the NYSE both in structure and in operation. The Japanese like to stress that everything they adopt from the West has "Japanese characteristics" and many of them savour the idea of their institutions having a unique Japaneseness. They positively encourage foreigners to think that this quality is something which they cannot hope to comprehend fully.

When foreign investors and fund managers began arriving in force in the Tokyo market after the relaxation of exchange controls in 1980, they found it inscrutable enough. Share prices could soar or collapse without apparent rhyme or reason and, apart from the sheer difficulty of understanding the Japanese language, foreigners found that capital market customs were very different from their own. To have any hope of picking the right stocks, you had to have the inside track, to know which stocks the major Japanese securities houses happened to be pushing at the time. Like the hapless odd-man-out in one of H.M. Bateman's famous cartoons, the butt of everyone's humour in the Tokyo market was the foreigner who bought on investment fundamentals.

As recently as 1982, one commentator in Tokyo (James Bartholomew of the *Far Eastern Economic Review*) wrote that: "A common assumption about the Japanese stockmarket is that it is clean and efficient as a Japanese TV set or a Japanese car. Equally, foreigners who marvel as one industry after another falls to a Japanese attack are tempted to transfer this respect for Japanese companies into a belief that it must be a good thing to buy the companies' shares." But, he concluded, "the reality is by no means so simple. Far from being as clean and reliable as a new Japanese car, the stockmarket is more like a second-hand model, to be inspected with caution and driven with care." Another foreign analyst in Tokyo added his opinion that "there is only one kind of dealing in this market — insider dealing."

No doubt there was truth in what both of them had to say. But things are changing. The sheer weight of foreign investment in the Japanese market in recent years and the remarkable degree of financial liberalisation which has brought foreign investment bankers and securities dealers into the Tokyo market — first as representatives of their head offices overseas, then as investment advisors and nowadays as securities dealers and fund managers — has inevitably brought about change. The foreigners no longer feel themselves to be the outsiders they were five or six years ago, at least as far as market practice is concerned, if not Japanese culture. Many, if not most, foreign fund managers operating in the Tokyo market have in fact enjoyed better performance and profit over time than have their Japanese counterparts.

There are still things to be wary of, things peculiarly Japanese which the uninitiated need to know about. There is still a fair amount of market "ramping" by groups who wish to support shares at a particular price for one reason or another. A few years ago, Yamaichi, one of the big-four securities houses in Japan, was

Table 1

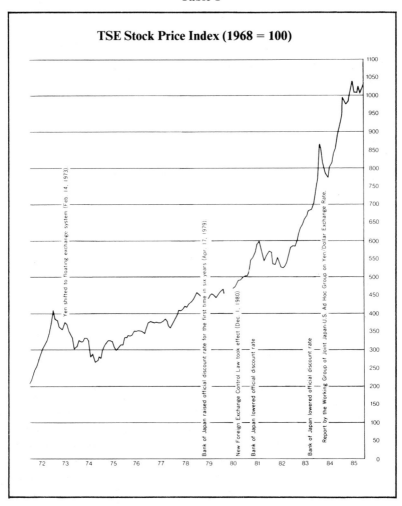

involved in a major market support operation which left it badly bruised. US investment bank Merrill Lynch and British stockbrokers W.I. Carr both lost heavily in mid-1986 when they bought securities in a firm called Nanka for a client who failed to honour the transaction. Both firms had to stump up cash and the Tokyo heads of both branches "took responsibility" (Japanese-style) and resigned. There are the so-called "seibi" groups who come together specially to conduct share ramping or shorting operations in smaller stocks. And there is still much "churning" of client portfolios by Japanese brokers intent on maximising their commissions. More about all this later.

The changes that have come about in the Tokyo market over the past three years parallel the remarkable strides that Japan has made in opening its financial markets to outside influence and participation since 1984 when the US put heavy pressure on Tokyo to liberalise. The administration of President Ronald Reagan found a sympathetic response in the internationalism (on financial and economic matters at least) of Japanese Prime Minister Yasuhiro Nakasone. Since then, Japan has gone "step by step but with big strides" as Tomomitsu Oba, special advisor to the Minister of Finance, expressed it to the author in the autumn of 1986. Recent progress in internationalising Tokyo's stock market is ample proof of this assertion.

Tokyo had a stock exchange as early as 1878, but it was nearly a century later that the Japanese market began opening up to the outside world and the real progress has been made in the past few years. Yen-based foreign bonds were listed for the first time in 1973 and a foreign stock section was established on the TSE in that same year. Even so, it needed the shock tactics of the US in the early 1980s to prise the market wide open to outsiders, just as US commander Matthew Perry had forcibly opened up Japan's foreign trade in the 1840s.

The present Tokyo Stock Exchange was founded in 1949, two years after the Japan Securities Exchange (a quasi-governmental organisation formed during the Second World War from the merger of all then existing exchanges in Japan) was dissolved. The TSE has since become far and away the biggest stock exchange in Japan. There are seven others — in Osaka (easily the second biggest), Nagoya (third biggest) and in Kyoto, Hiroshima, Fukuoka, Nigata and Sapporo — but the TSE accounts for the vast majority of trading done on all exchanges. In 1985, Tokyo did 83% of stock trading in Japan, both by value and by volume.

The really dramatic development in the Tokyo market over the past five years has been in the sheer volume of money going into stocks. The secondary market has grown much more rapidly than the primary-issue market while turnover has grown much faster in value than in volume terms. This indicates that the Japanese are becoming much more a nation of (stock) traders and speculators than they used to be. They buy stocks on credit as well as for cash, which is quite something for the financially-conservative Japanese. Margin transactions accounted for around 35% of individual investors' stock trading by value in 1985.

Between 1981 and 1985, the volume of stocks traded on Japan's stock exchanges as a whole grew by 14% (to ¥146 billion) while the value of those trades rose 61% (to nearly ¥95 trillion). Over the same period, the total number of domestic companies listed on the Tokyo Stock Exchange increased by around 5% to 1,476 and the

Table 2

Market Size of Major Stock Exchanges in the World

Stock Exchange		Tokyo	New York	U.K.
No. of Stock-Listed Companies	(Domestic)	1,444	1,490	2,171
	(Foreign)	11	53	582
No. of List Issues [Stocks]	(Domestic)	1,450	2,266	1,857
	(Foreign)	11	53	504
[Bonds]	(Domestic)	536	3,549	3,179
	(Foreign)	200	202	1,520
Total Market Value ($ mil.)	(Stocks)	644,412	1,529,459	236,321
	(Bonds)	371,070	1,021,791	240,910
Trading Value ($ mil.)	(Stocks)	271,076	764,738	42,266
	(Bonds)	150,570	6,984	168,529
No. of Member Firms		83	628	216

number of shares listed by some 17% to 259 billion. Again, the most significant feature was not the increase in the volume of shares traded on the TSE — which rose by 12% between 1981 and 1985 — but the value of those trades, which shot up by 60%. As a result, the price which investors have to pay for Japanese stocks compared to their earnings or after-tax profits (the price/earnings or P/E ratio) is the highest for any developed-country stockmarket and the highest among all Asian markets.

In 1985 the average P/E on the 22 stocks included in the TSE Index was 32. It moved even higher in 1986 as the Tokyo bull market progressed and it has rarely dipped below 20 in the past ten years. As prices have risen, so yields have declined. In 1985, the average yield on the 225 TSE Index stocks was slightly under 1%, having halved over the past ten years. This shows how much faster stock prices have risen than dividend payments.

Another remarkable factor has been the growth in foreign participation, which in proportionate terms has outstripped the growth of the market as a whole. The dramatic rise in the value of stocks traded in Tokyo broadly coincides with the period in which foreign investment took off. Annual foreign purchases of Japanese stocks increased by 75% between 1981 and 1985 (to ¥9.4 trillion). The real takeoff in foreign purchases came after the relaxation in exchange controls in 1980. Before that, in 1977, foreign purchases were ¥823 billion — less than one tenth of the level reached by 1985. It was estimated that foreign holdings accounted for around 7% of the total capitalisation of the TSE by the end of 1983, foreigners having been net buyers of Japanese stocks from the beginning of the 1980s. But they turned net sellers from 1984 up to the time of writing, so the proportion was thought to be nearer 4% by the end of 1986. Foreigners have been brisk traders, and their activity represents over one fifth of total stock trading by value in Japan. Europeans have been by far the biggest investors in Japanese securities markets, followed in most years by other Asians and then by Americans.

What is also apparent is that the growth in the pace of share trading by the Japanese themselves has kept pace with that of foreigners in recent years. This does not make the Japanese the most active stock traders in the region — far from it. The TSE turned over roughly a half of its equity capitalisation in 1985 and the ratio was similar in the immediately preceding years. Compared with, say Taiwan, that is modest but the interesting thing is that traditionally the Japanese have not been such active traders as the Chinese. Now they seem to be catching up.

A visit to the squat and granite-like structure which is the present TSE, in Nihombashi Kabuto Cho, reinforces this impression. (The present exchange is the most recent of a series of buildings which have housed the exchange since 1878 and was completed only in 1985). The main trading floor is a scene of rather un-Japanese pushing and shoving as hundreds of trading clerks try to catch the attention of the "saitory" dealers standing inside raised trading pits (actually more like large pulpits) matching buy and sell orders. The system is based on both "price priority and time priority." Behind the saitori stand the surveillance staff of the exchange monitoring deals to make sure that prices are properly entered. The really hectic activity centres on the 250 most-active stocks (a selection which changes from year to year) which are traded manually. Other issues — around 1,200 of them — are traded (by older clerks and saitory) in a more sedate computerised section known as the Computer-Assisted Order Routing & Execution System (CORES).

The market is two-tiered — first and second sections, according to the size and status of the companies listed. Around 1,500 stocks (those with a longer track record) listed on the First Section and 450 (with a shorter record) on the Second Section. First Section stocks account for around 90% of the total equity capitalisation of the TSE. If a company is de-listed for any reason it is usually

Table 3

Stock Trading Volume & Value in Tokyo

	No. of Trading Days	Volume (mils. of shares) Total	Daily Average	Turnover Ratio (%) (based on volume)	Value (¥ bil.) Total	Daily Average	Turnover Ratio (%) (based on value)
1981	285	107,549	377	50.0	49,365	173.2	58.4
1982	285	78,474	275	34.6	36,572	128.3	38.5
1983	286	104,309	365	44.3	54,845	191.8	48.8
1984	287	103,737	361	42.5	67,974	236.8	47.1
1985	285	121,863	428	48.0	78,711	276.2	44.7

Source: TSE

transferred to the separate Over The Counter (OTC) market so that shareholders can still trade. In comparison with the brisk and sometimes scrum-like activity at the Japanese share trading pits, the one pit devoted to foreign stocks (34 of them, traded manually) is an oasis of quiet. Nevertheless, trading in this "foreign" market is building up quite rapidly, as is the number of stocks listed.

Bond trading is also very big business on the TSE. The market for long-term government bond futures which was opened in October 1985 — an interest-rate futures market in effect — has already become one of the most active in the world. Of all secondary market trading in bonds on the Tokyo exchange, over 90% is in Japanese government bonds of one kind or another. Trading takes place in straight bonds issued by the central government, municipalities, banks and corporations. Convertible bonds, bonds with warrants and warrants themselves are also traded, along with some foreign currency bonds. Common stock accounts for around two thirds of the total market capitalisation on the TSE and bonds for the other one third.

All this puts Tokyo on a par with other major markets, but one factor which distinguishes the Tokyo market from other major markets is its relative narrowness in terms of the stock available for trading. This is by no means apparent at first sight. The number of companies listed on the TSE is very similar to that in New York. The respective numbers at the end of 1986 were 1,444 and 1,490. Admittedly, the number of issues by those companies were much greater in New York's case than Tokyo's — 2,266 against 1,450 — but that is not what makes Tokyo different to New York.

What does, is the close shareholding relationship which exists still among Japanese companies and which did not disappear with the formal dissolution of the Zaibatsu (bank-related industrial groups) after the Second World War. In many ways, the "Keiretsu" have become the modern-day successors of the Zaibatsu, and the web of interlocking shareholdings among Japanese companies seems as complex as ever. The difference is that under the Anti-Monopoly Law, financial institutions such as banks are not supposed to hold more than 5% of the shares of any one other company. Even this stricture, however, appears to be quite widely circumvented.

An entire book could be devoted to describing these cross holdings, but something can be said about their impact upon investment in the stockmarket. A popular view is that around 50% of the total 259 billion shares in issue on the TSE (many issues are duplicated on other Japanese exchanges) are in fact held by other corporations, listed or otherwise, and thus not available to the general investor. A senior investment strategist at one of the big-four local securities houses suggested to the author that the actual level accounted for by corporate cross-holdings is probably more than 70% and that "Japanese private [meaning institutional as well as individual] investors account for less than 30% of outstanding stock investments in Japan."

A sample survey of 1,806 Japanese companies made in 1985 by the National Conference of Stock Exchanges in Japan showed a very high concentration on share ownership in institutional and corporate hands compared with other countries. Fractionally under 40% of all stocks were in the hands of financial institutions (meaning banks and life assurance companies in the main) while a further 26% were held by "business corporations." Individuals and "others" held only 26% of the total — a proportion which the survey noted had been declining for the past nine years and which has now reached a record low. Foreign corporations held about 6%.

These semi-official statistics do not present quite the picture of concentrated share ownership that is suggested by talking with brokers and bankers in Japan. Much the same thing applies in South Korea where cross-holdings of shares in other companies by the "Chaebols" (broadly speaking, Korea's equivalent of Zaibatsu) are also generally believed to be much greater than suggested by official statistics of share ownership. The truth probably lies somewhere between popular impression and official assertion. Some holdings which are nominally by individuals probably disguise corporate holdings through nominees.

The prevalence of the cross-holdings is one reason why takeover bids occur so rarely in Japan. It is the norm for any company to have a stake in another one with which it has a client or customer relationship. Thus, a coal producer might have a shareholding in a steel company or a bank in a securities house to which it provides finance. This system of trading-partner relationship is, according to a Ministry of Finance (MoF) official, the "biggest barrier to takeovers here in Japan." In any case, he added, the Japanese don't like takeovers. They are considered as dirty. But he insisted at the same time that there are "no rules against takeover bids by foreigners — provided they are fair." Nevertheless, the adverse official reaction to the bid by a foreign group in 1985 to take over a Japanese concern called Minebea (which had itself launched a bid for another company called Sankyo Seiko) was taken as a sign that foreign takeovers are not really welcome.

Recent developments suggest that the forces of big Japanese business are becoming even more predominant in Japanese share ownership. A new generation of Japanese zaibatsu is in the making in the shape of the so-called Tokkin Funds, it is claimed. These are funds run by Japanese trust banks specially for the benefit of business corporations which have huge liquidity from export sales and need to find ways of investing it. (For many of Japan's big export houses hit by the strong yen, the profits they were expecting in 1986 would come from share trading rather than basic operations).

Many of these corporations have zaibatsu-like cross holdings in numerous other companies. Such holdings tend to be held at book value, so that if a company decided to sell its holdings at market value it would incur heavy capital-gains tax. By transferring holdings to the Tokkin funds (where they are effectively held at market value) corporations can deal without the same tax penalty. The Tokkin pay out dividends (including any capital gains) and

Table 4

Stock Trading Volume & Value on All Stock Exchanges								
							(mils. of shares, ¥ bil.)	
	All Exchanges		Tokyo		Osaka		Nagoya	
	Volume	Value	Volume	Value	Volume	Value	Volume	Value
1981	128,318	58,747	107,549	49,365	14,863	7,030	4,817	1,942
1983	122,320	65,333	104,309	54,845	13,469	8,350	3,375	1,665
1985	146,302	94,640	121,863	78,711	18,295	12,536	5,151	2,885

	Kyoto		Hiroshima		Fukuoka		Niigata		Sapporo	
	Volume	Value	Volume	Value	Volume	Value	Volume	Value	Volume	Value
1981	183	68	393	144	132	54	298	114	83	31
1983	244	104	331	149	149	61	341	120	102	39
1985	245	123	156	82	152	93	329	155	110	55

Source: TSE

these are tax-free in the hands of corporations.

There are suggestions that the Tokkin are becoming a cover for other activities. In fact some brokers say the Tokkin are the "new zaibatsu." They can buy and sell shares in other companies without disclosing the transaction and thus skirt around the Anti-Monopoly Law. "Banks here are building up zaibatsu-type holdings through the Tokkin," according to one Tokyo analyst. "The Tokkin is an ideal way to mount a takeover bid too." The Ministry of Finance does not appear to take this threat very seriously, arguing that the Anti-Monopoly Law prevents covert attempts to consolidate corporate power in Japan. Even so, the growth of the Tokkin funds has been remarkable and it seems odd that Japanese companies should be using them purely for trading cross-holdings which they value for strategic reasons. The total size of the Tokkin funds as of mid-1986 was estimated at around ¥16 trillion and was increasing at the rate of around ¥1 trillion a month.

These holdings represent what a Japanese broker calls a "source of energy for the Japanese economy." He commented: "The zaibatsu (sic) are very supportive. They never go into liquidation you will notice." Apart from their importance as stockholders, the Tokkin funds are becoming a major force in the market. One broker pointed to a sharp fall in the Nikkei Stock Average in September 1986 and attributed it almost entirely to the influence of a Tokkin contract expiring. Investments in the Tokkin are normally made for a contractual period of one year, expiring either in

Table 5

Stock Transactions by Investment Sectors in Percentage

(based on value)   (%)

	Corporations	Individuals	Foreigners
1976	39.5	55.5	5.0
1980	49.0	43.6	7.4
1985	48.7	37.9	13.4

"Corporations" includes securities companies, insurance companies, banks investment trusts business corporations and others.

Source: TSE

March or September.

Banks and business corporations have been slowly but surely increasing their share of total stock transactions in Japan but individuals are still the dominant force as far as trading is concerned. The proportion of total trading they account for — around 38% according to the TSE — is out of proportion to their importance among the totality of shareholders in Japan. (Again, the semi-official figures are at variance with market estimates that individuals account for around 50% of total share trading in Japan nowadays). This proportion is slowly declining however, as the securities houses and foreign institutions (now the third most important category) as well as financial institutions and business corporations, rise in importance as share traders.

Another new force to be reckoned with is the investment-trust movement in Japan. Investment trusts are fast becoming a real force in the Tokyo stock market. From just over ¥7,000 million (¥7 trillion) in 1981, their total net asset value rose to around ¥20 trillion by the end of 1985. The really astonishing growth came in 1986 as net assets rose by nearly ¥1 trillion a month. By the end of August they had reached ¥28 trillion or roughly one third the size of total assets held by US mutual funds worldwide. The reasons why are instructive as to the changing nature of Japanese society and attitudes to finance in particular. This in turn has pointers for the future development of the Japanese stock market.

The remarkable growth of Japanese industry in the post-war decades took place within a highly directed economy in which capital was channelled to manufacturing industry largely through the banks, while securities markets played a subsidiary role. Japanese bureaucrats like to describe this as the system of "indirect" financing (via banks) as against "direct" financing (where companies go to their shareholders or at least direct to the capital markets to raise funds).

A number of things have happened in recent times to alter this structure. The huge export surpluses which Japanese companies have earned abroad have won them a new independence from the banks — some of them are now more powerful financially than the banks themselves — and the liberalisation of interest rates on medium and large deposits has sent savers in search of new investment media. The investment trusts are a good example. From 1950 until the early 1970s the total net asset value of these funds grew very slowly and at the end of the 20-year period scarcely exceeded ¥1 trillion. By 1980 it had grown to around ¥6 trillion but did not really take off until interest rate liberalisation began to be felt in 1983. As rates have trended downward, the amount of money going into the investment trusts in search of higher returns has grown rapidly.

This process accelerated rapidly in 1986 as the official discount rate continued to ratchet downward. As it did so, the investment trusts began to rival the powerful trust banks (repositories of Japan's pension funds and other monies invested on behalf of the public) whose total assets as of mid-1986 were around ¥37 trillion. Tohru Takaoka, chairman and president of the Investment Trusts Association of Japan, reckons that in two or three years time, the net asset value of Japanese investment trusts (which are run by just under a dozen specially designated management companies) will have reached ¥50 trillion. This is almost equal to the present-day assets (¥54 trillion) of the biggest asset group among Japan's financial institutions, the insurance companies. The fact that individuals account for around 80% of total funds in Japanese investment trusts is a good indicator of the small-investor revolution that is taking place in the Tokyo stock market.

Not that this means that small investors will wrest power away from the banks and other financial institutions when it comes to the control of Japanese corporations. As one major securities house chairman in Tokyo expressed it to the author, "share ownership and management are separated in Japan. Shares carry automatic voting rights but in practice ownership and control are separate." And, despite the rapid growth of Japanese securities markets in recent years, the power of the banks is still very considerable. Ministry of Finance sources suggest that while Japan's bigger companies nowadays raise about 50% of their funds via "direct" means (from the capital market), only about 20% of their total outstanding funding is from that source. The rest is from the banks. Smaller companies still depend on banks for 100% of their financing according to the MoF.

The picture emerging from statistics provided by the Bank of Japan (the central bank) is one of even greater bank dependence than suggested by the MoF. In 1984 (the latest full year for which these figures were available at the time of writing) Japanese companies as a whole borrowed almost ¥21 trillion (largely from banks), which represented no less than 84.8% of their total financing. A far distant second as a source of finance was the local equity market which provided companies with ¥1.85 trillion or 7.6% of their total financing. Foreign currency bonds provided a further 5.8% and bond issues in Japan 3.5%. Net disinvestment of foreign debts (to the tune of 1.7%) brings the total to a level 100%. The ratio of borrowings (close on 85%) to total financing has been about the same over the past ten years. Even so, the majority of Japanese companies are nowhere near so highly geared or leveraged (in terms of debt to equity) as they were ten years ago. The ratio is roughly 1:1 now whereas it was nearer 10:1 as recently as 1977. The degearing process did not begin in earnest until the 1980s (chart).

What is changing is the increasing tendency by Japanese companies to look abroad for finance. Their total overseas financing doubled between 1982 and 1985, to ¥3.4 trillion. The bulk of this was in straight bond issues (¥1.67 trillion) convertible bonds (¥1.03 trillion) and bonds with warrants attached ¥679 billion). The bulk of these securities in the past couple of years have been issued in the Swiss market or in the Euromarkets, reflecting low interest rates there. Overseas equity issues have been falling steadily and totalled only ¥19.3 billion in 1985.

As Japanese companies have turned increasingly toward overseas financial markets, so their dependence on the domestic market

Table 6

Number of Companies Listed on All Stock Exchanges, End of 1985

	Tokyo		Osaka		Nagoya		Kyoto	Hiroshima	Fukuoka	Niigata	Sapporo
	1st Sec.	2nd Sec.	1st Sec.	2nd Sec.	1st Sec.	2nd Sec.					
No. of Listed Companies	1,052	424	776	260	394	97	232	184	232	195	189
Listed on Single Exchange	272	318	34	142	16	58	1	5	12	8	12
Listed on 2 or more Exchanges	780	106	742	118	378	39	231	179	220	187	177

Source: TSE

has diminished. The total amount of equity they raised in the domestic market fell from ¥1.73 trillion to ¥709 billion — a fall of over 40% — between 1981 and 1985. Issues of corporate bonds have also fallen sharply from ¥358 billion in 1981 to ¥252 billion in 1985. (This excludes the electric power companies in Japan, whose issues likewise declined over this period from ¥901 billion to ¥538 billion). The only category of Japanese domestic corporate financing which has been increasing is that of convertible bond issues, which rose dramatically from ¥364 billion in 1981 to ¥1.9 trillion in 1985. Convertible bonds are very popular with investors in Japan because they attract a Transaction Tax which, at just 0.045% is less than one tenth of the rate levied on ordinary shares. They are attractive from an issuers viewpoint too because typically they carry a coupon rate (yield on nominal value) of only around 1.5% whereas a ten-year government bond would probably pay three times that yield.

What do all these trends in corporate financing mean for the Japanese stockmarket itself? In a nutshell, they mean a great deal more money chasing a given number of shares. The number of shares listed on the TSE increased by under 17% (to 259 billion) between 1981 and 1985 while the value of trading in these stocks roughly doubled to nearly ¥80 trillion. Japanese companies preference for raising loans rather than equity, and for going offshore wherever possible, has to do with prevailing low interest rates of course.

Table 7

Foreign Companies Listed on TSE, End of 1985

Company	Nationality	Date Listed	Company	Nationality	Date Listed
Amex	U.S.A.	Nov. 14, 1985	*Philip Morris Sears	U.S.A.	Oct. 16, 1985
Bankamerica	"	Dec. 22, 1975	Sears	"	June 29, 1984
Chase Manhattan	"	Sept. 20, 1974	*Secruity Pacific	"	Sept. 4, 1985
Citicorp	"	Dec. 18, 1973	*Walt Disney	"	June 27, 1985
Dow Chemical	"	Dec. 18, 1973	*National Australia Bank	Australia	Sept. 6, 1985
First Chicago	"	Dec. 18, 1973			
G M	"	Dec. 20, 1974	*Bell Canada	Canada	Nov. 19, 1985
I B M	"	Nov. 27, 1974	*Dresdner Bank	Germany	Oct. 24, 1985
I T T	"	Dec. 16, 1974	Robeco	Netherlands	Dec. 8, 1976
I U International	"	Dec. 18, 1973	*Telefonica	Spain	Oct. 4, 1985
*3 M	"	Oct. 17, 1985	*Union Bank of Switzerland	Switzerland	Dec. 24, 1985

Source: Tse

An officer of Nikko Securities Corporation put all this into perspective. "In the past," he said, "the growth rate of stock prices in Japan was lower than that of GNP. Now stock prices are growing faster than individual financial assets, and those in turn are growing faster than GNP. The ratio of saving to disposable income has traditionally been high and now we have too much saving relative to investment. So liquidity is high. More money is going to the secondary market (the stockmarket in the main) yet capital raising is slow. The days of investment in huge industrial complexes is over and corporations have huge liquidity to invest. Government bond issues are static (because the government is trying to contain its debt-funded budget deficit) and companies do not need money. So, there is plenty of room for the stockmarket to grow and that is why so much is going into investment trusts and trust banks and city banks in Japan. But much of it is going offshore too, to the United States especially, into Treasury Bills and equities."

The tremendous growth in secondary market activity seen in recent times could slow, of course, if the government goes ahead with its plans to introduce a broad-based capital gains tax on securities transactions as part of an overall tax reform in Japan.

There are certain structural constraints too, on the growth of the market. The Ministry of Finance's secondary capital markets division, in conjunction with the surveillance department of the TSE, runs what it calls a "stock price check" when Japanese companies plan to issue new shares. The idea is to make sure that the price of the companies' stock — new issues are made at market value nowadays rather than at nominal or par value as they used to be — has not been ramped prior to the issue. A MoF senior official assured the author that this is done in the interests of investor protection. But at the same time he acknowledged that "it is a difficult gate to get through and there are many cases when we decline permission."

This rather paternalistic attitude towards investors — the idea that they must be protected from loss at all costs — is a common one in East Asian markets (with the exception of Hongkong) and one which seems likely to break down before long. Already it is being questioned in Japan. A former vice-minister in the MoF, now senior advisor to the Minister of Finance, told the author in September 1986 that he thought the time had come for investors to take more care of themselves in Japan and for the government to retreat from so much "administrative guidance" in specific cases to a policy of more generalised prudential supervision. For Japan, these are revolutionary thoughts.

If the MoF's hurdles have led to the scratching of new issue proposals by Japanese companies, they have certainly not affected the rate at which foreign companies are listing on the TSE nowadays. Their ranks are swelling rapidly. There were a score of them at the end of 1985, mainly from the US, and by mid-1986 the number had grown to 34. Securities houses expected the number to increase to 50 by the end of 1986 and to between 70 and 80 by the end of 1987, There are all sorts of reasons why this is happening. Most multinational corporations recognise the need to provide a listing for their stock in principal international markets nowadays. It makes for transaction costs for one thing. But in Tokyo the push to get foreign companies to list has special motivations.

For one thing, the amount of stock already listed on the Japanese stockmarket is simply not big enough to absorb the sheer amount of investment available, both from export-rich corporations and from an increasing number of wealthy Japanese looking for portfolio diversification in the local stockmarket. Nor does the rate of new share issues by Japanese coporations promise to make good this deficiency in the short term. Japanese securities houses too, are

Table 8

Leading Domestic Companies on TSE			
Rank	No. of Shareholders (thousands)		Market Value (¥ bil.)
1	Nippon Steel	448	Dai-ichi Kangyo Bank	3,922
2	Tokyo Electric Power	379	Sumitomo Bank	3,821
3	Toshiba	250	Tokyo Electric Power	3,744
4	Kansai Electric Power	237	Fuji Bank	3,501
5	Hitachi	234	Mitsubishi Bank	3,324
6	Chubu Electric Power	231	Toyota Motor	3,253
7	Mitsubishi Heavy Industries	220	Sanwa Bank	3,146
8	Nippon Kokan	185	Matsushita Electric Industrial	2,283
9	Tohoku Electric Power	162	Industrial Bank of Japan	2,240
10	Toray Industries	160	Hitachi	2,187

Source: TSE

very anxious to lure foreign companies into the Tokyo market —
because it promises more commission for them, at a time when
Japan (like New York ten years ago and London more recently) is
moving towards negotiated commissions for brokers. The fact that
often nowadays more Sony Corporation shares are traded in a
single day on the NYSE that on the TSE has not escaped the
Japanese brokers' attention. They want some more of the action in
US (and European) companies' stocks to compensate. All this, no
doubt, explains why Japan is happy to accept a US auditor's report
when an American company wishes to list on the TSE, whereas the
SEC in New York will not accept a Japanese auditor's report when
a Japanese company wishes to list on US exchanges.

The advent of major foreign participation in the Tokyo stock
market by investors, brokers and fund managers, as well as by
foreign campanies listing there, has set in motion far-reaching
changes. These have already affected the character of the stockmarket, the way business is done and to some extent the ethics of the
market. Before long it seems likely to alter the mechanics of stock
trading too, and the terms upon which deals are done.

One result of the foreign presence in the stockmarket has been to
make it more transparent, more susceptible to rational analysis.
Ironically, while foreign brokers and fund managers newly arrived
in the Tokyo market during the 1970s were feeling at their most
vulnerable, fearing they would never come to understand the
workings of the market, the Japanese themselves were also feeling
vulnerable to the foreign invasion. Japanese institutions observed
the techniques of fundamental investment analysis which the
foreigners were employing, and marvelled. "They decided that the
foreigners were very clever and tried to figure out what it was they
were doing," recalled one Tokyo broker. Technical analysis paid off
and foreign fund managers as a rule did better than did their local
counterparts (though it must be admitted that in some cases the
foreign firms were employing Japanese analysts and dealers to work
for them). Even now, the foreign funds still outperform Japanese
funds on the whole.

But Japanese fund managers often operate at a disadvantage.
The interlocking nature of corporate relationships in Japan can be a
major constraint. One example cited to the author was that of a
fund manager working for a Japanese insurance company that
wished to dispose of its holding in a local steel company, believing

this to be a good move on investment grounds. The fund manager then discovered that the company concerned — connected by a shareholding link — had just taken out a batch of life policies with his own company. In cases like this, according to Tokyo market practitioners, the fund manager has to consider his loyalty to the group as much as his fiduciary duty to policy holders.

Japanese fund managers also tend to be short-term traders, dealing in and out of the market rather than taking a long term view. Securities houses are more interested in commissions than in fees from managing funds. Japan's securities companies in aggregate derived 70% of their income from commissions of one sort or another in 1985 and only 12.5% from capital gains on securities held. Ironically, many if not most Japanese funds managers and brokers have as a result missed out on the gains which foreigners have enjoyed from riding the Tokyo bull market.

Staying in has definitely been a good strategy because the bull market in Tokyo stocks has (with a few ups and downs) been a long-running one. "It has really been going since 1974," one foreign broker assured the author in the latter part of 1986. This is broadly true because the last real bear market in Japan was in 1964. There were sharply different views at the time of writing (toward the end of 1986) about where the market was headed next. "We are headed into a serious bear market," one Amerian broker in Tokyo assured the author. "I can see the (Nikkei) index going all the way down to 10,000 in 1987 — and maybe lower." This was at a time when the market had recently breached 18,000 and was still in the upper 17,000s.

A Japanese securities house analyst was equally certain, however, that the Nikkei Stock Average would hit 22,000 at least by the spring of 1987. He based this not so much on a serious appraisal of economic fundamentals and corporate earnings prospects in Japan, as on a rather arcane chartist view that what he called the "deviation ratio" from the Nikkei's five-year moving average was due to move back up from virtually zero in 1986 to 100% in early 1987. This kind of highly theoretical analysis seems to appeal to the Japanese. Fund managers will suddenly seize upon a group of stocks said to have "hidden assets," even though those assets are highly unlikely ever to be realised to the benefit of the share price. "They indulge too much in group think," commented a director of a British merchant bank's Tokyo office.

Of course, much the same thing can be said about US analysts chasing a few blue-chip stocks on Wall Street. But the ability to look at real economic and financial fundamentals is something that seems to elude Japanese analysts. They prefer to watch a host of more technical ratios and chart patterns. Much the same sort of thing applies to Seoul now that South Koreans are discovering the joys of stock analysis. Foreign fund managers in the Tokyo market say that this sort of thing has brought then much comfort. While they may not be part of the Tokyo rumour mill and while they do not always get to hear about which securities house happens to be pushing which particular stock at any given time, they still do well enough over the longer term.

One foreign fund manager who concluded in 1985 that the falling oil price plus the rising yen would push the price of power generation down sharply in Japan — and thus the earnings of power corporations sharply up — was treated with great scepticism by his Japanese counterparts. Their charts suggested that power companies were a no-go area. Sure enough, when the earnings began to flow through in 1986, up went the share price. The message for foreign investors in the Tokyo market thus seems to be, look for value, rather than trying to second guess what the big Japanese players in the market are up to. Another foreign fund

Table 9

10 Most Active TSE Stocks (Volume and Value), 1985

Rank	Stocks	(mils. of shares) Volume	Rank	Stocks	(¥ bil.) Value
1	Mitsubishi Heavy Industries	4,068	1	Yamanouchi Pharmaceutical	1,871
2	Nippon Steel	4,044	2	Tokyo Electric Power	1,742
3	Asahi Chemical Industry	1,609	3	Mitsubishi Heavy Industries	1,454
4	Sanko Steamship	1,533	4	Asahi Chemical Industries	1,411
5	Mitsubishi Chemical Industries	1,435	5	Sumitomo Metal Mining	1,176
6	Tokyo Gas	1,325	6	Mitsubishi Estate	1,006
7	Nippon Express	1,306	7	Green Cross	983
8	Mitsubishi Estate	1,105	8	Kokusai Denshin Denwa	948
9	Nippon Yusen	1,075	9	Kuraray	855
10	Kawasaki Steel	931	10	Nomura Securities	792

Source: TSE

manager who spotted the fact that automboile giant Toyota was sitting on around US$11 billion in cash, and that its shares were priced in the market at only around twice their cash backing, likewise cashed in when the Japanese eventually latched onto the fact. As of 1986, many shares were selling even at below their cash value and cash is a lot more of a tangible benefit than "hidden" assets such as land when it comes to dividend potential.

Not that all the foreigners who have played the Tokyo market in recent years have got it right. Some of them, including professional fund managers, found themselves over-exposed to high-tech stocks at a time when many hi-tech products (semiconductors in particular) were in oversupply internationally. They could not get out without converting paper losses into realised losses and were thus unable to shift into other sectors. Financial and retail stocks, plus special situations such as pharmacueticals, communications services and construction stocks, seemed set to show the best profits in 1987.

Just as superstition and folklore has a way of retreating before the inexorable advance of science, so much of the mystery that once surrounded the Tokyo stockmarket has been dispelled by the advent of rational analysis. "Tokyo has an undeserved reputation for being a managed market," in the opinion of one long-staying foreign fund manager, "a lot of things have changed. The more you look at this market the more it seems to make sense. Instead of throwing up your hands in disgust and saying, 'I don't understand this,' you try to understand it over time."

As one small example he cited the fact that wherever a listed company in Japan makes a scrip issue (variously known too as a "bonus" or "free" issue) to its shareholders, they regard this as a good thing and the price of the stock goes up. Western analysts would say that this is illogical, because the price of the shares should automatically adjust (downward) to reflect the extra number in issue. In fact, the Japanese reaction is quite logical. Japanese companies usually pay the same percentage dividend on the new bonus shares as they did on the existing shares (as do most Western companies) so the investor's overall income rises. When the price of a Japanese stock rises following a scrip issue, analysis shows that the rise usually corresponds with the increase in income, to give a constant yield. The reaction is thus not only logical, it is quite mathematical.

But probably the most important change to occur in the Tokyo market has been the reduction in the ability of local brokers to push stocks. This is largely a result of the sheer volume of new money (especially foreign money) coming into the market and because there are just too many sophisticated investors around nowadays. Market ramping still goes on but on a much smaller scale than before. One of the bigger securities houses with a widespread network of branches might be able to despatch its salesmen and get the price of a particular stock up (perhaps when the company is contemplating a new issue) but that sort of tactic works best when everyone is playing the same game. The advent of many new foreign players in the market, including half a dozen foreign brokers and investment banks who now have seats on the TSE, has made it harder for the Japanese institutions to be sure that everyone will join in the game.

There are still the "Seibi" groups, or pools, to contend with. These groups of speculators come together in specially formed syndicates to try and corner the market in the shares of some smaller or medium-sized company. Typically they all agree to buy the stock concerned until other investors are drawn in, by curiosity or through rumours planted in the market and in the Japanese financial press. Once the share price is launched on an upward

Table 10

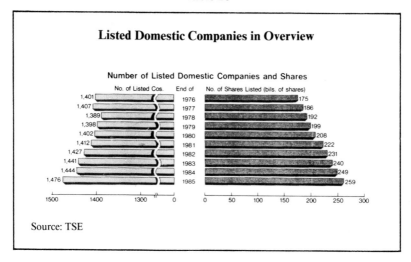

Source: TSE

path, the syndicate starts feeding out stock until it has sold out completely. Those investors (not part of the original syndicate) last in and last out are the suckers. Another Seibi group tactic is to find stocks where investors have gone short and to start buying, thus forcing the shorts to buy from the Seibi members to cover their positions. But things can and do go wrong. Often individual members of a seibi group will secretly start selling out before the rest of the group. In one case involving a company called Meiji Tekki, the price was pushed so high that no-one else wanted to buy. The syndicate was left high and dry.

Spurious investment advisors who formerly dominated the Tokyo scene are slowly disappearing too. (Investment advice, unlike fund management and broking, is not something which Japanese have been able to charge for and even if they could few Japanese would be prepared to pay for it). Under a new law which was scheduled to come into effect around the end of 1986 (literally translated as the Law Concerning Investment Advisory Companies) investment advisors in Japan will in future have to register with the MoF as "Toshi Komon" or "investment businesses."

There will be two types, one which can only give advice but not execute orders on behalf of their clients or undertake discretionary management of funds, and a second one which can carry out all of these functions. The Ministry of Finance says it is willing to register any Japanese or foreign group which wishes to carry on either type of business, provided the applicant is "credible" from the point of view of background, staffing, resources and so on. Most foreign investment banks and brokerages in Japan are expected to go the Toshi Komon route, except for the eight or so who have been granted special licences to deal in trust business — hitherto the exclusive province of trust banks and insurance companies. Toshi Komon will in any case be allowed to advise on the investment of trust funds, if technically not to execute such business.

It was the so-called Toshi Journal scandal in the early 1980s which acted as a catalyst for reform of the law. The Toshi journal was a publication — one of many of its kind in Japan — which gave investment advice to readers. Later however, it graduated to offering to manage their money for them. When the journal proved not only unable to achieve the sort of investment performance it promised but also unwilling or unable to return investors money, there was a major outcry. There were a series of scandals involving investment advisors who collected money from the public but failed to return it. This is part of the darker side of Japanese financing, like the still thriving business of the Sarakin (loan sharks) who lend money at extortionate rates and then pressure debtors (sometimes to the point of suicide) into repaying. Another unsavoury activity is that of the Samaiya who threaten damaging publicity against companies unless they pay. This kind of extortion threat is sometimes carried to the point of disrupting shareholders' meetings.

What of insider dealing (dealing for individual profit on the basis of privileged information not available to the generality of a company's shareholders)? Though reckoned by some to be a way of life in the Tokyo stock market, it is in fact officially proscribed under the rules of the Tokyo Stock Exchange. The trouble is, as one foreign broker in Tokyo put it, "the authorities here have a hard time trying to decide what is inside information and what is not. In the United States everything is inside information unless it is in *The Wall Street Journal,* but not here." In Tokyo inside information tends to come more from brokers than from companies and while certain clients do profit from dealing on such information, foreign brokers and fund managers do not worry too much about it. They still feel that they do best by taking a longer term view than by trying to emulate those dealing quickly in and out of the market on the basis of leaked information.

Table 11

Total Bond Volume

(¥ bil.)

	No.of Listed Issues	Government Bonds Block Trades	Total	Convertible Bonds	Yen-Based Foreign Bonds	Others	Total	Tokyo OTC Markets 'Repos'	Total
1981	572	2,236	2,387	3,102	15	74	5,578	141,531	288,429
1982	641	3,983	4,172	2,383	14	72	6,641	135,274	327,108
1983	659	8,573	8,792	6,592	13	52	15,448	137,205	385,097
1984	736	22,337	22,601	11,713	13	33	34,359	148,703	692,470
1985	854	39,152	39,428	22,165	20	29	61,642	251,577	2,164,669

Source: TSE

Insider dealing is also addressed in Japanese law. In order to prevent any officer or major shareholder of a company availing himself of sensitive information obtained through his office or position, the Securities Exchange Law provides that the company may, within such a person's profiting from this information, require him to account to the company for the profit. This law also contains provisions covering the unjust use of secret information or fraudulent action for the purpose of inducing securities transactions. Subject to these provisions, company directors are allowed to deal in the shares of their companies.

The Ministry of Finance is reticent about discussing insider dealing. The official attitude seems to be that not many cases are reported and therefore not much of its goes on. "I am of the opinion that the performance of the Tokyo Stock Exchange in this respect is rather better than that of overseas markets," one senior MoF offical declared rather stiffly to the author. Questions about insider dealing in the Seoul stockmarket elicit a similar response from officialdom there: New York or London are worse offenders they say. They may be right, but there is undoubtedly an anxiety in Tokyo as much as in Seoul to sweep such things under the carpet rather than have them out in the open.

One thing which has helped to reduce the scope for insider dealing in Tokyo is the advent of very good stock information services such as the "Quick" (teletype) machine service offered by Nihon Kezai Shimbin (Nikkei). This carries not only comprehensive stock quotations but also most of the financial news that goes into the group's financial publications. Jiji Press and Kyodo also offer good services. In fact they are so good that a broker in New York or the City of London connected to Tokyo via one of the special services can sometimes be better informed about what is going on in the Tokyo market than are local practitioners. The same does not hold true of the financial information services available to Tokyo from these other two major financial centres. The amount and quality of brokers' research in the Tokyo market has improved greatly in recent years with the introduction of Western-style research but that produced by Japanese securities houses often tends to have a market rather than company-specific flavour. To some extent this reflects differences in Japanese accounting practices.

There is a certain ambivalence in the attitude of the MoF toward the development of the stockmarket in Japan. The MoF has always had to perform a delicate balancing act in trying to foster the development of the securities markets while not discriminating against the banking sector. There are separate banking and securities "bureaux" within the Ministry which have often been in an embattled situation, with the Minister or his immediate deputies having to arbitrate.

As Tsuneo Fujita, a senior official of the MoF (also a member of the Policy Board of the Bank of Japan) put it: "The Securities Bureau is a strong supporter of the idea of developing capital markets in Japan. But there are possible conflicts. The interests of securities and banking are different. Expansion of the capital markets means a reduction of the power of banks over manufacturing industry." Though Fujita did not say so, the clear implication is that the MoF sees itself facing an increasingly difficult task in holding the ring between banks and securities houses. The banks are still very powerful and, as noted earlier, Japanese companies as a whole are still criticially reliant upon them. So, any over-rapid development of securities financing which jeopardised the position of the banks would not be in the interests of "Japan Inc."

It required the influence of the powerful Ministry for International Trade and Industry (Miti) rather than the MoF to promote the growth of Japan's highly successful Over the Counter (OTC) market in the early 1980s. Miti is not caught between the banks and

Table 12

			Corporate Financing			(¥ bil.)
	Stocks	Industrial Bonds	Foreign Currency Bonds	Borrowings	Foreign Debts	Total
1976	934	662	299	14,888	381	17,164
%	(5.5)	(3.9)	(1.7)	(86.7)	(2.2)	(100.0)
1980	1,441	563	214	15,399	760	18,377
	(7.8)	(3.1)	(1.2)	(83.8)	(4.1)	(100.0)
1984	1,850	858	1,420	20,767	-412	24,483
	(7.6)	(3.5)	(5.8)	(84.8)	(-1.7)	(100.0)

Note: Figures in parentheses indicate percentage to total.

Source: Bank of Japan.

securities houses to the extent that MoF is. As a result of the OTC coming into being (and subsequent competitive moves by the stock exchanges of Tokyo, Osaka and Nagoya to ease the requirements for listing on their second sections) the stockmarket as a whole in Japan began to cater for the needs of small to medium-sized companies wishing to have their shares traded publically, instead confining this privilege to the major corporations.

The (Tokyo-based) OTC market had 140 stocks being traded as at the the middle of 1986 and during 1985 turnover totalled ¥183 million. Both quoted and unquoted shares can be traded in the OTC market. The Japan Over the Counter Trading Company acts as intermediary for OTC issues between securities companies. All the securities houses are members of the market. The self-regulatory organisation which runs the market is the Securities Dealers' Association and in July 1984 the OTC market Automated Quotation System (akin to NASDAQ in the US) was introduced. The market is regarded more as a testing ground for a company, preliminary to a full listing on one of the stock exchanges proper, than a competitor to the main markets, as is the case in New York.

The Ministry of Finance meanwhile does not believe that the securities industry in Japan is yet ready to be exposed to the full force of competition from the banks. Article 65 of the Securities and Exchange Act, which is Japan's equivalent of the Glass-Steagall Act in the United States, prevents any one institution from engaging in both lending and underwriting securities. In other words, it separates the function of commercial banks and securities houses. As Japanese banks increasingly conduct securities business overseas through offshore subsidiaries and as foreign banks enter the securities business in Japan itself through shareholdings in purpose-built affiliates, the pressure to loosen or even scrap Article 65 grows.

Tomomitsu Oba, special advisor to the Minister of Finance expressed his personal opinion to the author during 1986 that he saw "no danger in scrapping Article 65." But securities officials within the MoF do not agree. If Article 65 went, banks would quickly take over a great deal of securities business but securities houses could not hope to compete in banking because of their inadequate branch networks, argue the officials. Already, the Japanese city banks (the 13 major commercial banks in effect) are major shareholders in Japan's leading securities houses, though the same does not apply when it comes to securities houses interest in banks. This continuing tussle between banks and securities firms in Japan could limit the future rate of growth of the capital markets in general and in particular the rate at which companies are encouraged (or allowed) to reduce their dependence upon banks and turn to the stockmarket for equity or bond finance.

There are just over 200 securities companies in Japan, roughly one half of which are members of the TSE. The others are members of the various regional exchanges, though there is of course some overlap of membership between the TSE and the rest. The 206 firms in existence today are a dramatic reduction on the 1,100 or so in the early post-war period, and competition threatens to produce further consolidation in future. The big four — Nomura, Daiwa, Nikko and Yamaichi — already dominate the market heavily. They account for an estimated 40-45% of total turnover on the TSE. (For comparison, the six foreign firms which had seats on the TSE by late 1986 are estimated to account for around 1% of turnover in that market). The dominant position of the big four will almost certainly increase in future because of their huge capital base which enables them to underwrite and distribute stocks as well as provide brokerage services.

To put this in perspective, Nomura, Daiwa and Nikko occupied top position in the entire Japanese corporate-earnings league in

Table 13

New Share Offerings, All Listed Companies

	Rights Offerings		Public Offerings		Private Placements		Total	
	No.of Cases	Amount Raised (¥ bil.)	No. of Cases	Amount Raised (¥ bil.)	No. of Cases	Amount Raised (¥ bil.)	No. of Cases	Amount Raised (¥ bil.)
1981	67	496	233	1,197	20	37	284	1,730
1982	43	221	*192	* 969	13	18	*227	*1,208
1983	17	133	68	444	22	118	97	695
1984	23	90	*127	* 811	18	66	*154	* 967
1985	39	186	99	489	18	33	139	709

Notes: 1. Those issued in foreign countries excluded.
2. * Including preferred stocks.
Source: Yamaichi Research Institute

1986, with the two big electric power companies, the Bank of Japan, NTT (the national telcommunications corporation), auto manufacturer Toyota and the two biggest city banks trailing behind. Nomura, Nikko and Daiwa are bigger in terms of worldwide assets than US giant Merrill-Lynch, which explains why they feel quite safe from any future threat of a foreign takeover (even if it were possible in Tokyo).

This also explains why the big-four securities houses say they are confident they could survive competition from the Japanese banks, even if Article 65 went. But, they say, Article 65 should stay — for the protection of the smaller securities houses. This is not altogether disinterested beneficence on their part. The big four admit that through shareholding links they are able to ensure that smaller brokers remain "friendly." This helps when it comes to deciding what tactic to adopt in support of the stockmarket as a whole (or of any particular sector or stock) if the need arises.

Table 14

Shareownership by Type of Investors, All Listed Cos.				
	Mils. of Share		Percentage	
	1982	1985	1982	1985
Govt. & Local Govt.	480	504	0.2	0.2
Financial Institutions	89,155	102,288	38.6	39.6
All Banks	39,891	47,361	17.3	18.3
Investment Trusts	3,039	2,801	1.3	1.1
Annuity Trusts	953	1,319	0.4	0.5
Life Insurance Cos.	29,022	32,827	12.6	12.7
Non-life Insurance Cos.	11,302	12,312	4.9	4.8
Securities Finance Cos.	1,755	1,808	0.8	0.7
Other Financial Institutions	3,194	3,862	1.4	1.5
Business Corporations	60,732	66,971	26.3	25.9
Securities Companies	3,973	4,913	1.7	1.9
Individuals & Others	65,619	67,862	28.4	26.3
Foreigners	10,718	15,626	4.6	6.1
Corporations	10,625	15,506	4.6	6.0
Individuals	93	120	0.0	0.0
Total	230,677	258,164	100.0	100.0

Source: TSE

A MoF official acknowledged to the author that he saw a problem with what he termed the "monopoly position" of the big-four securities houses. Despite the law that no financial institution may have a shareholding of more than 5% in another, the big four do have de-facto control of many other securities firms, via board representation. "Of the 200 or so securities companies in Japan, all are under the influence of the majors to some extent," commented this official. "Some are under the influence of banks. Very few are independent." By setting up so-called research affiliates (which many of the big securities houses have done in recent times) they can breach the 5% rule. "They could use this to influence stock prices," added the MoF man.

In order to try and prevent such market manipulation, the Ministry intends strengthening its inspection of dealings, though because its monitoring staff (of three) is too small relative to the size of the task, the MoF will have to rely on the TSE to use its own surveillance staff of around 20 to do some of the work. Financial bureaucrats in Tokyo see no contradition in asking the TSE, essentially a private corporation, to carry out this role of official policeman. "The TSE was formed under a special law. It should be considered as part of the private sector but it should also act in the public interest," an official said.

Foreign brokers in Tokyo have rather unflattering things to say too, about Japanese securities houses. They claim that some of them try to "unload their positions" onto foreign fund managers. This is no doubt true, though the more honest among the foreign fund managers in Tokyo admit that they try to do the same thing themselves, onto the Japanese brokers.

There was a something of a scandal a few years ago involving several Japanese securities houses which went in for short-selling of clients' stock. As a result, rules were brought in forbidding employees of securities houses from selling short. (As a general rule, Japanese investors are allowed to go short — usually by renting stock from the Japan Securities Finance Corporation — though foreigners are not. Likewise, foreigners are not permitted to deal in securities on margin whereas Japanese are). A number of prominent securities houses were involved too, in what was known as the Kyodo-Shiro affair in 1973. It was as a result of this particular securities-financing fraud that the securities houses were asked to establish internal surveillance departments, to monitor price movements in relation to possible price manipulation and insider dealing.

There are other gripes against the Japanese securities houses. It is claimed that they make Tokyo a "broker-driven" market "The Japanese securities houses churn portfolios like mad," claimed a foreign securities analyst. "They churn the Tokkin funds they manage and there is much churning of investment-trust stocks too. Some are liquidated and new ones formed especially so that the managers can get front-end fees." The bigger securities houses readily acknowledge their over-dependence upon commission income. A senior executive within one of the biggest houses commented to the author: "We don't like to be dependent upon equity commissions. We would like to increase our bond dealing (formerly the exclusive province of the big banks) and move into corporate finance services domestically and internationally." In other words, the big houses want to increase their fee-based income and to become full-fledged investment banks.

One thing which is going to force such change upon the securities houses is the approach of negotiated commissions in Japan's stockmarket. "We have to expect negotiated commissions in the future," according to Masaharu Yonezawa, a general manager with Yamaichi Securities. "Institutions have given lower (than published) rates for block trades since 1983 but still our rates are expensive compared with New York." An augury of things to come was seen in October 1986 when the TSE announced that it was preparing to lower fixed-commission fees for trades of more than ¥10 million. It was hardly coincidence that this announcement came just days before the Big Bang in London which abolished fixed commissions there. The prospect of losing business to London (in trading of Japanese stocks) worries Tokyo.

The prospect of lower commissions does not please everyone however, including some of the foreign operators in Tokyo. Those overseas institutions which have established branch offices in Tokyo enjoy a 73% discount on published commission rates when dealing with a Japanese broker. (A representative office qualifies a foreign institution for a discount of only 20%, though some say that, with rebates, it can be nearer 50%). But if fixed commissions go, so does much of the advantage of waiting three years for a branch licence in Tokyo. Some may consider it worthwhile in that event paying the ¥1 billion or so needed to buy a seat on the TSE.

(When the TSE allotted ten seats for foreign brokers on the exchange during February 1986 — of which half a dozen had been taken up by October that year — the cost per seat was around ¥500 million for a special participation fee plus another ¥500 million for deposit money. This was substantially below the figure of ¥1.6 billion paid in April 1985 when Daifuku Securities sold its TSE seat to Utsimaya Securities).

Another thing which is going to have to change in Tokyo is the rather arcane system of market making by the Saitory members. Ordinary members of the TSE act as dealers as well as brokers and around 20% of total transactions are on members' own account. Saitori members act as intermediaries for matching transactions between regular members. But they do not take positions. A saitori member is prohibited from dealing on his own account. In a sense they have privilege without responsibility.

There are four Saitori members on the TSE compared with 83 regular members. The "intermediary clerks" employed by the saitory, are stationed at trading posts on the stock exchange floor where they marry buy and sell orders placed by the trading clerks of

Table 15

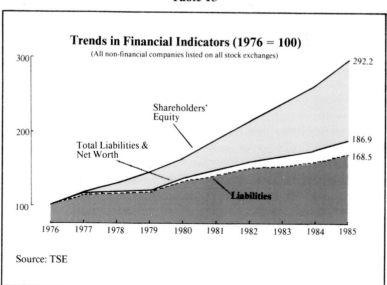

Source: TSE

the regular members. Trading clerks can deal among themselves but usually deal via the Saitory. Given the "tremendous number of orders flowing into the trading floor, the economic need for saitori members is obvious," says the TSE. Many people disagree. The big securities houses say that the saitory members are no longer necessary now that trading on the TSE is largely computerised.

Some Japanese brokers argue too, that the Saitory system is inadequate for present-day needs. A lot of block-trades are matched between institutions nowadays and then simply put through the stock exchange on a pro-forma basis without Saitory intermediation. One obstacle in the way of reform is that the Saitory members employ a total staff of around 400 (nearly half the size of the TSE's own staff) and the unemployment problem that would arise from abolishing the system would not sit well with the tradition of lifetime employment in Japan.

The Japanese market relies to some extent on the system of automatic price limits on stock movements to take the place of specialists who would normally act as a buffer between buyer and seller. This (also very Japanese) system means that stocks are permitted to move only within prescribed price increments, which in turn relate to the price of the stock. The system does not guarantee that a seller can get out at the limit price when stocks are falling. But, argue its defenders, it does ensure that potential sellers are brought into the market by giving notice that a stock is "limit down." Ditto when prices are moving up. This helps iron out major

Table 16

Amount of Shareholders' Equity and Total Market Value (¥ tril.)

(all TSE companies)

End of

1981 — Shareholders' Equity 41.1 — Total Market Value 91.9

1985 — Shareholders' Equity 62.5 — Total Market Value 190.1

0 10 20 30 40 50 60 70 80 90 100 110 120 130 140 150 160 170 180 190 200

Source: TSE

price fluctuations in the absence of specialists absorbing large movements through their own book. There are a number of stocks which are permitted to move without limit, however.

Table 17

Brokerage rates, May 1985

Stocks and Subscription rights

Trading value	Commission as percentage of trading value
Up to Yen 1 MMllion	1.25%
Over Yen 1 MM and up to Yen 3 MM	1.05% + Yen 2,000
Over Yen 3 MM and up to Yen 5 MM	0.95% + Yen 5,000
Over Yen 5 MM and up to Yen 10 MM	0.85% + Yen 10,000
Over Yen 10 MM and up to Yen 30 MM	0.75% + Yen 20,000
Over Yen 30 MM and up to Yen 50 MM	0.65% + Yen 50,000
Over Yen 50 MM and up to Yen 100 MM	0.55% + Yen 100,000
Over Yen 100 MM and up to Yen 300 MM	0.45% + Yen 200,000
Over Yen 300 MM and up to Yen 500 MM	0.35% + Yen 500,000
Over Yen 500 MM and up to Yen 1 billion	0.30% + Yen 750,000
Over Yen 1 billion	0.25% + Yen 1,250,000

Notes: Commission on trading value less than Yen 200,000 is fixed at Yen 2,500. Includes preferred stocks and foreign stocks.

Source: TSE

Changes as at October 1986

Trade size	New commission rate	Current commission rate
¥ 10-30 million	0.7% + ¥25,000	0.7% + ¥20,000
¥ 30-50 million	0.5% + ¥85,000	0.65% + ¥50,000
¥ 50-100 million	0.3% + ¥155,000	0.55% + ¥100,000
		Less than ¥300 million: 0.45% + ¥200,000
¥ 100-500 million	0.25% + ¥235,000	More than ¥ 300 million: 0.35% + ¥500,000
¥ 500 million-1 billion	0.2% + ¥485,000	0.3% + ¥750,000
Over ¥ 1 billion	0.15% + ¥985,000	0.25% + ¥1.25 million

Source: Nihon Keizal Shimbun.

If, as seems likely, Tokyo moves eventually to a system of single capacity (broker cum jobber) market makers, then the big securities houses will need to increase their capital accordingly. At present, their position-taking is limited by a net capital rule, as in the US. Few (except presumably the Saitory members themselves), seem happy with the present system which, if nothing else, ensures that the match-makers receive large reward in return for taking little risk.

Another area where Tokyo recognises it will need to introduce reforms, in order to come into line with international practice, is that of stock-index futures trading. The Japanese capital is one of the few major trading centres in the world where such instruments are not available. Singapore beat Tokyo to the post by launching a stock-index futures contract based on the Nikkei average early in

Table 18

Breakdown of Income of All Securities Companies, 1985

Extraordinary Profit 0.1%

Non-Operating Income 0.5%

Gains on Securities Dealings 12.5%

Interest or Dividend Received 7.0%

Margin Transactions 9.9%

Financial Revenue 16.9%

Commissions Received 70.0%

Current Income

Other Commissions 19.5%

Brokerage Commissions 50.5%

Source: Japan Securities Dealers Association.

1986. Osaka, which used to have nearly 30% of total stockmarket business done in Japan but later lost much of it to Tokyo, is trying to fight back by launching an index futures contract based on a package of shares. This was expected to materialise some time in the early part of 1987. Modelled broadly on the Toronto system, the Osaka contract for 50 shares (which can include delivery of the physical stocks) is permitted in Japan under the Securities Transaction Law because of its special nature. But, as yet, a fully-fledged index contract (without the option of delivery on the underlying stocks) is not permitted. The law is, however, expected to be changed before long so that the TSE can compete internationally.

Yet another area where reforms affecting stockmarket investment are on their way in Japan is that of accounting and auditing. The present system is rather complex. There are three types of corporate auditor. There are the so-called "statutory" auditors who are nominally elected by a company's shareholders at their annual meeting but who in reality are nominated by the company president. Their role supposedly is to ensure that company directors perform their fiduciary duty on behalf of shareholders. But the grace-and-favour nature of their appointment means that their loyalties are potentially divided.

There are internal auditors, whose function is much the same as that of internal auditors anywhere — to check a company's operations and controls — and then there are the independent

Table 19

Number of Member Companies in Each Stock Exchange

(the end of May, 1986)

	Tokyo	Osaka	Nagoya	Kyoto	Hiroshima	Fukuoka	Niigata	Sapporo
Regular Members	93	55	35	20	16	19	16	13
(Main Office Memebers)	(76)	(29)	(13)	(6)	(2)	(1)	(5)	(1)
(Branch Members)	(17)	(26)	(22)	(14)	(14)	(19)	(11)	(12)
Special Members	—	—	1	1	1	1	1	1
Saitori, Nakadachi Members	4	1	3	—	—	—	—	—
Total	97	56	39	21	17	21	17	14

Source: TSE

outside accountants (Certified Public Accountants or CPAs). The CPAs undergo a fairly rigorous training and are no doubt professionally competent. The trouble is that their appointment as auditors to a company often has to be with the endorsement of the statutory auditors (who typically are not trained accountants but retired directors). The whole structure thus has a rather incestuous nature which does not give confidence that shareholders always get an objective or "true and fair view" of their company's affairs.

The fact that two sets of accounts are required in Japan — one for shareholders, prepared under the Commercial Code and another for shareholders and creditors, prepared under the Securities Exchange Act, complicates matters further. However, as in other areas, the accountancy and audit profession in Japan seems likely to have reform thrust upon it quite soon as a result of the increasing internationalism of the Tokyo market.

The MoF set up an ad hoc committee toward the end of 1986 called the "group for the study of the disclosure system." It promises to bring greater transparency to the accounting system in Japan. One of the things it was expected to tackle is the question of consolidating companies' accounts. Technically speaking, all companies which are required officially to submit financial statements (which includes all those listed on Japanese stock exchanges and on the OTC market) have, since 1983, been required to equity-account the earnings and consolidate the assets of their subsidiaries and affiliates, within the parent company accounts. This applies to subsidiaries owned by more than 50% and affiliates which are between 20 and 50% owned. But the complex web of cross

Table 20

During	Stocks					Bonds
	Purchases	Sales	Net Balance	Purchases	Sales	Net Balance
1976	912	945	-34	920	392	527
1980	2,873	1,688	1,185	3,601	2,352	1,249
1985	9,381	10,161	-780	25,194	24,045	1,149

Foreign Investment in Japanese Securities

(¥ bil.)

Source: Bank of Japan

shareholdings among Japanese companies in general is so structured that stakes are dispersed and thus fall below the level where
consolidation is necessary.

Apart from this, many Japanese companies have long been in
the habit of setting up subsidiaries or associate companies mainly
to provide continuing employment for directors and other staff
retiring from their main function. These "loyalty" companies have
often been loss makers rather than profit earners. Thus, there is real
uncertainly as to what the impact on group earnings would be if
Japanese companies were to go in for real consolidation. Some
subsidiaries and affiliates would no doubt contribute profits while
other would bring their losses into the parent company accounts.
However, fuller equity accounting does seem to be the way of the
future. Because of structural changes in the Japanese economy, big
companies are finding increasingly that they cannot afford to fund
unprofitable subsidiaries. They are also eager to adopt a "matrix or
network" system of corporate organisation which will better enable
them to diversify their activities. Monitoring these diverse activities as profit centres will require consolidated accounting.

Basic Data:

Tokyo Stock Exchange

Trading system

All securities, whether money-market or capital-market issues, must be traded through an authorised securities dealer, all of which are members of the Japan Securities Dealers Association.

The trading of shares is carried out under the Zaraba method, which is an open outcry method. Prices are first established at the beginning of the trading session, based on orders which have reached the floor before the opening of business. Other investors then enter the market with further buy or sell orders which are matched by open auction. Selling orders at the lowest prices and buying orders at the highest prices take precedence over other orders. A special auction is held to determine the opening and closing prices of specific shares, usually those of large companies which are widely traded, as designated by the stock exchange. This is known as the group auction method, whereby competing prices are fixed amongst sellers and separately amongst buyers, and then between both buyers and sellers. Contracts are settled at a price which is close to the highest bid and the lowest offer prices.

The Japanese brokers take the responsbility of making the markets. Banks are not allowed to trade on the exchange and must go through a broker.

Settlement and transfer

Japan has a book entry clearing system, whereby securities companies, financial institutions and others open accounts with a depositary institution by depositing their stock holdings with it. Securities transactions are subsequently cleared by simple entry on the books of these institutions rather than by actual movement of certificates.

Settlement can be effected in four different ways:
—Regular settlement: delivery is due on the third business day following the day of the contract. This is the most widely employed procedure, used for approximately 99% of stock transactions.
—Cash: delivery is due on the day of the contract but it can be made on the next business day if this is agreed by both parties of the contract.
—Special agreement: delivery is due on the fixed date agreed on by both parties of the contract, which may not be later than 14 days following the day of the contract.
—When issued: delivery is due on the fixed date as determined by the exchange. This kind of transaction is employed only for new shares and subscription rights where there is a fixed issue date but certificates or warrants have not yet been issued.

Dividends

Dividends from a Japanese corporation paid to foreign shareholders are subject to Japanese withholding tax at 20% of their gross amount. Reduced tax treaty rates may apply if the shareholder is a resident of a country with which Japan has a tax treaty.

Capital Gains

In the case of a non-resident individual investor, capital gains from the sale of shares in a Japanese corporation are exempt from Japanese taxation unless the investor, together with his relatives, has:

a) owned at least 30% of the total issued shares at any time during the year of sale or in the two preceding years;
b) sold at least 5% of the total issued shares during the year;
c) sold at least 15% of the issued shares within the three years.

Exchange controls

The government's attitude to foreign investment in Japan is flexible. Restrictions still exist with respect to non-resident purchases of Japanese equities but these have been liberalised by the exchange control regulations which became effective in December 1980.

There are no limitations on the repatriation of capital and earnings under the Foreign Exchange and Foreign Trade Control Law, provided that the underlying transactions are proper and legal.

Although regulations regarding foreign investment in shares of Japanese companies have been significantly liberalised since the new exchange controls were introduced, specific restrictions still exist. The new rules define Japanese companies into two categories for foreign investment purposes. Companies may be classified as being in the "national interest" (industries such as mining, agriculture, nuclear power, gas, railways, banks, aircraft, pharmaceutical industries and oil refineries). In this case their foreign shareholding is limited to 25%. Other "non-strategic" companies have no such limitation.

When an acquisition of shares in a listed corporation is made through an authorised security company in Japan and the acquisition represents less than 10% of the corporation's issued capital when aggegated with the existing holdings of the investor and its related parties, formalities are minimal.

Shareholder protection codes

The TSE Regulations attempt to ensure fair and orderly transactions in listed securities and the protection of investors.

The exchange conducts strict examinations of the periodic reports submitted in accordance with the provisions of the SEL. The exchange also takes steps to ensure the full disclosure of financial statements of listed companies.

Market indices and their constituents

The Nikkei-Dow Average Share Price Index is calculated on a formula similar to that for the Dow Jones average in the United States. The calculation, made on a daily basis, uses the share prices of over 250 companies listed on the first section of the exchange relative to a base of 4 January 1968=100.

Although the Index is adjusted for rights issues and share splits, it has several failings as a reliable indicator of total stock market movements. In particular, it is only an arithmetic average, so small and large companies are given equal weighting. This means that volatile movements in the share prices of small companies, with a listed number of shares available for trading, can have a disproportionate effect on the Index. Additionally, it includes less than 25% of total shares in the first section.

A more recent index, the TSE Stock Price Index, was devised to remedy the defects of the Nikkei-Dow Index. This is a weighted average of all the shares listed on the first section of the Tokyo Stock Exchange. It has been calculated retrospectively to have the same base as its precedessor: 4 January 1968=100. It is revised to take account not only of rights and split issues but also of new listings. Sub-indices are also calculated for groups of small, medium and large companies defined by issued capital, for specified industrial groups, and for 300 designated shares that are traded on the second section of the exchange.

Source: G.T. Guide to World Equity Markets.

South Korea: The One Most Likely To?

For the many Western Investors who face East nowadays when they think about markets for the future, South Korea has become Mecca. Tokyo is now a mature market — the world's biggest after New York — and, as such, it no longer exerts the fascination of the unknown. What does is the Korean Stock Exchange (KSE) in Seoul. The market is still closed to direct foreign investment and is likely to remain so until late 1987 at the very earliest, and quite possibly until well into the 1990s. Yet, it has the excitement of performance as well as the lure of being largely untrodden territory. After languishing for four or five years, the market came suddenly to life in 1986 with what looked like being one of the strongest bull markets in its relatively short history.

South Korea is the biggest of the so-called "New Japans" in terms of its economy which, while still only around one tenth the size of Japan's, is by far the biggest in Asia after India. Yet by comparison the KSE (the only stockmarket in the country) is a midget. The capitalisation of the market (as at the end of 1985) was only one fifth that of Hongkong, a half that of Malaysia and considerably smaller than that of neighbouring Taiwan — all much smaller economies. One reason for this is precisely because Korea has an exclusive little market from which foreign investment has been largely excluded.

Behind the barriers which the Koreans have maintained around their stockmarket since its founding in 1956 (three years after the end of the Korean War) stands a wall of fear. Koreans are — as were the Japanese a decade or so ago — suspicious and fearful of outside influence in general and of foreign investment in particular. They are much happier to borrow liberal amounts from foreign banks to finance their development rather than allow foreigners to own their equity assets, even if this does mean a heavy external debt burden for the country.

To put this in perspective: South Korea's foreign debt grew from US$27 billion in 1980 to around US$47 billion by mid 1986.

Meanwhile the outstanding value of all securities quoted on the KSE grew from just US$2.8 billion in 1980 to a still modest US$7.25 billion at the end of 1985. In other words, debt still figures

Table 21

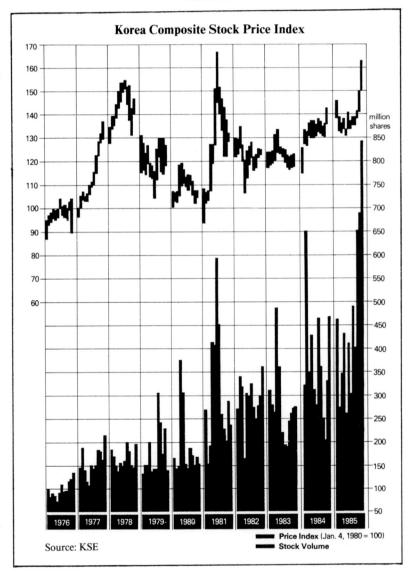

very much more heavily than equity in Korea from a national point of view as well as from the standpoint of individual corporations. Putting it another way, the capitalisation of the stockmarket at the end of 1985 was equivalent to only 8.8% of Korea's GNP whereas foreign debt represented 56.5% of GNP. How far these ratios improve in future depends criticially upon the government's attitude to the stockmarket as well as to foreign borrowing.

The irony of the South Korean stockmarket is that foreigners have up to now been more enthusiastic about it than the Koreans themselves — at least those Korean bureaucrats who shape its destiny. And it must always be borne in mind that in Korea the bureaucracy (in this case the Ministry of Finance) shapes the destiny of most things. Foreigners have, for instance, been happy to pile into special Korea investment trusts (the only way they can get into the local stockmarket as yet) with little idea of the stocks those trusts were going to invest in, or the returns they could expect. They were equally happy to accept penal conditions on Korea's first convertible bonds, launched in 1985.

The reason for this is quite simple. It has to do with the parallels which foreigners like to draw between Korea and Japan. As Karl Ferris Miller, an American broker of long standing in Seoul, puts it: "If you had put your money in the Tokyo Stock Exchange in 1960, you would be a wealthy man now. We are flooded with representatives from foreign securities markets who think that the same thing will happen here." Such optimism appears to be well founded, on paper at least. Figures compiled by the International Finance Corporation (the equity financing arm of the World Bank) show that US$100 invested in the Korea Stock Exchange in 1975 would have been worth $845 by the beginning of 1986. That figure is adjusted for fluctuations in the value of the US dollar against the Korean won and was roughly double the gain that would have been achieved on a comparable investment in the US Standard & Poors 500 index or in the Capital International World Index over the same period.

Yet, despite this very robust performance by their stockmarket over the past decade, Koreans continue to agonise over how far and how fast to open it up to the outside world. Senior financial bureaucrats repeatedly emphasised during conversations with the author how fragile (they think) the market is compared with developed stockmarkets and how carefully it has to be nurtured before it can be left to the mercy of international investment flows. The vision some of them like to conjure up of rapacious foreign speculators bent on ravishing their market is not only at odds with the facts, it is also ironic. The Korean stockmarket had a history of volatile price movements, rampant speculation and insider dealing well before foreigners came on the scene.

Korea's bureaucrats have apparently failed to realise that the foreign investors who are presently so keen on getting into their market — certainly those from the United States and from principal European centres — are much more likely to be rather dull pension funds or insurance companies intent only on securing long-term portfolio diversification and steady growth in their assets rather than speculators bent on pumping hot money into the Korean market — and out again just as quickly. And they apparently fail to see any inconsistency in allowing foreign multinational companies to hold majority stakes in Korean ventures and not allowing foreign portfolio investors to hold minority stakes in companies listed on the KSE.

A less charitable, but possibly valid, interpretation is that Koreans do realise all of these things but prefer to keep their stockmarket in the domestic domain where the government can control it and where, if anyone is going to make money it will be Koreans themselves. This was true of the Tokyo stockmarket until the late 1970s and the reluctance of the broking establishment there to allow foreign competitors into their market — at least until the

Table 22

		Stock Trading Volume			
Year	Trading Days	Trading Volume (mil. shrs.)	Daily Average (mil. shrs.)	Sales Value (bil. won)	Turnover Ratio (%)
1976	298	591.8	2.0	628.7	53.7
1980	291	1,645.3	5.7	1,134.0	44.4
1983	295	2,750.7	9.3	1,752.6	53.87
1984	293	4,350.3	14.8	3,118.2	74.28
1985	294	5,563.8	18.9	3,620.6	66.06

Note: Turnover ratios are based upon sales value.
Source: KSE

US and other foreign governments made them realise that they had to if they wanted to enjoy access to overseas markets — is reflected in Korean attitudes today. Koreans also like to assure some Westerners that their aversion to foreign ownership of their assets stems from the period of Japanese colonialism in Korea (from 1910 to 1945). There is probably some truth in this because the indirect (investment trust) route to foreign investment which the Koreans have permitted so far has been aimed mainly at US and European investors. But it is hardly a valid, long-term posture.

In some respects the Korean market is possibly more transparent than the Japanese market, on which it is modelled. There is not so much "collusion" (to move share prices) between Korean brokers as there is between their Japanese counterparts, according to foreign brokers who know the market at first hand. "There is too much competition among brokers to allow that," says one. Some would argue, however, that the herd instinct among Japanese brokers is often mistaken for collusion. Whatever the case, the fact is that Korean brokers do not seem to have quite the same herding or colluding instinct as do the Japanese.

This independent streak among securities houses in Korea was compromised only once when Sam Bo Securities — at that time the biggest — collapsed in 1983 and was absorbed (with official persuasion) by Daewoo Securities. Sam Bo's president was forced to sell most of his personal possessions to help pay off the firm's debts and, it must be said, investors suffered no serious losses. But just where the brokers' fierce pursuit of their own interests leaves their client interests in day-to-day business is an interesting question. Probably the most truthful answer is that Korean investors at large are not unduly worried if the broker makes more than they do — just so long as they make something themselves.

Korean securities houses do not send out door-to-door salesmen to do a heavy selling job on a particular stock they want to push as is sometimes the case in Japan. And the foreign fund manager is less likely to become the meat in the sandwich of concerted share-ramping operations, as happened in the early days of foreign penetration of the Tokyo market. The individual investor is more likely to come under pressure from his bank manager to buy new shares being issued by the bank itself than he is from some hard-selling securities house salesman. Most of the big securities houses are linked to chaebols (big business houses) of the same name.

Daewoo, for instance, is controlled by the Daewoo industrial group, though Korean banks are also large shareholders. The tied securities houses claim to respect certain "Chinese-wall" type separations in dealing with their parents. Daewoo, for instance, would not be allowed to underwrite and market an issue of new shares by member companies of the Daewoo "family" (though it could act as lead manager for any bond issue the Daewoo group makes).

The Korean stockmarket is peculiarly susceptible to manipulation in the sense that its size and liquidity are constrained by factors other than the relatively lowly valuation put on stocks. Though there are some 8,300 million shares technically being traded on the KSE (from the 369 issues of 345 listed companies) the number actually available for trading by investors in general is very much smaller. Cross holdings by chaebol companies in each other are widely thought to reduce the amount of free stock available by roughly a half. If the holdings by the (nowadays powerful) invest-

Table 23

Ranking	Companies	Listed Shares (mil. shrs.)	Market Value (bil. won)	(US$ mil.)
1	Hyun Dai Motor	228.7	458.8	515.4
2	Yu Kong	212.3	394.6	443.3
3	Hyun Dai Engineering & Construction	250.0	273.8	307.6
4	Kia Industrial	120.0	176.4	198.2
5	Gold Star	200.0	175.8	197.5
6	Sam Sung Electronics	110.0	137.5	154.5
7	Lucky	160.0	125.6	141.1
8	Sam Sung Semi-Conductor & Telecommunication	60.0	118.5	133.1
9	Dae Woo Heavy industries	97.0	115.2	129.4
10	Dae Woo	150.3	89.6	1007
11	Korean Air	120.0	70.5	79.2
12	Sun Kyung	50.0	67.7	76.1

Leaders in Market Value

At the end of 1985, the market value of the top 30 companies amounted to Won 2,929.9 billion, representing 44.6% of the market value of all listed companies. In 1984, the top 30 companies accounted for 38.8% of the total. Hyun Dai Motor Company had the biggest market value of Won 458.8 billion, 7.0% of the total.

Source: KSE

ment trusts and brokerage houses are also excluded, then the "floating supply" of stock probably is only around 20% of the total listed. A quarter of this may easily change hands in just one day. That explains why the KSE may easily turn over one and a half times its capitalisation a year — a very high ratio compared with other Asian markets. As a result, liquidity is a problem. "When prices are rising, it is hard to get in and when they are falling it is impossible to get out," observed one foreign analyst.

Getting more companies to list their stocks would help alleviate this situation, especially if they were smaller or medium-sized companies not linked to chaebols. Every year the MoF sets targets for new company listings. These are usually very ambitions. The target for 1986, for instance, was 59 and even though half way through the year only 15 had in fact come to market, even this is high by the standards of most markets in the region. Now the government is also pushing foreign joint-venture firms in Korea (Fuji Film is one example) to list on the KSE.

Often companies have to be bullied into listing. This is partly because they simply do not like the public exposure that comes along with a stock exchange listing. Korea's accounting and auditing standards may have been somewhat relaxed by Western standards up to now. But the pressure from even the limited number of foreign fund managers who are involved in the market nowadays is leading to the growth of a financial research industry and will ultimately lead to higher accounting and auditing standards. Another problem is the undervaluation of equity, rendering the cost of equity capital high relative to debt. Taxation is the biggest distortion in the cost of capital because interest payments on borrowed capital are tax-deductible whereas dividends on equity shares are not. It might be supposed that redressing this imbalance is a straightforward technical issue. In fact, it is a political one. "The government here thinks that if you give a tax credit on dividends you are benefitting the capitalists," complained one analyst. Finance Minister Chung In Yong explained during a conversation with the author. "We cannot give too many favours to people investing in shares or in the capital market. We must take an equitable approach on the one hand for wage earners paying high tax and privileges to those investing in the capital market."

Tax is not the only problem. In most Western capital markets, a company going public would pitch the price of its shares at whatever level the market would stand. This would usually be comfortably above the nominal or par value of the shares (used for purposes of determining how much capital should be issued). In Korea things are different. The authorities have an obsession with par values and often companies have been forced to issue new shares either at par or at least at a price nearer par than market value. The SEC blandly denies this and says that companies "are encouraged to issue new shares at current market price." The SEC agrees that it vets new issues but claims this is simply to see that the valuation has been properly done, and that the Korean Securities Dealers Association makes the pricing decisions.

Even if companies are free in theory nowadays to make new issues at market value, many of them hesitate to do so for fear that the issue will flop. Korean investors have been brought up on a diet of cheap new issues. The same applies to rights issues. Lucky Goldstar, a leading Korean electronics concern, decided to raise money by way of a rights issue when the market price of its shares was Won 2,200. The new shares were issued at only Won 500 each, which was less than a third even of their par value. Major shareholders in Korea do not like having to fork out new money for rights shares any more than do their counterparts in other markets.

Table 24

Aggregate Market Data For Listed Securities (as of May 1986)					
STOCKS					
Classification	No. of Companies	No. of Issues	No. of Shares (mil. shrs.)	Capital Stock (bil. won)	Market Value (bil. won)
1st Section	257	270	6,459	3,861	8,322
2nd Section	88	99	1,805	974	1,106
Total	345	369	8,264	4,835	9,428

BONDS			
Classification	No. of Issuers	No. of Issues	Nominal Value (bil. won)
Public	15	945	5,140
Corporate	1,247	2,832	7,441
Total	1,262	3,777	12,581

Source: KSE

But they have had it too good for too long. For the same reason, bonus or "scrip" issues are very popular in Korea, especially as the market price of the old shares does not automatically adjust downwards in line with the issue as it would in other markets.

A few years ago, when the bottom fell out of the Middle East construction boom and the share prices of leading Korean construction firms crashed (along with their profits) demonstrators picketed the stock exchange, demanding that the government put share prices back up again. At the same time, however, Koreans are inveterate speculators and gamblers. They are, as one foreign banker in Seoul commented to the author, "natural traders." This is not an uncommon paradox in East Asia. Every taxi driver and amah (domestic servant) in Hongkong for instance will happily stake their own (and their family's) savings in the stockmarket, yet when a major local bank (Hang Lung) collapsed in 1983 shareholders picketed the government there to compensate them for money they had lost on their Hang Lung shares.

Stock watching is a serious business for many Koreans — certainly for the more wealthy who can afford to live off their investments. For them the daily routine of office work is replaced by the routine of sitting in a broker's office staring at electronic screens which monitor the every movement of the stocks listed on the KSE. Myong Dong ("Wall Street") is where the big deals take place but brokers offices can be found throughout Seoul's scattered business district and they are usually playing to a full house. It is not an unpleasant life for those market watchers managing their

Table 25

				Turnover
End of	No. of Companies	No. of Shares (mil. shrs.)	Capital Stock (bil. won)	Market Value (bil. won)	Ratio of Listed Shares (%)
1976	274	1,583.3	1,153.3	1,436.0	50.6
1980	352	3,875.6	2,421.4	2,526.5	43.9
1983	328	5,444.0	3,238.8	3,489.6	56.3
1984	336	7,406.9	4,336.1	5,148.4	69.2
1985	342	7,955.3	4,665.4	6,570.4	77.3

Key Statistics for Listed Stocks

Source: KSE

portfolios from the comfortable offices of big brokers like Daesin Securities. They sit drinking coffee (courtesy of the broker) trading in and out of the market on the thinnest of margins. The scene is the same at numerous other brokers' offices. Occasionally some spice is added. Daeyu Securities, for instance, is said to have big overheads so it goes for high turnover, using some unorthodox methods to achieve it. Daeyu employed at one of its offices a corps of miniskirted girls to skip around at table-top level marking up prices on traditional boards — to the delight of its clientele, the male element at least.

If Korea's financial bureaucrats do not yet trust the stockmarket, that did not prevent the government from adding a traditionally Korean touch of bravado when commissioning a new stock-exchange building a few years ago. The smart, if somewhat stark building in Yoido Dong replaced the old exchange in Myong Dong. It is, as one American broker in Seoul noted, "a miniature of the New York Stock Exchange." It is not all that miniature. It is one of the largest stock exchange buildings in the world. It is also one of the most modern in Asia, with a high degree of computerisation and a central depository system.

The government, which owns 68% of the KSE (the remainder being held by 25 Korean securities houses) flew in three former presidents of the NYSE to help with its design. This trio subsequently went on to design a stock exchange for the EI Salvador capital of San Salvador though it never opened. The KSE building was designed with the listing of 1,000 companies in mind, though so far it has attracted only one third of that number.

Not surprisingly, the exchange is not always busy. "I can tell how much market activity there is from the amount of time traders spend out at the back of the exchange playing baseball," noted an American broker whose office overlooks the KSE building. The market did not have an appearance of hetic activity, even during the bull market of 1986 — one of the most protracted Korea has ever known — when turnover was hitting around 45 million shares a day or more. Representatives of the 25 local securities houses mill around the trading posts on the exchange floor feeding in orders from the 240 branch offices which brokers have throughout the country. Though it is the country's only exchange, the KSE mirrors the relative lack of priority accorded to the market in national financial development.

Table 26

Korean Securities Market Data

	1975	1984
Equities		
No. of Companies Listed	189	336
No. State Owned Entities Listed	6	0
No. of Multinational or	10	32
Joint Venture Companies		
No. of Shares Listed (million shares)	825	6,326
Market Value of Shares Listed (Bn Won)	916	5,148.5
No. of Shareholders (000)	291	760
Share Ownership		
Individuals (%)	53	56
Institutions (%)	32	42
Government (%)	14	0
Foreigners (%)	1	2
Annual Turnover of Shares (%)	51	72
Annual Turnover of Shares (Bn Won)	48.3	42.8
Annual Sales Volume (mn shares)	311	4,350
Annual Sales Value (Bn Won)	334	3,118
General Index of Shares Prices	89.7	131.9
(Base Date: January 4, 1980)		
Average Dividend Yield (%)	13.7	6.1
Average Price Earning Ratio (x)	5.3	4.5
New Issues		
Number	62	n.a.
Amount Offered (Bn Won)	39.9	81.3
Amount Subscribed (Bn Won)	39.9	81.3
Rights Issues		
Number	68	n.a.
Value (Bn Won)	82.9	397.6
Total Corporate Funds raised from Equities (Bn Won)	122.8	478.9
Debt Securities		
Listed Government or Public Bonds		
Annual Number of Issues Listed	78	272
Annual Listed Amount (Bn Won)	61.7	1,415.1
Annual Sales Volume (Bn Won)	12.9	499.6
Average Yield of Public Bonds (%)	21.1	13.7
Total Amount of Funds	n.a.	2,068.7
Raised from Public Bonds		
Listed Corporate Bonds		
Number of Issues Listed	71	908
Annual Number of Issues	67	441
Annual Issue Amount (Bn Won)	33.5	1,859.9
Annual Listed Amount (Bn Won)	32.5	1,415.1
Annual Sales Volume (Bn Won)	0.6	593.5
Average Yield of Corporate Bonds (%)	20.1	13.6
Total Corporate Funds Raised from Bonds (billion won)	33.5	1,859.9

Rumour has traditionally driven the market more than investment fundamentals, owing to the preponderance of individuals rather than institutions investing. Every broking house has its "rumour men" whose function is simply to circulate among brokers and dealers collecting all the rumours for the day and relaying them back to head office where they form an important input for investment decisions. Lucky Securities even has a "rumour room" for collating such activity.

Many would claim that another major factor which drives the Seoul market is insider dealing — not so much by the legendary "big hands" but more nowadays by the securities houses themselves. Securities house staff are not supposed to deal on their own account but it is generally acknowledged that they do — just about all of them. They use nominee or even numbered accounts and attempts by the government to require "real-name" accounts appear to have come to little so far. "Insider dealing is rampant and brokers trade actively on their own account," declared one scandalised British merchant banker in Seoul. "There is gross insider dealing by [company] directors." Not everyone agrees. For one, the local Securities and Exchange Commission doesn't. An official there told the author: "The scope for insider dealing in the Korean securities market is very narrow because the aggragate capitalisation of the market is only US$10 billion." This is not an altogether convincing argument.

Korea's Securities Transaction Law (modelled along Japanese lines) empowers the SEC to bring those suspected of insider dealing before the courts, and the Securities Industry Act (based on US legislation passed in 1934) also contains clauses to regulate insider dealing. But much of the regulation is done through "administrative custom" rather than according to statute law. Remarkably, no actions for violations of the insider dealing rules have yet been brought before the courts. Asked whether this could possibly mean that there is no such thing as insider dealing in the Korean market, an SEC official replied: "In my private opinion, there is a possibility of insider trading." Though the SEC has powers to look behind transactions and determine who beneficially owns shares held in brokers' accounts, it rarely does so. "In regulating the market we generally use persuasion or moral suasion rather than legal powers," said the SEC official. He described this as a mixture of "self-regulation and Korean custom."

A meeting took place in the early part of 1986 between SEC officials and the heads of the leading securities houses, apparently so that the broking chiefs could be ticked off for getting a bit too blatant about insider dealing. It seems likely that what provoked this little chat was a complaint from the manager of one of the foreign funds operating in Seoul. It seems he told the authorities he was sick of dealing on the "outside" when everyone else was dealing on the "inside." A few months later, the president and two other employees of Hyundai Securities were arrested for allegedly trading in bonds at artifically low prices in return for payoffs. Such disciplinary action has been extremely rare up to now.

Meanwhile the influence of the so-called "big hands" has declined. Chief among these was the so-called "Kwanghwamun Bear" (named after the city road intersection from where he directed his operations). Just why this big market operator (whose real family name was Koh) was called the "bear" when in fact he was as often bullish as bearish is a mystery but his name has passed into local folklore. Having made a minor fortune in real-estate dealing, he then went on to bigger things in market manipulation. But nowadays the official Securities Supervisory Board is too active for the likes of the Kwanghwamun Bear.

The crucial test of Seoul's intentions on foreign investment in its stockmarket will come in October of 1987. Foreign investors and fund managers have become fixated with that date because it is the month when the convertible bonds (CBs) issued (in May 1986) by Samsung Electronics Company (a member company of one of Korea's biggest business groups or "chaebols") become eligible for conversion into ordinary shares of the company. That seemingly technical event in fact has great significance. The investment institutions in New York and London which bought these convertible bonds or those of Daewoo Heavy Industries (another chaebol) issued around the same time, assume that, come October 1987 (or November in Daewoo's case), they will be free to convert their bonds. They will thus become the first foreign holders of individual Korean ordinary shares. (There are of course numerous foreign institutions and individuals who hold Korean stocks via one or other of the special trusts set up in recent years but, for now, foreigners are prevented by the Foreign Exchange Control Act and the Securities Exchange Act from holding shares directly in Korean corporations). They also assume that if they are free to hold such shares, then they will also be able to sell them — and to buy other Korean stocks with the proceeds.

Things do not look so clear cut and simple from the viewpoint of the Ministry of Finance in Seoul. Senior officials there (including even Finance Minister Chung In Yong himself during a conversation with the author in August 1986) say that Korea cannot commit itself to a major market opening of this kind until sometime "in the 1990s." This could, of course, mean 1990 or 1999 but neither Chung nor any of his aides will say when. This is curious because back in 1981 the government set itself a definite timetable for opening up its stockmarket. The first stage has, in fact, been achieved: namely the setting up of the New York-listed Korea Fund and of other investment trusts between 1981 and 1984. The second stage — scheduled for 1985/1987 — allowing foreigners to invest in listed Korean securities "on a limited basis," could also be said to have been achieved with the issuing of convertible bonds. But the third stage, scheduled for 1988-90, permitting foreigners to invest in securities listed on the KSE "on a comprehensive basis", now looks highly problematical. This must also throw some doubt upon whether the fourth and final stage, allowing Koreans to invest freely in foreign securities, can be achieved "in the early 1990s" as planned.

Bureaucrats try furiously to fudge this issue, claiming that the overall programme is ahead of schedule. But their claim that the intention of opening up the market to direct participation by

Table 27

Yields and P.E. Ratios				
	Yield (%)			Price Earnings Ratio
End of Period	Public Bonds	Corporate Bonds	Stocks	
1976	21.8	21.7	12.9	6.6
1980	28.9	27.6	21.5	2.5
1983	13.97	14.17	7.6	4.3
1984	15.62	14.97	5.2	4.8
1985	12.55	13.50	6.1	5.7
Source: KSE				

foreigners is unchanged, is at odds with official statements. Asked how they reconcile the idea of foreign holders being able to convert their bonds into ordinary stocks (thereby becoming direct participants in the market) with the idea that foreigners at large will still be excluded, officials simply say that the two things are "different." Pressed in a conversation with the author over how this inconsistency could be reconciled, one very senior official at first looked tense and then, in a face-saving (and characteristically Korean) gesture, burst out laughing. The matter was "not yet decided" he said and made it clear that further questions would not be welcome.

Even Korean stockbrokers are at odds over the timetable for liberalisation. "It is very natural to expect opening of the market [to foreign investors] in october 1987 if policies are to be consistent," commented one to the author (in 1986). Another declared with equal conviction that it would be "ten years before the market is fully open to foreign investors."

All this points to a deeper uncertainly on the part of Koreans about the degree to which foreigners should be involved in their economy. Although foreigners often find Koreans to be more open and "less inscrutable" than the Japanese or the Chinese, the Korean temperament can be highly unpredictable. This can manifest itself from time to time in anti-foreigner sentiment and in resentment against foreign economic influence. There have been various demonstrations of popular feeling against liberalisation of Korea's financial system along Western lines. In the early part of 1986, a joint-venture bank involving the Bank of America and several Korean partners (the Kor-Am Bank) felt the brunt of demonstrators' resentment against what was seen to be the privileged position of foreign banks. None of this is meant to suggest that South Korea is an inherently unstable place or that foreigners need to be unduly nervous of investment in the local stockmarket. But it does provide clues as to why the government may be dragging its feet over opening the stockmarket and why it has to be sensitive to popular feeling on such issues.

The market is, of course, still young. Founded in 1956, three years after the armistice of the Korean War, the present exchange was initially a tiny market whose function was to finance the war-torn country's reconstruction through the issue and trading of government bonds. (Korea first had a stockmarket in 1911 but it was closed during World War II and thereafter existed as a

securities club or informal market among securities houses until
1956). As the size of the economy expanded and the government

Table 28

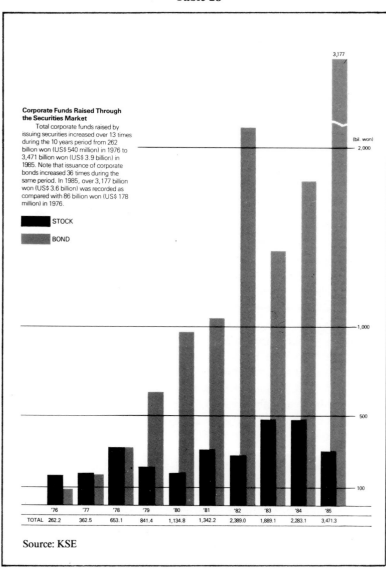

Corporate Funds Raised Through the Securities Market

Total corporate funds raised by issuing securities increased over 13 times during the 10 years period from 262 billion won (US$ 540 million) in 1976 to 3,471 billion won (US$ 3.9 billion) in 1985. Note that issuance of corporate bonds increased 36 times during the same period. In 1985, over 3,177 billion won (US$ 3.6 billion) was recorded as compared with 86 billion won (US$ 178 million) in 1976.

STOCK
BOND

	'76	'77	'78	'79	'80	'81	'82	'83	'84	'85
TOTAL	262.2	362.5	653.1	841.4	1,134.8	1,342.2	2,389.0	1,889.1	2,283.1	3,471.3

Source: KSE

pushed through an almost ruthless programme of industrialisation (to compensate for the fact that much of the country's pre-war industry was in what is now Communist North Korea) the need for mobilising domestic capital became greater and the stock exchange grew. As noted, that growth nowhere near kept pace with the growth in foreign debt. The market remained very small until the late 1960s and lacked both a regulatory agency and legislation governing market trading. More rapid growth came in the early 1970s, though again it did not keep pace with the growth in the economy under the impact of Korea's successive five-year plans.

In some ways the market did expand impressively. The number of listed companies on the KSE grew from just 34 in 1968 to 352 by the end of 1980 (though it has since declined somewhat). That is about the same number of listings as in Hongkong whose stockmarket capitalisation was around five times that of Seoul at the end of 1985. It is nearly three times as many companies as are listed on Taiwan's stock exchange. So why does the market remain so small in relation not only to Korea's GNP and to levels of foreign debt but also by comparison with neighbouring markets where often there are far fewer companies listed?

There are a number of reasons. One is that Korea has chosen to develop its bond market ahead of its equity market — again reflecting the national preference for debt. But the most obvious factor is that the weight of investment available in other, more open, markets simply does not exist in Korea. One indicator of this is the price/earnings ratio of Korean stocks which, at an average of around 5.5 in 1985, was only one third of that in Hongkong. In general, the higher the price/earnings ratio (p/e) the higher a company's shares are valued by the market. The fact that ratios are so modest in Korea points to a shortage of investment relative to the number of stocks listed. It certainly does not point to high average earnings (after-tax profits) among Korean companies — another factor which could depress the p/e ratio.

In fact, Korean companies have traditionally operated on very thin margins, because of the country's need to import most essential raw materials and the high cost of inputs such as fuel and power. The average Korean company too, has much higher debt levels than its Western counterpart or even than corporations in the once-highly-geared Japanese corporate sector. This too, helps to depress earnings. Yet another indicator of how lowly the South

Korean stockmarket rates its companies is the high yield on Korean stocks — meaning not that dividend payouts by companies are high but that share prices are low relative to the level of payout.

All of this makes a nonsense of the official claim in Korea that there is a "supply-side" problem with the number of companies listed on the stockmarket rather than a demand-side problem of insufficient investors and insufficient funds. The KSE has a relative abundance of listed stocks and even if the 30 biggest of them do account for around 45% of the total market capitalisation, this is still a much better market spread than in Hongkong where a score of companies account for over 80% of the total market value of listed stocks. The fact is that there is a demand-side problem. Too much of Korea's savings goes into banks or debt instruments of one kind or another rather than into equities and the favouring of foreign lenders over foreign portfolio investors also deprives the stockmarket of needed capital.

Once again, this is ironic because not only are foreign investors beating at the door of the KSE trying to get direct access but also the level of national financial savings is running at record high levels nowadays. This is partly a reflection of the swing back into surplus in South Korea's trade balance during 1985/86 — for the first time in 20 years — and the achievement of an overall current account balance for the first time in a decade. (This in turn is thanks to the so-called "Three lows" — low oil prices, lower international interest rates and the low level of the Korean Won

Table 29

Key Statistics for Listed Bonds

(In bil. won)

End of	No. of Issuers	Public Bonds No. of Issues	Par Value	No. of Issuers	Corporate Bonds No. of Issues	Par Value	Total Par Value
1976	8	254	280.1	105	180	118.4	398.5
1980	7	230	895.4	434	1,004	1,649.3	2,544.7
1983	14	627	3,026.4	734	1,680	4,371.1	7,397.5
1984	14	916	4,193.6	1,065	2,168	5,286.6	9,480.2
1985	12	979	4,737.8	1,213	2,749	7,263.2	12,001.0

Source: KSE

relative to the Japanese Yen). Admittedly, the stockmarket rose strongly throughout most of 1986 under the impact of all this liquidity but even without foreign investors in the stockmarket the Korean government is highly fearful of letting it rise too far. As a result, Korean corporations continue to be deprived of a realistic valuation for their shares and the opportunity to raise new equity capital at a cost which compares favourably with (tax-favoured) debt issues.

This is very characteristic of the "command economy" which the Korean government likes to operate. The military-dominated and highly autocratic government feels it must regulate at every turn and protect domestic investors from the possible consequences of their own speculative folly. The official order of priorities is neatly summed up in a comment made to the author during 1986 by Paik Won-Ku, head of the powerful Securities and Insurance Bureau of the Ministry of Finance. "We want to stabilise and develop the stockmarket," he said. That order of priorities reflects the cautiousness of the bureaucracy: first keep the market stable and second let it grow.

Government officials blandly deny that they intervene in the stockmarket to control it. They point to the limit-up mechanism operated by the market, which restricts daily price rises to a (variable) percentage of the stock's value. That, they say, is sufficient to keep the market from becoming overheated. The reality is rather different. The presidents or senior executives of

Table 30

Bond Trading Volume

(In bil. won)

| Year | Nominal Value | | | Market Value | | |
	Public Bonds	Corporate Bonds	Total	Public Bonds	Corporate Bonds	Total
1976	37.1	6.7	43.8	30.0	6.7	36.7
1980	267.4	643.3	910.7	246.0	643.9	889.9
1983	1,294.2	2,163.2	3,457.4	1,321.9	2,026.4	3,348.3
1984	973.6	1,419.6	2,393.2	899.2	1,352.8	2,252.0
1985	780.9	2,998.1	3,778.9	660.1	2,918.0	3,578.1

Source: KSE

Korea's 25 or so leading securities companies (who dominate trading) regularly get telephone calls from the Ministry of Finance "advising" them on whether to adopt a buying or selling posture in order to stabilise market movements. They rarely disobey.

A particularly interesting example of this came in April of 1986 when the Composite Index (the leading measure of KSE activity) plunged suddenly and mysteriously early one morning on what local newspapers termed "black rumours." A government decision to recall loans made to stockbrokers was one explanation. Another was that there might have been an attempted coup in the highest levels of the military/political establishment in Seoul. Whatever the truth of the matter, brokers estimated that people in the know about what was going on must have placed sell orders as early as 3 a.m. that morning — in order to be at the head of the queue of sellers when trading opened. But then the market recovered as quickly as it had crashed. The Ministry men had been on the phone — and the securities houses had come to the rescue.

More subtle methods of controlling the stockmarket are being used nowadays. When the market is heating up, the government increases its issue of so-called Monetary Stabilisation Bonds, directing the securities houses to put their liquidity into these instruments rather than into the stockmarket. If the market is looking depressed, the tactic can be reversed. But no-one believes that the time-honoured tradition of phone calls and ministerial "guidance" is about to end yet. Officials admit that there are still "telephone calls from the Ministry to the securities houses," but they argues that these are becoming less frequent now that other methods are being tried.

Despite government intervention, there is little evidence to suggest that the Korean stockmarket has been inherently more stable than others in Asia. Thailand's market, which is a good deal more open and free than Korea's, has been a model of stability by comparison. Some brokers in Seoul argue that even the limit-up mechanism on the stock exchange is counter-productive and that it has the effect of lengthening boom and bust tendencies (while prices adjust by the maximum permitted increment to underlying funda-. mentals) rather than eliminating them. The limit mechanism also has the effect of driving some business outside the market, though the number of deals done off market does not appear to be high.

One seasoned foreign broker in Seoul summed up the situation with the comment: "The MoF's idea of an overheated market is different from mine. I cannot think of any one occasion when government intervention was warranted." Korean analysts see things differently. "The government has had very bad experience with the market in the past so has to be cautious," noted one. This "bad experience" is partly to do with price volatility, though it can be argued that governments elsewhere in Asia — in Singapore/ Malaysia for instance — have coped with much greater market swings. The individual investors who dominate the KSE — individuals account for well over a half of total share ownership — appear to believe that the market should be stable on the downside but not on the upside. In other words, they want the best of both worlds.

Table 31

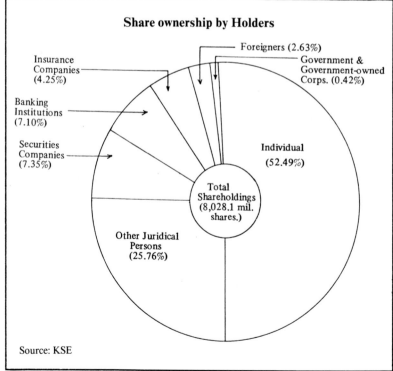

Source: KSE

How soon these disadvantages to equity share issues are re-
moved in Korea will naturally influence the growth of the stockmarket. Foreign investors who are poised to move into the market
along with the growing body of local institutional investors will not
want to find themselves bidding up the value of a limited amount
of scrip against each other. Otherwise that scrip will quickly
become overvalued and the market saturated. They will want
access to a diversified range of assets — something which will also
make equity capital more widely available to Korean business as a
whole. But first the government has to realise that enlarging the
market and making it play a more more meaningful role in the
national finances rests as much on reforming the (taxation and
issuance) rules as on simply coercing companies into going public.

What Korea can boast is a well developed bond market — both
in corporate and government instruments — certainly by comparison with Taiwan or Hongkong. The market is more akin to Japan's
in its size and degree of development, bearing in mind the
enormous difference in the size of the two economies. This has
been conscious government policy and does provide a solid base for
future growth of the stockmarket. And Korea has shown a
remarkable ability to innovate financially with its decision to issue
convertible bonds in the Euro-markets for foreigners.

As noted, the bond market dwarfs the equity market in Korea. In
terms of new funds raised in the stockmarket during 1985, public
offerings of bonds accounted for Won 3,177 billion while equity
issues (by way of public offerings and rights issues) totalled just
Won 260 billion. In other words, debt securities accounted for
91.5% of total corporate financing through the market. By the end
of 1986, 3,728 bond issues from 1,225 issuers were listed on the
KSE, with a total face (par) value of Won 12,000 billion. Corporate
bonds accounted for just over 60% of this total and government
bonds for the remainder.

This compares with the total par value of Won 4,665 billion of
listed ordinary shares (of 342 companies) whose total market value
was Won 6,570 billion. However, such is the high turnover ratio of
ordinary shares, that trading in stocks during 1985 at Won 3,621
billion actually exceeded slightly the Won 3,578 billion of turnover
in bonds. This is consistent with what one foreign broker described
to the author as the "alarming" amount of turnover or "churning of
portfolios" that goes on in the Korean market.

The bias in favour of the bond market and against equity shares has contributed to the over-geared position of Korean corporations (debt relative to capital and reserves). Whereas a debt: equity ratio of one to one might be regarded in many Western markets as the maximum desirable, Korean companies have long lived with ratios of four or five to one or even (as Deputy Prime Minister and chief government economic advisor Kim Mahn Jae admitted in an interview with the author) of up to ten to one. Kim acknowledged that this is "very bad."

Some Korean analysts say it is not as bad as it looks. "If you look at a Korean balance sheet compared with a US one, it is highly leveraged but if you understand Korean practice you feel more comfortable," suggested one.

The absence of a developed hire-purchase sector in Korea means that manufacturing companies often have to finance consumer finance operations themselves (resorting to commercial paper issues to fund it) and this impacts adversely on their balance sheets. The same goes for companies having to provide their own factoring services. The point is that the debt load is spread wider and more evenly than if it were a case of straight borrowing for asset finance or working capital. Even so, the fact remains that Korean companies in general are too highly geared for comfort — and for their own safety, as was seen when the collapse in international construction and shipbuilding hit Korean companies during the mid-1980s. Many of them had to be baled out by the banks (which then in turn had to be baled out by the government). One such, Kukje, collapsed altogether in 1985 when it diversified from light engineering and footwear manufacture into contracting.

Another problem in Korea is the lack of consolidated company accounts — including subsidiary as well as parent-company figures. As a result, the widespread cross guaranteeing of debt among chaeobols and other connected groups is not generally known about. This can be dangerous. A company with an apparently healthy balance sheet could be pushed to the wall if the (undisclosed) debt guarantees it has given to an affiliate were called. This is not a problem unique to Korea. Taiwan's Cathay group was pulled down by just such problems and when Hongkong Land company got into serious trouble in the early 1980s its sister company Jardine Matheson was technically bust by the size of its obligations to Land. But in Korea the practice seems almost standard.

Legally the position in Korea is that one company may not own more than 10% of another but it can provide cross guarantees of debt without limit. Local accountants and auditors do not look beyond the single company picture. As one put it: "Our accounting system here is of good quality and our CPAs (Certified Public Accountants) are quite good but they concentrate on individual companies and don't have the capability to see whether they are related. The CPAs know about the cross-guarantees but they are not able to prepare a matrix showing them." Meanwhile Korean banks,

Table 32

Securities Companies' Trading Volume		
	Total	
Securities Companies	Sales Value (bil. won)	Market Share (%)
Daehan	216.5	1.5
Ssangyong	1,215.5	8.4
Hanshin	814.5	5.7
Daeshin	1,215.6	8.4
Daewoo	2,292.2	15.9
Shinyoung	459.9	3.2
Taipyung	232.8	1.6
Seoul	315.2	2.2
Hanyang	217.2	1.5
Hanil	236.3	1.6
Kunseul	63.5	0.4
Lucky	1,522.5	10.6
Bukuk	107.6	0.8
Shinhan	108.8	0.8
Daeyu	130.4	0.9
Dongnam	338.4	2.4
Hanheung	133.3	0.9
Dongsuh	1,379.0	9.6
First	651.6	4.5
Shinheung	97.8	0.7
Yuwha	204.8	1.4
Tongyang	514.6	3.6
Dongbang	448.7	3.1
Kukil	942.9	6.6
Coryo	537.8	3.7
Total	14,397.4	100.0

who also presumably are aware of these guarantees, are "very secretive" about providing information to outsiders, presumably because they want to safeguard their own position rather than tipping off other creditors or investors about the true liabilities of a company.

The independent rating agency, Korea Business Research & Information Inc, (KBR) set up in 1984 as a joint venture between Korean partners and the Washington-based International Finance Corporation (IFC — an arm of the World Bank) is trying to make all this more transparent. The agency has been busy rating the various debt instruments of some 300 Korean companies and may soon move on to rating preference shares too. It was set up partly to prepare the way for foreign investors who will eventually come into the local stockmarket demanding a good deal more information than do locals — and partly to help Korean companies planning to issue securities overseas (in Tokyo for instance) achieve a recognised credit rating.

This information in available only to KBRI clients at present (banks and business companies) though it may be more widely published eventually. KBRI president and chief executive officer Lee Hun Jai thinks that Korean investors are not yet sophisticated

Table 33

Established Funds by Management Companies

(In bil. won)

Name of Company	Stock Funds		Bond Funds		Total	
	Amount	Composi-tion (%)	Amount	Composi-tion (%)	Amount	Composi-tion (%)
Koreal Investment Trust Co.	396.2	44.0	1,948.8	39.7	2,345.0	40.4
Daehan Investment Trust Co.	354.7	39.4	1,847.2	37.7	2,201.9	37.9
Citizens Investment Trust Mgt. Co	148.7	16.6	552.7	11.3	701.5	12.1
Korea Merchant Banking Co.	—	—	93.0	1.9	93.0	1.6
Korea Kuwait Banking Co.	—	—	101.3	2.1	101.3	1.7
Saehan Merchant Banking Co.	—	—	84.9	1.7	84.9	1.5
Korea French Banking Co.	—	—	122.5	2.5	122.5	2.1
Asia Banking Co.	—	—	77.5	1.6	77.5	1.4
Korea International Merchant Banking Co.	—	—	76.0	1.5	76.0	1.3
Total	899.6	100.0	4,903.9	100.0	5,803.5	100.0

Source: Korea Investment Trust Company

enough to use such information. Lee told the author that if the government were to decide that the opening of the capital markets [to outsiders] was not practicable then a rating system would not be so essential. A straw in the wind maybe.

There have been others too, suggesting that market opening may be delayed. There is the fact that some of the convertible bonds issued by Korean companies contain a put option — in other words, a means through which the investor can dispose of his bond before maturity and at a guaranteed price. Some take this to be a let-out should the government decide not to permit the conversion of such bonds into ordinary shares after all. Toward the end of 1986, the finance ministry informally told major corporations that they should not after all go ahead with plans to issue more convertible bonds for the time being. Goldstar Company and Hyundai Engineering and Construction had been planning such issues in 1986. It was unclear at the time whether the government move was because it wanted to limit all forms of foreign capital inflow for a time — in the light of a much improved balance of payments position — or whether it reflected official embarrassment at being unable to resolve the issue of whether full market opening would coincide with the conversion of bonds.

Korean officials do not readily accept the case for allowing more foreign participation in their market. Finance Minister Chung In Yong argued to the author that the ratio of foreign to total investment in the Korea Stock Exchange is about 3% or 6% if the shares held by company owners to maintain control are excluded. This, he added, is "about the same proportion as in Japan." That may be true, but the fact is that the Korean market is a great deal smaller than the Japanese market, not just in absolute terms but relative to the size of the economy.

Even before they do let in foreigners, some Korean analysts are beginning to think about mechanisms for preventing foreign dominance of their market. An executive at Korea Investment Trust Co (KITC) one of the biggest investment trust groups in Korea suggested: "We [should be] concerned when a foreigner buys more than 10% of the total market capitalisation of a company." Various schemes are being played with, such as (probably unworkable) one to limit foreign ownership to 10% of the total capitalisation of the Korean stockmarket. Probably a more practicable arrangement would be to limit foreign ownership to 10% of the total number of shares issued by any individual Korean company.

The amount of money raised by ordinary shares issues in Korea is not only very small in relation to bond issues it is also minute compared with the total flow of funds through the system. Local bureaucrats appear to have failed to recognise the importance of institutional capitalism as distinct from individual capitalism as a factor for boosting the stock market and for reducing corporate debt. Kim Mahn Jae admits that Korea's level of financial savings has reached "explosive levels" now — levels that have "great implications for the development of our capital markets."

But it is a long jump from admitting this to actually permitting capital market institutions the freedoms they need to grow and develop. If anything, the Korean government appears to be intent on increasing rather than decreasing the role of the banks in the economy. This is partly a matter of necessity. The slump in international contracting and in shipbuilding hit Korea's banks (as well as their corporate clients) very hard. As a result, the government had to inject huge sums into the banking system in 1984-85 so that the banks in turn could inject it into industry. The banks badly need recapitalising as a result. In order to help their strapped position, the government has allowed them to raise interest rates in order to attract back funds from the free sector of the debt market (the money markets) where funds have flowed in recent times. This does not seem to augur well for the growth of equity financing.

Insurance companies, which would normally be significant participants in most equity markets, are insignificant in this respect in Korea. Equity holdings account for only around 5% of their total assets. They tend to make large direct loans to industrial companies instead, a practice which even Kim Mahn Jae admitted was "potentially dangerous" [for policyholders]. Two thirds of the life assurance company assets of Won 6,500 billion at the end of 1985 were in the form of loans, some to policyholders but many direct loans to companies.

Pension or provident funds do not appear at all as investors in the Korean stockmarket because they are virtually non-existent, with the exception of a couple of official pension funds serving teachers and the armed forces. Private pension funds do not exist yet. There is a plan to create a national social security/pension fund system in 1989 but it will invest largely in housing and other infrastructures. Investment trusts are the biggest investors, holding around Won 5,000 billion of investments at the end of 1985, though the bulk of this was in bonds rather than equities, again reflecting the composition of the stockmarket. Investment and finance companies held just Won 252 billion of securities at this time. (For perspective, the total outstanding loans of Korean commercial banks at this time stood at over Won 20,000 billion).

As players in the stock market though, Korean investment trusts

Table 34

1. Performance of Funds Available to Foreign Investors
30 June, 1986

Fund Name and Manager	30 Jun Won	US$	Price % Change in USD terms since:			
			One Month	Three Months	Six Months	Twelve Months
Korea Intn'l Trust (KITC)	16,650.1	18.73	3.0%	11.1%	48.6%	81.3%
Korea Trust (DITC)	22,360.0	25.22	0.7%	12.6%	48.3%	71.6%
Seoul Int'nl Trust (KITC)	14,587.1	16.41	2.0%	11.8%	41.1%	
Seoul Trust (DITC)	13,341.0	15.05	-2.4%	7.7%	31.5%	
Korea Growth Trust (CITC)	13,688.4	15.40	2.9%	13.5%	38.1%	
Korea fund NAV:		22.34	2.7%	24.9%	66.5%	94.6%
MARKET PRICE:		33.38	3.5%	41.3%	89.3%	126.3%
PREMIUM TO NAV:		49.4%	48.3%	32.1%	31.4%	28.5%
Composite Index 1/		243.06	5.6%	21.5%	49.4%	74.6%
Exchange Rate Won/US$		892.1	887.4	886.1	891.4	876

1.   Composite Index has been adjusted to show % change in dollar terms.
2.   Quotations given represent NAV for all funds except Korea Fund for which the market price on the NYSE is given.
3.   Korea Fund size was increased by US$40 million in May 1986 by public offering at US$32.25 ($31.75 nett). As a result, the NAV of existing shares increased by approximately 15%.

2. Performance Since Inception

	Issue Price US$	Issue Date	% Increase			Exch Rate On Iss Date	Cumulati Dividend US$
			Won Terms	USD Terms	USD Inc Divs		
Korea Intn'l Trust (KITC)	9.94	19/11/81	142.8%	88.4%	109.7%	690.0	2.11
Korea Trust (DITC)	14.95	27/11/81	116.8%	68.7%	87.7%	691.9	2.84
Seoul Int'nl Trust (KITC)	9.95	19/4/85	70.4%	64.9%	64.9%	860.5	
Seoul Trust (DITC)	9.95	30/4/85	55.8%	51.2%	58.2%	865.9	0.69
Korea Growth Trust (CITC)	9.95	29/3/85	61.3%	54.8%	59.1%	853.0	0.43
Korea Fund (Scudders)	12.00	22/8/85	MKT PX 178.1%	178.1%	178.1%		
	11.16		NAV 100.2%	100.2%	100.2%		
	12.00		Issue PX				

Table 34 *(Continued)*

3. Market Value of Funds

	30 Jun US$	Outst Shares (Mil)	Value US$ Mil
Korea Intn'l (KITC)	18.73	2.60	48.7
Korea Trust (DITC)	25.22	1.75	44.1
Seoul Int'nl Trust (KITC)	16.41	3.00	49.2
Seoul Trust (DITC)	15.05	3.00	45.1
Korea Growth Trust (CITC)	15.40	3.00	46.2
Korea Fund (NAV)	22.34	6.26	139.8
Total			373.2
As % of Market Capitalisation — (US$ 11.02 Bil)			3.4%

4. Issuing Details Of Funds

Name	Value	Manager	Underwriters	Year End	Ends	Type
Korea Trust	$25m	DITC	Merrill Lynch	Jun	—	Open
Korea Int'l Trust	$25m	KITC	Credit Swisse -First Boston	Mar	2001	Open
Korea Fund	$100m	Scudders	First Boston	Mar	—	Closed
Korea Growth Trust	$30m	CITC	Jardine Fleming Sec	Dec	2005	Open
Seoul Trust	$30m	DITC	Prudential Bache	May	2005	Open
Seoul Int'l Trust	$30m	KITC	Vickers da Costa /Baring Brothers	Jun	2005	Open

NOTES
1. KITC — Korea Investment Trust Company
   DITC — Daehan Investment Trust Company
   CITC — Citizens Investment Trust Company
2. KT and KIT originally US$15m each but expanded by $10m at end of 1983.
3. Korea Fund was originally US$60 million, but was increased by $40 million in May 1986.

5. Investment Trust Companies

	Shrhldrs Equity Dec 84	Profit Yr to 31Dec 84	Funds Managed US$ Mil	Staff	Branches	Funds Under Management Int'l	Bond	Equity
KITC	55.0	9.9	2,300	1,134	23	2	14	14
DITC	56.7	8.8	2,100	1,000	24	2	12	17
CITC	15.2	1.2	700	490	16	1	12	9

Source: W.I. Carr

are big, along with the securities houses. Brokers describe the investment trusts and the short-term investment finance companies (money market operators in effect) as a "tremendous force" in the market especially the investment trusts which can (and do) invest up to 35% of their total assets in the stockmarket. (These are not to be confused with the Korea Securities Finance Corp (KFSI) which exists to provide margin financing for securities transactions, something which securities houses do too).

There are nine major fund management companies, though only three — Korea Investment Trust Co (KITC), Daehan Investment Trust Co (DITC) and Citizens Investment Trust Management Co (CITMC) — specialise in investment trust business. The remaining six companies are in the merchant banking business. The total assets of these three funds at the end of 1985 amounted to Won 6,351 billion, of which Won 5,232 billion was represented by bond funds and Won 1,1184 billion by stock (ordinary share) funds. This reflects yet again the predominance of the bond market in terms of size in Korea. In fact, the big-three trusts accounted for 43% of all bond holdings in Korea by the end of 1985.

These three funds are responsible for managing much of what foreign money has come into the Korean stockmarket so far. (It is worth noting that the US$250 million or so which has come to Korea via this route pales against the total US$7.4 billion capitalisation of the KSE at the end of 1985 — and of course is minute compared to South Korea's more than US$45 billion of foreign borrowings from banks and export credit agencies).

KITC operates Korea International Trust (KIT), a fund of US$25 million, and the Seoul International Trust (SIT), a US$30 million, vehicle with a 20% bond component. DITC has the US$25 million Korea Trust (KT) and the US$30 million Seoul Trust (ST), again with a 20% bond component. Citizens (CITMC) has the US$30 million Korea Growth Trust (KGT). These are all "open-ended (unit trust-type) funds for investment only by foreigners. In addition, there are two smaller funds intended for foreign and domestic investment. One is the Korea Small Companies Trust run by the KITC and the other is DITC's Korea Emerging Companies Trust. Both are of around US$6 million and both are "closed-ended" (mutual fund-type) funds listed on the KSE. Most of these funds are traded in the City of London via International Depository Receipts (IDRs) and have a variety of US, European and

Japanese managers and underwriters. Some of them, such at the KIT and the SIT, generally trade at a premium to net asset value, which is unusual for vehicles of this type. They are unusual animals in other respects too. Though nominally open-ended, they are in practice closed-ended and the managers have to wait for existing investors to redeem units before they can sell units to others. They do not expect the funds to become truly open ended — to have the normal freedom to issue new units at will — until the Korean stockmarket is fully opened to foreigners.

The best known of the Korea vehicles for foreign investment is the Korea Fund which was established in May 1984 and was listed three months later on the New York Stock Exchange (NYSE). It is managed by Scudder, Stevens & Clark in New York. This investment counselling firm also acts as investment advisor to the Korea Fund, with Daewoo Research Institute, a subsidiary of Daewoo Securities Co acting as advisor to the manager. The Korea Fund was launched at US$60 million but subsequently raised a further US$40 million during 1986 bringing its total funds up to US$100 million. The Korea Fund has been enormously successful from the view point of its promoters — so successful that according to one foreign broker (not involved with the Fund)," foreigners are rushing to buy the Korea Fund without having the first idea of what it is investing in."

Not surprisingly, plans are afoot for another Korea Fund-type of vehicle. This, though, will be listed in Europe rather than the US and will sell mainly to European investors. This European fund will be a much more Korean affair, though in the sense that Korean securities houses will probably have control of it. The local partners were expected to be Ssangyong Securities, Daeshin Securities, plus Dogsuh and Lucky. British merchant bank Baring Brothers and US investment bank Merrill Lynch were hoping to be the foreign partners. Neither, however, appeared to be delighted with the idea that Koreans would want control of the management company and there were suggestions that the Korean securities houses might stuff the new fund full of the stocks they were anxious to offload themselves. For their part, the Koreans argued in return that they need to have the inside track on management of such an international fund so that they could gain the necessary experience needed to manage foreign money in the Korean market.

Given Korea's reputation for horse-trading in business (and for face-saving), it seemed likely that some deal would ultimately be worked out that satisfies both foreign and local partners in the European Fund. Seoul, in any case, has to have regard for foreign feelings on such issues because of the anxiety now by Korean securities houses to set up representative offices in London and elsewhere. The European Fund seemed likely to be greeted as enthusiastically by investors, just as its predecessor the Korea Fund was. But whether the foreign investors love affair with Korean stocks will continue to burn with such ardour in the future if it is not requited by a full opening of the Korean Stock Exchange, is a matter of some doubt. Korea could be in danger of playing too hard to get.

Basic Data:

Stock Exchange building in Seoul

Official Exchange Index

The Composite index and several sectorial indices are published daily. Each index starts from 100, setting January 4th, 1980 as the base day.

The Composite index: Minimum in 1985 : 131.40 (20/5/1985)
Maximum in 1985 : 163.37 (26/12/1985)
26/12/1985 : 163.37

Types of shares

All Korean shares have a nominal value, and may be either bearer or registered shares. The equity instruments most commonly traded in the securities markets in Korea are common shares and cumulative and participating preferred shares. Convertible bonds may also be listed on the Korea Stock Exchange. Shareholders of common shares are entitled to nominal voting rights, usually one vote per share.

Trading system

Share transactions on the stock exchange are effected through one of the 25 securities companies which act as brokers but may also buy and sell as principals. Once placed with the office of a securities company, a customer's order is electronically transmitted to the trading floor. The order is then submitted to an appropriate trading post by a floor representative of the member firm concerned. The exchange operates on a continuous trading basis under the principle of the double auction. An exchange employee acts as an auctioneer and determines the price by matching the best bids and offers. The opening prices are determined by all bids and offers submitted to the trading post in the first five minutes of the trading session. Trading in equities takes place in lots of 100 shares; the trading unit for bonds is normally Won 100,000 at par value. Trading of odd lots is not handled on the exchange.

Membership and Organisation

The Korea Stock Exchange is a non-profit corporation, whose capital stock is contributed by the government and 25 member firms.

Exchange transactions

Regular-way transactions	:	Settlement is due on the 3rd business day from the day of the transaction.
		Stocks, bonds traded in the last one hour in the afternoon session, and investment trust.
Cash transactions	:	Settlement is due on the day of the transaction.
		Bonds traded in the morning session and first one hour in the afternoon session.

Brokerage rates

Stocks: 0.7 — 0.9% of the sales value.
Bonds and investment trust: 0.3% of the sales value.

Taxation

Corporate tax	:	20-30% for the listed companies, and 33% for the large unlisted companies.
Dividend income tax	:	Dividend from the listed companies: — 10% final withholding tax for minority shareholders, and 10% withholding tax and taxation on aggregate income for majority shareholders.

Dividend from the unlisted companies:
— 25% withholding tax and taxation on aggregate income.

Securities transfer tax : Tax for the listed securities: 0.2%.
Tax for the unlisted securities: 0.5%.

Restrictions regarding investment in Korea securities for foreign investors

Only with the permission of the Ministry of Finance. Taxation on income depends upon international tax agreements between Korea and the country of residence of the foreign investors.

Taiwan: Not yet for Widows and Orphans

The Taiwan Stock Exchange, in the words of one foreign fund manager, is "not the place to put your life savings if you're a widow or orphan." He was being polite. A local banker, citing what he called the "extraordinary high turnover ratios" on the Taiwan Stock Exchange, declared that the market is "more of a gambling game than a vehicle for serious investment." Stock turnover on the exchange is certainly very high. It far outstrips that on any other Asian stock exchange (except for Tokyo) and exceeds by three or four times the level of Hongkong, which is a bigger market by far in terms of the number of stocks listed and their aggregate market value. The Taiwan market managed to turn over some US$8.3 billion worth of equities in 1984, for instance — nearly three times the amount turned over in either the Seoul or Singapore stockmarkets, which again are much bigger in terms of the number of companies listed.

Some might argue that this high turnover and the (characteristically Chinese) speculative flavour of the Taiwan market are the ideal combination to ensure the liquidity needed by buyers and sellers of stock. But that would be missing the point. The lack of meaningful information on corporate performance in Taiwan means that stock selection is often little more scientific than sticking a pin blindly into a racing tip list. Gambling is the name of the game and stocks are treated much like casino chips by local investors.

Yet, there is a strange dichotomy between the speculative nature of the Taiwan stockmarket and the strict regulatory framework surrounding it. Price movement restrictions mean that share prices are not permitted to move up or down more than 5% a day on the previous day's close (2% either way for bonds). This is obviously an obstacle to free trading, though transactions can be done outside the market.

Apart from the preponderance of individual investors in the stockmarket — as distinct from investment institutions which give markets elsewhere more stability — there is a paucity of listed companies. This accounts for why the same relatively few stocks change hands so often 'thus boosting turnover' in order to satisfy demand for gaming chips. It also means that many of the companies responsible for Taiwan's much-lauded "economic miracle" are not represented in the stockmarket. The securities authorities are trying to remedy this — fostering more corporate disclosure, less insider dealing, a greater institutional presence, and bringing more companies to market. But the pace of reform has been slow so far.

History will show the arrival of foreign investors in the market to be the chief catalyst for reform. This is ironic, because for years the Taiwan authorities kept the stockmarket completely closed to outside investment, fearing (they claimed) a disruptive impact on the market. In reality, long-term institutional investment from the West promises to give the Taiwan market a breadth, depth and stability which it has lacked for years and which has discouraged some of the bigger corporate concerns in Taiwan from seeking a listing.

But for the moment, the Taiwan market is very much a sideshow compared to the spectacular performance of the economy, the emergence of nearby and to Hongkong as a regional and international stockmarket. One reason for this is that, unlike Hongkong, Taiwan retains strict foreign exchange controls and restrictions on capital movements. Another is that the fortress mentality of Taiwan, besieged as it feels itself to be by neighbouring mainland China, has excluded the foreign influences which enabled other stockmarkets in the region to develop to international size.

Unlike those markets which developed as a result of foreign colonial links, not only in Hongkong but also in Singapore and Malaysia, Taiwan's stockmarket is very much a home-grown affair. The market had its origins in 1953, four years after General Chiang Kai Shek's Kuo Min Tang regime (fleeing before the Communist armies of Mao Tse Tung) arrived in Taiwan. At that time the KMT government embarked on a programme of land reform — known as "Land to the Tiller" — to help boost food production and to free agricultural labour for industry. Landlords dispossessed of land under the scheme were compensated with Land Bonds as well as with shares in government-owned enterprises such as Taiwan Cement, Taiwan Paper and others. These securities, worth some NT$2.2 billion in all (at 1953 values) joined the government's

"Patriot Bonds" in circulating among the public. There was no stockmarket at the time, so trade was carried on by a number of brokerage houses — a kind of early over-the-counter market.

It was not until 1958 that the government decided the time had come to establish a formal securities market — for the purpose of "providing sufficient funds for future economic growth." Teams were sent to the US and Japan to study securities market development. But rather than set up a formal stockmarket first and then regulate it later, Taiwan took the opposite path and established its own Securities and Exchange Commission (SEC) in 1960 to regulate securities transactions. The Taiwan Stock Exchange (TSE) came into being one year later — in 1961. This dirigiste approach has carried over to the present day, with the SEC maintaining a firm hold over the TSE.

The bureaucratic desire to channel entrepreneurial activity is also apparent in the structure of the Taiwan Stock Exchange. Instead of being funded by the stockbrokers (securities dealers) who operate it — on the basis of "seat money" — the TSE is a private

Table 35

TAIWAN STOCK EXCHANGE WEIGHTED STOCK INDEX

Source: "1985 SEC Statistics", Securities and Exchange Commission.

corporation whose stockholders are banks plus private and public companies. Thirteen of the 27 brokerage firms operating in the market are banks (which in turn are just about all government owned or controlled) while the other 14 are companies licensed to do securities business. There are additionally 12 "traders" — securities investment companies and trust companies.

The exchange is, as one insider puts it, very much "controlled by the government." Government control is exercised through the SEC, whch has itself been under the direct control of the Ministry of Finance since 1981. The US investment bank Prudential Bache, noted in the prospectus for a Taiwan investment-fund issue that most members of the TSE's board of directors were businessmen or representatives of financial institutions. "This is an unhealthy situation," commented Pru-Bache, "and the government should modify the Securities Transaction Law to require that one-third of the directors and supervisors be experts, scholars and prominent citizens in society."

The SEC chooses the top officials of the stock exchange — the shareholders electing the other directors and the chairman is chosen at "even higher" levels of government. This is a shorthand way of saying by the ruling KMT party. Everyone, including the TSE president, is subordinate to the chairman. Much depends upon the actual chairman as to how much power he wields.

But as in Singapore (another tightly-administered society), the desire by officials in Taiwan to be in control of the stockmarket does not mean that is in fact well regulated. Far from it. There are oddities and quirks — and sometimes abuses — in the operation of the market which foreign investors would do well to be aware of. These do not, of course, necessarily outweigh the potential rewards of investing in one of East Asia's fastest growing economies, but they do caution against any over-simplistic assessment of Taiwan as one of the "new Japans" of the investment world.

In fact, Taiwan is in some ways one of the old Japan's of the region. Years of occupation of the then island of Formosa by Japan left the firm footprint of Japan on Taiwan's financial system. The financing of industry is heavily dominated by the (mainly state-owned) commercial banks, as it was in Japan for a long time and still is to some extent. The result in Taiwan has been relative under-development of the stockmarket and an almost total lack of development in the bond market.

By the end of 1985 there were 127 companies listed on the TSE, which is the only stock exchange in Taiwan. This is less than a third of the number (455) listed in South Korea, an economy which is only 25% bigger than Taiwan's. Growth in the number of companies listed has simply not kept pace with the expansion in the economy. To some extent this reflects the situation whereby a great deal of Taiwan's remarkable economic growth in recent years has been accounted for by relatively few companies, operating in export markets such as the United States. But it also has to do with the fact that a good deal of economic activity is concentrated in the hands of state-controlled firms which do not enjoy a stock exchange listing. Taiwan's industrial base is represented too, by small to medium-sized companies, to a far greater extent than is South Korea where the so called Chaebols — roughly equivalent to Japan's huge Zaibatsu groups — are predominant.

Table 36

The 20 Largest First Section Listed Companies	By capitalisation, Based on Closing Price 1985 30th November NT$
Taiwan Cement	24.00
Asia Cement	21.90
Wei-Chuan	20.60
Wey-Wang	20.40
Formosa Plastic	29.10
Nan-Ya Plastic	28.30
USI Far East	26.90
China Gulf	28.10
Far East Textile	17.20
Taroko Textile	16.30
Taiwan Glass	28.90
Tong-Yuan	29.00
Taiwan Fluorescent	27.00
Sampo	14.30
Kolin	24.10
Nan-Chow Chemical	28.90
Yuen-Fong Yu Paper	26.50
Cathay Construction	26.30
Pacific Construction	15.50
Far East Department	18.40

Source: TSE

There are a dozen major corporations, such as public utilities and other enterprises, which are owned by the state. The only one which has a stock exchange listing is China Steel Corp. and even then the shares are hardly ever traded. This relatively large government preemption of industrial activity is justified on the ground that these are activities in which private investors are unable or unwilling to take part. There is probably some element of truth in this, given the traditional Chinese predilection for small business but the "government knows best" philosophy (again akin to Singapore) is another factor.

What stocks are listed on the TSE represent a broad range of industrial and commercial activity. But in terms of turnover, the action tends to be concentrated in textiles (companies like Chung Shing Textile and Taiwan Fabric), electricals (Tatung), plastics (Nan Ya Plastic and China Gulf Plastic), pulp and paper (Chen Loong), automobiles (Yue Loong Motor) and construction (Kuo-chan Development). That is in the so-called First Section of the market. In the Second Section (in which different listing criteria apply) the big — turnover sectors are again textiles (Hualon-Teijran), paper and pulp (Taiwan Paper) and a handful of others in the electronics and mining industries. Banks figure in both sections of the exchange but, judged by turnover, they are not popular stocks with investors.

Why are there not more stocks listed in the TSE? According to exchange officials there are at least 300 more companies not presently listed which would meet the requirements if they were to apply. Yet, on average, only around six new listings a year are granted (though in 1985 the total did rise to ten, counting both listings and approvals). There are three basic reasons why Taiwan companies are reluctant to seek a stockmarket listing. In order of importance these are: first, their dislike of having to reveal too much about their corporate or financial affairs to outside share-holders; secondly, the fact that they have been weaned on a tradition of (short-term) bank borrowing and, thirdly, the relatively low valuation they are permitted to put on their assets for purposes of marketing them to the public via the stock exchange.

The first is a matter of deep-seated psychology and it is common to Chinese entrepreneurs throughout the region. Hongkong, for instance, has managed to achieve a reasonable degree of disclosure of financial information by listed companies but any suggestion that proprietors or directors should disclose their shareholdings and dealings for long met with fierce resistance. Such requirements do not appear even to have been contemplated in Taiwan yet, and even getting companies to reveal (reliable) routine financial information is a very real problem. Things are, however, improving slowly.

Present TSE rules require all listed companies to submit annual and half-yearly financial statements of results, though, this does not yet include the need to consolidate subsidiaries' results in the parent company accounts. Thus, published accounts are often misleading, with assets or liabilities hidden outside the parent company. But consolidated accounts will be required by the SEC in "due course." Another problem is that the Certified Public Accountants (CPAs) who are required to audit company accounts have in some cases a reputation for being what can politely be termed unprofessional. The Examination Yuan (one of the five branches of government in Taiwan along with the legislature, executive, judiciary and "control" branch) has the duty of licensing CPAs and there are widespread allegations that political favour weighs as heavily in the balance as professional capability. Retired military personnel, ex-judges or other officials due for retirement or relocation, may wind up as CPAS, it is often claimed.

Table 37

Listed Company Shares — 1985

	First Section	Second Section	Full Delivery Section	Total
Number of Listed Companies at year end	65	39	23	127
Number of Listed Stocks at year end	66	41	23	130
Trading Value for year (NT$ million)	152,375	39,138	3,715	195,228
Trading Volume for year (million of shares)	9,472	3,989	1,073	14,534
Market Capitalisation at year end (NT$ million)	377,039	36,909	1,758	415,706

Source: Edited by NITC research staff, based on "Status of Securities Listed on Taiwan Stock Exchange" published by TSE, January to December 1985.

This is denied by the SEC, which nevertheless allows that there is plenty of room for improvement in financial disclosure. A senior official assured the author early in 1986 that the SEC is "working towards improving standards of financial disclosure and accounting principles." He claimed that the "majority" of CPAs currently auditing accounts are properly qualified but noted that there was a "continuing review" of the examination system going on. To give the SEC credit, it has recognised the fact that lack of disclosure and reliable financial information is a major obstacle to investor confidence in the Taiwan stock market. By pushing for reform, the SEC is trying to force traditional family-controlled companies to modernise their management. And, once the principle of obligatory disclosure has been established, crossing the next hurdle of stock exchange listing will not be so frightening for companies which at present are able to keep themselves to themselves.

If this is the stick which will eventually beat more companies toward going public, there is also a considerable carrot now being dangled before them. The advent of increased foreign investor interest in the Taiwan stockmarket and the launching of a number of special investment trusts aimed at foreigners is already having the effect of driving up share prices. It should thus become more attractive in time for private companies to market their assets via a stock issue to investors.

Table 38

Trading Volume

Total trading volume for both equities and bonds on the Exchange in 1985 totalled NT$196 billion, of which less than 1 per cent, consisted of bonds. Listed bonds include 35 Government and 2 corporate bonds.

Listed Bonds — 1985

	Government Bonds	Corporate Bonds	Total
Number	35	2	37
Issuing Amount	74,645	400	75,045
Total Outstanding Value (NT$million)	54,750	150	54,900
Total Trading Value (NT$ million)	1,078	—	1,078

Source: "Year Book of Financial Statistics of the ROC, 1985", MOF.

They may well be more anxious to do so, anyway, in the wake of the so-called Cathay affair in 1985 when the collapse of a leading financial group and the subsequent after-shock led to a rapid withdrawal of bank and finance company loans to many medium-sized companies. With these lifelines withdrawn, many of them had to go to the government to be baled out and it is unlikely that the lesson about over-dependence upon debt and under-availability of equity was lost on them. Taiwan companies as a whole may not be so highly geared as are their South Korean counterparts, but they are certainly highly leveraged compared with Western companies.

The third problem over Taiwan companies going to market — the undervaluation of their assets upon listing and consequently the relatively high cost of equity capital — is more intractable. Stockmarket sources say that while companies can nowadays list their assets at a premium to book value (for purposes of deciding their worth upon flotation) these premia are still restricted. Share underwriters use a combination of asset value and earnings to decide the worth of a company in Taiwan, but the local SEC will usually not put its chop of approval on the prospectus without reducing the underwriter's valuation. Again, as in Singapore (where new issues are often astronomically over-subscribed, reflecting their relative under-valuation) the authorities in Taiwan are loath to trust the market's judgement. The SEC, however, disclaims any knowledge of interference. "Issue prices are decided by the company and its underwriter. We only check the facts," an SEC official assured the author.

If more companies do not come to market quite soon, there is a danger of the stockmarket becoming almost irrelevant to the Taiwan economy. That ecomony has been one of the fastest growing in the world during the past ten years and yet not only has the number of companies listed grown slowly (only 25 were added to the list between 1980 and 1985) but also the amount of new money raised through the stock exchange by those companies which are listed has been modest. New issues for cash (as distinct from "free" issues by way of stock dividends) have averaged around NT$5 billion a year (or US$131 million at current exchange rates) over the past ten years (excluding 1980 when an uncharacteristic surge of new issues for cash raised nearly NT$21 billion). By contrast, outstanding loans from banks to private-sector companies in Taiwan have much more than doubled over the past ten years —

from some NT$200 billion to around NT$530 billion. Total debt which private companies owe to banks is also well over double the issued capital (NT$218 billion) of all companies listed on the stock exchange.

Measures like giving companies a 15% reduction in business tax if they agree to list their shares on the stock market, and exempting shareholders from capital gains on listed company shares, are going to have only a limited effect in boosting the size of the Taiwan stockmarket. So too, probably will the imposition of capital gains tax on transactions in unlisted companies' shares, which are quite frequent in Taiwan.

Meanwhile, the size of companies listing on the TSE is getting bigger nowadays. They used to come with as little as US$10 million of paid-up capital but Formosa Fibre was listed fairly recently with capital of US$250 million. Even so, the problem, as expressed by one TSE official, is that, "we do not see any large — world scale — enterprises being formed in Taiwan." Taiwan needs new company formation on a large scale (plus technology transfer) if it is to survive competition from South Korea and other NICs (Newly Industrialising Countries) in Asia and elsewhere. This official expressed the hope that the exchange would have 300 stocks listed by around 1995. But that looks very ambitious given the present rate of new listings.

Table 39

Taiwan Stock Exchange Yearly Turnover Values

Year	Stocks (NT$ million)	Bonds (NT$ million)	Total (NT$ million)	Total (US$ million)[1]
1972	54,051	144	54,195	1,355
1975	130,336	1,485	131,821	3,474
1980	162,113	1,310	163,423	4,545
1981	209,217	404	209,621	5,547
1982	133,875	590	134,465	3,448
1983	363,845	3,913	367,758	9,121
1984	324,475	937	325,412	8,228
1985	195,228	1,078	196,306	4,926

Source: "Year Book of Finance Statistics of the ROC, 1985", MOF.

The fact that Taiwan is not getting new industries at the rate it needs has to do in part with enterpreneurs' reluctance to move out of the profitable milch-cow industries (fibres and textiles and heavy goods, plus consumer electronics which have brought them much profit in export markets) and into new, high technology-based industries. This may have to do with Taiwan's current unease about its future vis-a-vis an emergent Mainland China but it also has to do with the fact that the local capital markets, including of course the stockmarket, do not provide an efficient channel yet for export earnings to be channelled back into new industries. That is also one reason why Taiwan has built up such massive (around US$40 billion) foreign-exchange reserves in recent times.

Unfortunately, the SEC (which speaks with the voice of the Ministry of Finance — the second most powerful economic organisation in Taiwan after the Central Bank of China) does not appear to see the task of enlarging the size of the market through new listings as its major priority. Under its present chairman (as of 1986), Shen Pei-ling, a former computer expert at the MoF, the SEC appears intent on pushing through total computerisation of all dealings on the stock exchange, much to the dismay of most exchange officials.

The TSE has been instructed by the SEC to computerise all dealings, not only in the smaller, Category B stocks (which are already computerised) but in the much bigger Category A stocks too. Some further explanation of the difference between the two categories is needed at this point. Categories A and B are also known as First and Second Sections respectively. A Third Section was added in July 1984 but so far no stocks have been listed under it. The criteria for paid-up capital, pre-tax and net profits, net worth, number of shareholders and so on, are different under the two main categories.

If a First Section company fails to maintain the requirements for a period of two consecutive years, it is placed in the Second Section, and likewise Second Section companies can be promoted to the first division. Firms are not de-listed if they fail to meet the requirements on them but are relegated to a strange sort of limbo where they are designated as "full delivery" shares. This is rather akin to the practice in Tokyo of shifting stocks which can no longer meet the requirements of the big board onto the unlisted or over-the-counter securities market. (Taiwan has had an over-the-counter

market since 1982 but at present trading on this market is limited
to government bonds, corporate bonds and bank debentures).

As at the end of 1985, there were 65 listed companies in the First
Section (with 66 stocks listed), 39 in the Second Section (with 41
stocks listed) and 23 in the Full Delivery Section. Category A is
obviously where the action is. During 1985, class-A companies
turned over 9.5 billion shares with a total trading value of NT$152
billion and a total capitalisation of NT$377 billion. Class-B
companies turned over just under 4 billion shares with a trading
value of NT$39 billion and a capitalisation of NT$37 billion. The
Full Delivery Section turned over just over a billion shares with a
trading value of NT$3.7 billion and a capitalisation of NT$1.76
billion. The turnover in this latter section was remarkably high in
relation both to number of stocks and their capitalisation.

The move to computerise dealings in the First as well as the
Second Section is thus going to have a major impact on the Taiwan
Stock Exchange. It could, as one exchange source put it, turn the
whole place into a "morgue." Already the computer room where
category B stocks are traded has an air of almost total somnolence
even when the main (category B) market is enjoying a bull market.
Orders are simply matched by computer for B stocks (plus bank
stocks listed in the First Section) whereas the main stock exchange
floor — in the Young-Teh Building at the corner of Nan Hai Road
and Roosevelt Road — is often a hive of activity. Each of the

Table 40

Shareholder Characteristic of Listed Companies							
	1965	1970	1980	1981	1982	1983	1984
			Percentage of capital				
Government and Govern-							
ment Agencies	43.0	20.2	25.5	27.6	28.6	28.9	26.0
Financial Institutions .	2.9	8.9	4.7	4.6	6.2	8.5	9.8
Foreign Institutions ...	1.2	3.1	3.5	3.6	2.4	2.4	3.0
Corporation and other							
Juristic Persons	8.6	10.5	12.5	13.7	12.7	13.1	14.9
Individual Investors ..	44.3	57.3	53.8	50.5	50.1	47.1	46.3
Total	100.0	100.0	100.0	100.0	100.0	100.0	100.0

Source: "Year Book of Financial Statistics of the ROC, 1985", MOF.

brokers or traders has a dozen or so representatives on the exchange floor and orders are executed by trading clerks. Share prices flash on an electronic display board linked to brokers' offices and there is usually much arm waving and scurrying about.

All this could change if the SEC has its way and all orders are computer-matched. Originally the target date was the end of 1986 but this appears to have slipped somewhat. Taipei could become the only stockmarket in the world (with the possible exception of Toronto) to kick stockbrokers off the floor completely. There is more than just an obsession with hi-tech behind all this. Basically the bureaucrats at the SEC do not trust brokers. They are convinced that the broker or trader on the floor has more scope to manipulate orders — by buying in from a seller and then adding on a margin before passing the stock on to a buyer — than would be possible

Table 41

	Trading Turnover for 1985		Market Capitalisation at 31st December, 1985	
	NT$ million	%	NT$ million	%
Cement Industry	10,989	5.63	32,231	7.75
Food Industry	11,985	6.14	13,337	3.21
Plastics Industry	19,339	9.91	52,869	12.72
Chemical Industry	11,621	5.95	7,346	1.77
Textile Industry	54,115	27.72	67,847	16.32
Electric Machinery and Machinery Industry	12,173	6.23	15,580	3.75
Electric Appliance, Wire and Cable Industry	12,864	6.59	13,514	3.25
Glass and Porcelain Industry	4,350	2.23	6,297	1.51
Paper and Pulp Industry	11,552	5.92	20,542	4.94
Steel Industry	2,959	1.52	60,511	14.56
Rubber Industry	5,475	2.80	3,441	0.83
Automobile Industry	9,438	4.83	6,783	1.63
Electronic Industry	7,797	3.99	3,555	0.86
Construction and Plywood Industry	10,105	5.18	10,299	2.48
Ship Transport Industry	404	0.21	114	0.03
Tourist Industry	1,900	0.97	2,186	0.53
Bank and Insurance Industry	5,178	2.65	96,057	23.11
Department Store and Trade Industry	1,230	0.63	2,597	0.62
Others	1,752	0.90	600	0.13
Total	195,226	100.00	415,706	100.00

Industry Analysis:

under a computerised system. Brokers in Taiwan are licensed to act as middlemen only, while traders buy and sell only for their own account, but the SEC does not believe that such separation of functions is adhered to. (Reforms evisaged for the future in Taiwan would open the registration of traders and brokers to the public and would allow a new class of dealers, able to act both as brokers and traders). In point of fact, the fully computerised market could well become more subject to manipulation than it is at present. If local brokers suspect that a major buyer (such as one of the newly-created foreign or local investment trusts) is in the market and they choose to collude on their offer price for a particular stock, there could well be an in-built basis for a false market. The SEC does not see things this way. A senior official there declared to the author his belief that "machines are more efficient than manual markets" and that computerisation of the Taiwan market will "decrease manipulation."

This official also claimed that manipulation in the Taiwan stockmarket is "not too serious compared with other countries." Asked which countries he had in mind, he singled out the United States where insider dealing is a "major industry" in his view. A new Securities Industry Act for Taiwan is before the Executive Yuan (government branch) and is expected to become law in 1987. Among other things, this should outlaw insider dealing, providing jail sentences of up to five years and forcing inside traders who have profited by their special knowledge to compensate their "victims" financially.

There is one possibly unique bit of manipulation which goes on in the Taiwan stockmarket. As noted above, there are a number of companies (24 as of early 1986) which are classified as requiring Full Delivery, in other words shares must be delivered and payment made on the spot when the stocks of any of these companies are dealt in. It is argued that a listed company needs to be able to continue trading of its shares even if it has fallen from grace and no longer qualifies for trading in the main sections of the stock exchange. Otherwise shareholders would be locked into their investment. Some of the companies in Taiwan's Full Delivery section have not simply fallen from grace however; they have stopped doing business altogether. The bizarre phenomenon exists of active trading in the shares of companies which are bankrupt in all but name. Some have sought the protection of the courts against their creditors but have not been declared formally bankrupt. Their factories may have been sold and the nameplate taken down — but they still exist as far as the stock exchange is concerned.

Why, especially when it can be assumed that the hapless original shareholders have long ago cut their losses and moved on to other things? The answer is that syndicates of wealthy investors have devised an ingenious way of making money out of these ghost stocks. They will typically buy a parcel of shares in the defunct company and sell to another syndicate, which will then sell it back again, and so on. This game of pass the parcel goes on until unsuspecting smaller investors decide they want to get in on the action and start buying too. Once they do, the syndicates bale out, leaving the small fry to burn as the stocks fall to their inevitable doom. The SEC has tried to clean up this particular bit of nastiness in the past, and this resulted in SEC officials being roughed up — presumably by syndicate hit-men. The SEC denied all knowledge of

Table 42

Bond Market

Volumes of outstanding bonds

31st December	Listed Public Bonds		Listed Corporate Bonds		Total Listed Bonds	
	NT$ million	US$ million	NT$ million	US$ million	NT$ million	US$ million
1975	10,142	266	2,678	71	12,820	337
1980	19,902	553	3,050	85	22,952	638
1981	22,282	588	3,100	82	25,382	670
1982	38,462	969	3,700	94	42,162	1,063
1983	43,662	1,084	2,250	56	45,912	1,140
1984	34,822	881	800	19	35,622	900

Source: 1984 SEC Statistics

Average annual yields for issues of public and corporate bonds

Year	Public Bonds (%)	Corporate Bonds (%)
1980	11.35	11.85
1981	11.97	12.86
1982	12.06	14.07
1983	11.51	14.24
1984	10.79	13.38

Source: 1984 SEC Statistics

any such incidents to the author. Losing face is not something that Taiwan officials like any more than do Chinese elsewhere.

The Taiwan stockmarket is peculiarly susceptible to syndicate activity because of the relative lack of institutional investors in the market. By the same token, the small investor occupies an inordinately important role in the market. This explains the sensitivity of officials to offending the small investor. Reliable sources retail shocking tales of the way in which certain financial journalists in Taiwan are able to hold SEC officials and others to ransom. Rather than have a journalist write something about him which will damage his reputation in the eyes of profit-obsessed local investors — even if this is simply carrying out his duty — an official will grant favours (which can include pecuniary benefits) to the commentator concerned. Again, this is a very sensitive subject upon which the SEC denies all knowledge. But there seems little doubt that such abuses are quite widespread.

As one foreign investment bank noted: "Most of the investors in the [Taiwan] stockmarket are individuals; institutional investors hold less than 20% of total shares. This indicates that the local stockmarket is vulnerable to speculation and manipulation. The establishment of domestic investment-trust companies to funnel capital of small investors into the market in a proper manner is needed."

According to SEC officials, individual investors account for 45% of total trading on the TSE. The other 55% is accounted for by securities companies, banks, trust companies and other institutional investors. Nevertheless, the SEC admits that even its (conservative) estimate of individual investor activity points to room for improvement. Individual investors' contribution to turnover needs to be reduced to 35-40% of the total, says the SEC, noting that in Tokyo the level is nearer 25% (but also that Tokyo is now anxious to increase its level of individual investor participation).

If there is one thing upon which all shades of opinion — both local and foreign alike — in the Taiwan market are agreed, it is the need to develop a sound fund-management and advisory industry to increase institutional participation, iron out the volatility in the market and put it on a sounder footing for the future. One manifestation of this volatility is that the TSE is capable of turning over virtually its whole capitalisation in some years — 1983 and 1984 were good examples — whereas in others (such as 1985)

Table 43

Government Enterprises

In 1985, Government consumption accounted for 16.6% of GNP. In addition to normal Government services, the Government has invested in a number of enterprises such as public utilities, other key enterprises which private individuals or organisations are either unwilling or unable to undertake, and enterprises operated with pooled capital partially provided by private individuals or organisations. Government enterprises, operated under the supervision of the Ministry of Economic Affairs, include:-

Taiwan Power Company	Solely responsible for the development and supply of power in Taiwan.
Chinese Petroleum Corporation	Exploration, production, refining, distribution and marketing of gas and oil.
Taiwan Sugar Corporation	Operates 25 sugar mills, three alcohol distilleries, three by product factories, 32 pig farms, two cattle ranches and other activities.
Taiwan Fertilizer Company	Produces urea, ammonium sulphate, nitrochalk, calcium superphosphate and compound fertilisers.
Taiwan Aluminium Corporation	The sole primary aluminium producer in Taiwan.
Taiwan Metal Mining Corporation	Exploits mineral resources and conducts smelting operations. Production includes gold, silver and electrolytic copper.
China Shipbuilding Corporation	Shipbuilding, ship repairing and machinery manufacture.
Taiwan Machinery Manufacturing Corporation	Manufactures heavy industrial equipment.
China Steel Corporation (listed)	Steel mill operations.
BES Engineering Corporation	Civil and building construction, industrial district and community development.
China Petrochemical Development Corporation	Petrochemicals manufacturing subsidiary, is Petroleum Corporation of China.
Taiwan Alkali Company	Subsidiary of China Petroleum Corporation producing caustic soda, liquid chlorine and other chemicals.
China Phosphate Industrial Corporation	Produces dicalcium phosphate and related products.

turnover can slump to less than half the market capitalisation. Likewise, the volume of stocks traded are prone to sudden spurts and lags.

A modern fund-management industry is in the making. It consist of a pioneer group, International Investment Trust or IIT set up in August 1983 by overseas and local interests, plus three similar funds which were either newly under way or about to be at the time of writing (mid-1986). In addition, eight investment advisor's licences have been given out to various firms and a couple of foreign merchant banks have set up offices — little more than listening posts at this early stage — in Taipei.

The trouble is that these new groups are in a sense "all dressed up with nowhere to go." As Mark Mobius, president of IIT put it to the author early in 1986, "there is a shortage of stock here for the serious investor." He was not exaggerating. Out of the 127 companies listed on the TSE, maybe only 30 are suitable by virtue of their size and marketability for inclusion in a portfolio designed for a major institutional investor, especially one like IIT which has to answer both to its own shareholders abroad and to the overseas holders of units in its funds. There is an obvious danger in these circumstances of IIT and the other fund-management groups setting off a bull market when they enter the ring and causing the price of any particular stock to rise or fall sharply whenever they indulge in a spot of portfolio diversification. It also means that smaller investors in Taiwan are likely to spend most of their time in future trying to second-guess the tactics of the new funds.

Mobius sympathises with the SEC for being less eager than the TSE to list more companies at present, pointing to the fact that there are a score or so listed already which "should not be" (the so-called Full Delivery stocks). Rather than simply enlarging the list of companies quoted, Mobius has been urging the authorities to adopt a more rational approach to the development of the capital markets as a whole in Taiwan and the stockmarket in particular. This is a criticism common to various foreign observers of the Taiwan scene who complain that "unlike the South Koreans who have a definite plan [for capital market development] the Chinese [in Taiwan] are ad-hoc in their approach."

These critics had a rare opportunity to air their grievances and suggestions publically in 1985 when they were invited to make submissions to an Economic Reform Committee set up under

Table 44

Stock Categories

As at the beginning of 1984 the Exchange had three categories of stocks, those listed in the First Section, those listed in the Second Section and those listed in the Full Delivery Section. New regulations promulgated on 1st July, 1984 added a Third Section but no companies have yet been listed under that Section. Requirements for the First and Second Sections are as follows:-

	First Section	Second Section
Paid-Up Capital	Not less than NT$200 million.	Not less than NT$100 million.
Pre-Tax Net Profit and Operating Income	(1) Minimum over 10 per cent. of paid-up capital for past two years, OR (2) minimum NT$40 million, being not less than 5 per cent. of year end paid up capital for past two years, OR (3) either (1) or (2) above in each of the last two years.	(1) Over 10 per cent. of paid-up capital in the most recent year, OR (2) an average of not less than 5 per cent. in the two most recent fiscal years, with the most recent year greater than the previous years.
Net Worth/Total Asset Ratio	One-third or more for preceding year.	Not Applicable.
Current/Assets/ Current Liabilities Ratio	Over 100 per cent.	Not Applicable.
Number of Shareholders	Over 2,000.	Over 1,000.
Distribution	Not less than 1,000 shareholders should each hold from 1,000 to 50,000 shares and the total number of shares held by those shareholders should be more than 20 per cent. of the total issued shares or 20 million shares.	Not less than 500 shareholders should each hold from 1,000 to 50,000 shares and the total number of shares held by those shareholders should be more than 20 per cent. of the total issued shares or 10 million shares.

government auspices to work out a long-term strategy for economic and financial development. The committee was headed by the reform-minded C.C. Chao, former head of China Steel and now head of the Council for Economic Planning and Development. Chao was all for extending the life of the committee but apparently ran up against opposition from conservatives like Prime Minister Yu Kuo Hua (who is a former head of the central bank) on the ground that "too much democracy" can be a bad thing. Whether the committee will prove to be a real instrument for reform or merely a cosmetic exercise in consultation, remains to be seen.

A good intermediate step toward strengthening the stockmarket in Taiwan would be to encourage many more local companies to issue bonds initially rather than equities. Presently, only a handful of corporate bonds are in issue and when companies such as Asia Cement or Far Eastern Textile do issue them they are bought by banks and kept in their vaults until maturity. A few trust companies buy them too, but there is no active secondary market. Statistics for 1985 show only two corporate bonds in issue with an outstanding value of only NT$150 million. Likewise, there were only 35 government bonds listed (outstanding value NT$54.8 billion) reflecting the central government's reluctance to run a budget deficit.

Promoting a corporate bond market would have the effect of stabilising the financial position of many companies, weaning them away from the potentially dangerous dependence upon short-term bank financing and replacing that with longer-term debt. Issuance of corporate bonds would also not involve the loss of control which so many company proprietors in Taiwan seem to fear. Nor would it necessarily involve the same degree of financial disclosure demanded in the prospectus for a full public flotation. But it would provide investors in the Taiwan market with a new set of financial instruments to help expand and stablise their portfolios. It would also make known to investors — local and foreign alike — the names of companies which are at present strictly private, in every sense of the term.

The collapse of the Cathay Group in 1985 badly affected confidence in the stockmarket. This was largely because of the widespread practice of cross-guarantees on corporate debt in Taiwan under the present system. Thus when Pao Ling Paper (a Cathay-linked company) got into trouble so did Lien Hwa, an industrial gases group with an apparently clean and debt-free balance sheet. The cross-guarantees had not been disclosed. Increased reliance on public bond finance (plus better disclosure) would reassure investors worried about the prospect of more Cathay-type crashes and reverberations through the stockmarket.

A better-structured and more balanced capital market should emerge eventually in Taiwan, on the sock of the new fund — management industry. IIT was the first joint-venture (foreign and

Table 45

Investment Trusts

Kwang Hua Securities Investment and Trust Co.

Shareholders:	%
Ta-Hwa Investment Co. Ltd.	35
Huei-Hong Investment Co. Ltd.	28
Rue-Tai Investment Co. Ltd.	5
Pacific Leasing Co. Ltd.	2
Interallianz Bank Zurich A. G.	10
MIM (Asia Pacific) Holdings Ltd.	10
Hoare Govett Asia Ltd.	10
	100

National Investment Trust Co. (Cheng Hung)

C. C. Hong, Chairman Richard Hong, Vice President

Shareholders:	%
National Holding Co. Ltd.	21.2
Bank of Communications	10.0
Chinese Automobile Co. Ltd.	10.0
National Leasing Co.	10.0
Shanghai Commercial & Savings Bank	7.5
Yu Fong	4.75
Shin Yi	4.75
Shiu Feng Chemical Products	3.0
National Capital Management Corp.	3.0
Richard Lu	1.0
K. C. Wang	1.0
Yuen Yu Enterprises	0.5
Prudential Bache Securities Co.	7.9
GT Management Asia	7.9
BT Foreign Investment Corp.	7.5
	100.0

Taiwan) investment group to be established. It has a broad range of local and overseas shareholders. In October 1983, IIT launched the Taiwan (ROC) Fund, at that time the only authorised vehicle for portfolio investment in the Taiwan stockmarket and the sole vehicle for investment by non-resident foreigners. The fund is listed on the London Stock Exchange, though not actually traded. Vickers da Costa, one of IIT's shareholders makes a secondary market in the shares.

The first issue by the fund raised US$41 million and an additional US$40 million was raised in December 1984. The fund has been successful and most investors are staying in for the long term. Few holders have redeemed their units and most are ploughing back their dividends. Anyone who bought the units in 1983 would have been approximately 40% better off two years later, in US dollar terms.

Three additional fund management groups have since been set up: Kwang Hua Securities Investment and Trust Co., National Investment Trust Co., and Chung Hwa Securities Investment Trust Co. All three, like IIT, have a broad spread of local and foreign shareholders. The first of the new three to go public was Kwang Hua with the launch of its Formosa Fund early in 1986. This US$25 million investment trust is traded overseas through Depositary Receipts issued by the Brussels office of Morgan Guaranty Trust Company of New York. Second to go was National Investment Trust Co. with its (also US$25 million) Taipei Fund — again traded via Depository Receipts issued through Morgan Guaranty in Brussels.

Chung Hwa (China) Securities Investment and Trust was expected to launch its fund around the end of 1986. The partners in Chung Hwa, especially Merrill Lynch, were said to be anxious to get approval for a US$60 million fund rather than the US$25 million fund granted to the other two groups, so that it could be listed in New York (anything less would not be viable). But it seemed likely the Taiwan SEC would want the third group to go with US$25 million initially, like the other two. Both funds already established at the time of writing were moving cautiously into the market and maintaining a high degree of liquidity.

An interesting sidelight to the formation of the new investment management groups was the eagerness of local interests to participate. They had, as one foreign broker noted rather wryly, apparently "confused the profits of the funds with those of the fund-management groups." The political connections of some of these local shareholders worries some foreigners. There is a fear that they could try to influence the funds toward buying the stocks of companies they are connected with. "There have been some problems already given the commercial ties of our shareholders," a foreign broker noted. "We must not let anything happen which could damage the reputation of these funds."

The MoF has specified that all the funds must run domestic as well as foreign funds. This is an attempt to accustom the Taiwan public to investing longer-term through investment or unit trusts holding a wide portfolio of stocks, rather than jumping in and out of single, speculative situations. Whether the tactic will work depends largely on how successful the managers are in producing returns which are big enough to attract locals away from their usual gambling games in the stockmarket or even on the local kerb (money-lending) market.

One curious phenomenon in Taiwan is the practice of making so-called Company Loans whereby employees deposit money with their employers (who are often fully borrowed already on their bank lines) and receive returns of 25% per annum on the money. The trouble is, they do not always get it back, as was again evidenced in the case of the Cathay group collapse. Even so, stockmarket funds will be hard put competing with such potentially rewarding, if often risky, ventures.

IIT was first off the mark again at the beginning of 1986 in setting up such a domestic fund. By May, subscriptions had reached NT$1.2 billion and were expected to hit NT$2 billion by the end of the year. National Investment Trust and Kwang Hua were also expected to launch their domestic funds by the end of 1986. The response generally looked encouraging. According to David Hsu, vice president and manager of the investment department at Kwang Hua, his group was having to turn away locals wanting to buy into the Formosa Fund — these funds are reserved for foreigners. If Hsu's optimism about the domestic funds proves to be justified — as well as that of Mobius who points out that "there is a whole middle class here in Taiwan not involved in the stockmarket, so there is tremendous potential" — then the Taiwan market may be moving toward a new kind of stability.

The truth of this is borne out by the preponderance of small people — the proverbial amahs (Chinese servants) and taxi drivers — who are to be seen crowding round the teletype displays of share prices in brokers offices around Taipei. Some will trade (remarkably large sums of money) daily, waiting for the slightest upward move in a share price before cashing in their chips. Lending to finance share speculation in Taiwan is supposed to be the monopoly of the official Fu Hwa Securities Finance Corp. In reality, just about every broking firm lends margin money (illegally) to its clients for this purpose. Likewise, many foreigners (especially Hongkong Chinese) are able to invest on the TSE via the currency black market, despite the fact that this is legally prohibited.

The government made it a condition of licensing the new fund-management groups that they carry out financial research into listed companies. Slowly but surely a new industry is emerging as a

Table 45 *(Continued)*

Chung Hwa Securities Investment Co.

Shareholders:
Merrill Lynch International
Fidelity International
Bangkok Bank
Yamaichi Capital Management
Chung Hwa Development and Trust

International Investment Trust (IIT)

Shareholders:
Bank of Communications
Bank of Taiwan
Central Trust of China
Citicorp International
Credit Suisse First Boston (Asia)
Farmers' Bank of China
Gartmore (Hongkong)
International Commercial Bank of China
Lazard Brothers & Co.
Nikko International Capital Management Co (Europe)
Robert Fleming (Hongkong)
United Merchant Bank
United World Chinese Commercial Bank
Vickers da Costa International
Wardley Investment Services

Sources: Various

result, with groups like Kwang Hua employing computer-literate business graduates to get into the new business of fundamental analysis. Instead of producing the rather meaningless reams of graphs and charts on "head-and-shoulder patterns" in the market, these people are actually getting down to the real business of visiting companies and asking meaningful questions. Whether they will get meaningful answers, initially at least, is open to considerable doubt but it seems likely that as the share rating of the better and more open companies improves, then the black sheep will be forced to come into the fold too.

Stockbrokers Vickers da Costa has been doing research on the Taiwan market for some time. So it seemed fitting that Vickers should be one of the first two foreign groups to be granted one of the eight investment licences so far awarded in Taiwan. Hongkong-based merchant bank Jardine Fleming (JF) got the other foreign licence. Local groups account for the other licences which have been taken up so far. JF's general manager in Taipei, Blair Pickerell, freely admits that his Taipei office is a cost rather than a profit — centre for JF at present, and likely to remain that way for a considerable time as the market grows.

The day is probably still quite distant when foreign brokers will be granted seats on the Taiwan Stock Exchange or, indeed, when they can engage in share underwriting business. Underwriting is something of a farce at present with underwriters, in fact, conducting a "lottery" among family members of an issuing group who buy and sell to one another in order to get the share price up above the artifically low levels fixed by the SEC for flotations.

Market reforms will become increasingly necessary as Taiwan slowly dismantles its cumbersome controls on outward portfolio investment. A number of Trust Funds for Overseas Bond Investments were created in 1986, allowing locals limited freedom to invest (indirectly) in foreign bonds and other instruments. As this chink in the armour of "Fortress Taiwan" slowly widens there will be increasing temptations for Taiwan investors to put their money offshore. That potential outflow could more than offset the inflow of foreign funds, given the sheer size of Taiwan's foreign-exchange reserves. So the Taiwan stockmarket must make sure it marches in step with other markets, not least neighbouring South Korea and Hongkong.

Basic Data:

Placing orders at the Trading Posts

Securities Traded

The Exchange has listings of company stocks, government bonds (issued by the central, provincial and municipal governments), bank CDs, Central Bank Savings Bonds and corporate bonds.

Trading Units

Stock certificates in listed companies originally varied in par value size from NT$1 to NT$300 and in board-lot size from 100 to 10,000 shares. Since 1979, however, public companies have been required to change their share certificate and board-lot size to meet the SEC's Rule of Certificate Unification which specifies a NT$10 par value certificate and a 1,000 share board lot.

Commissions and Securities Transaction Tax

Brokerage commissions for stocks are 0.2% while commissions for bonds are 0.1 per cent. A securities transaction tax of 0.3% (levied on the seller) has been suspended for the period from 24th June, 1985 up to 30th June, 1986.

Large Transactions

There are limitations on large volume transactions of 300 trading lots or more, or if the amount of the transaction exceeds NT$3 million.

Price Limits

There is also a restriction on price fluctuations to 5% on either side of the previous day's closing price in the case of stocks and 2.5% in the case of bonds.

Types of Settlement

There are two types of settlement for transactions:-

> Regular: Settlement made in cash with delivery of the share certificate through the Exchange Clearing Department on the next business day following the transaction day.
> Cash: Settlement made by cash and share certificate delivery through the Exchange Clearing Department on the same day of the transaction or next day only if agreed by both parties.

Mechanics of Trading

Execution of share transaction on the Taiwan Stock Exchange is handled by floor specialists, who are employed by the exchange, and who match buy and sell orders delivered to them through the floor representatives of brokerage firms acting on behalf of the individual client.

Company Reports

Each listed firm must submit annual and semi-annual financial statements. In February 1981, the Government announced moves to require major companies to disclose more financial data to the public. At that time the Government said that all firms, listed or unlisted, with a capital of more than NT$200 million would be required to issue detailed public financial reports.

Securities Financing

Margin credit is presently given for up to 50% of the purchase cost for First Section stocks and 40% for Second Section stocks.

Stock Exchange Indices

The Exchange has a Weighted Stock Price Index which is comparable to the Standard and Poor's Index in the US and Tokyo Stock Exchange Index insofar as it takes a wide selection of listed shares and weights them according to the number of shares outstanding. It is compiled using the "Paasche Formula" by dividing the market value by the base day's total market value for the index shares. In 1966, when the index was first started, the number of shares for inclusion numbered 28. The number was subsequently increased to 41 in 1972 and 108 in July 1983.

Hongkong: The China Syndrome

When Britain signed the official accord with China in September 1984, agreeing to hand back sovereignty over the Crown Colony of Hongkong as from 30 June 1997, that set the seal on the ultimate fate of the local stockmarket to an extent which was not fully appreciated at the time. It meant that the Hongkong stockmarket could expand eventually to become the principal fund-raising centre within an economically powerful China — perhaps the primus inter pares among a number of Chinese stockmarkets. Or it could decline into obscurity and eventual oblivion under the yoke of Chinese Communism.

It must be admitted that, from a purely historical perspective, the prospects do not look very good. Shanghai, which was a thriving centre of commerce in the days when Hongkong was little more than a trading backwater, had an active stock exchange from 1919. The Communists under Mao Tse Tung, quickly closed down this symbol of Shanghai's thriving capitalism.

In addition to Shanghai's, no fewer than 150 other stockmarkets opened in China during the 1920s — only to disappear once the communists took over. The heirs to Mao are still in charge in Peking. It might reasonably be asked why there should be any more reason to be optimistic about the survival of the Hongkong market within China than there was about Shanghai and other markets spawned during China's brief flirtation with capitalism in the 1920s and 1930s. The answer has to be subjective as much as objective.

China has "guaranteed" the continuation of Hongkong's capitalist way of life for 50 years beyond 1997 — a unique charter for the future of any country, as Peking officials like to point out. Sceptics who witnessed the inexorable squeeze on Shanghai's businessmen after 1949 are wont to respond that death can come not by one blow but also through "a thousand pinpricks." Of course, Shanghai's future was not guaranteed through a treaty lodged with the UN, as is Hongkong's. But that does not reassure those entrepreneurs who fled to Hongkong from China, some of whom are now preparing to decamp again before 1997.

There are some grounds for optimism, however. China, under paramount leader Deng Xiao Ping, has become a good deal more liberal economically than it was under Mao and seems more concerned with emulating the giant economic strides made by Japan than with continuing to emulate the Communist USSR. So, it seems reasonable to suppose that China's economic liberalisation will continue beyond the death of Deng, and with it the need for capital, including equity finance.

Within a couple of years of the signing of the Sino-British accord, Hongkong began to assess how its stockmarket might play a part in raising local and foreign equity capital for the benefit of China as whole. Even as Dr Ronald Li, first chairman of the unified new Stock Exchange of Hongkong (created in 1986) and his colleagues were considering how to raise Hongkong's profile within greater China, the cities of Shanghai, Canton (Guangzhou) and even Peking were initiating their own moves. By September 1986, Shanghai had opened a rudimentary form of stock exchange again (operating from a branch of the People's Bank of China and listing just two stocks initially) and the city of Shenyang had done likewise. Guangzhou, Chongqing, Wuhan and Changzhou were expected to follow suit. Hongkong does not need to worry for a long time about competition from the re-born bourses of China. In fact, the longer they continue to thrive, the better it will be for Hongkong.

The Hongkong stockmarket has achieved a remarkable preeminence among other Asian markets (except of course Japan's) given the relatively small size of Hongkong's economy. Among the

Table 46

HANG SENG INDEX — JAN 1971 TO SEPTEMBER 1985

TURNOVER HK$ MILLION

Source: Stock Exchange of Hong Kong

world's major stockmarkets, only New York, Tokyo and London, plus all the exchanges put together in each of Australia, Canada and West Germany, rank ahead of Hongkong in terms of equity turnover. (There is one other exception, and that is Taiwan which, as noted elsewhere in this book, achieves remarkable levels of turnover in some years).

In terms of equity market capitalisation, Hongkong's market was worth HK$270 billion (or some US$35 billion) at the end of 1985. This compared with S$71 billion or US$32 billion for Singapore and A$103 billion (US$72 billion) for the Australian Associated Stock Exchanges. Comparitive figures for equity turnover in 1985 were: Hongkong, HK$76 billion (US$9.7 billion); Singapore, S$6.3 billion (US$2.8 billion); Australia, A$22.5 billion (US$15.8 billion) and Tokyo US$478 billion equivalent. All of these figures are naturally influenced by prevailing exchange rates but they do offer an order of magnitude.

Because of Hongkong's total absence of exchange controls and lack of interest on the part of the authorities in who owns what financial assets and who is hiding behind nominee interests, the Hongkong stock exchange has achieved an especially wide following in the region. The so-called Overseas Chinese or "Hua Chao" — emigrants who left China over a period of a century and more and established a multitude of small businesses and larger dynastic enterprises throughout South East Asia — find Hongkong the natural place to put their money. This can either take the form of anonymous "transaction balances" which move freely in and out of the Hongkong banking system or speculative investments in the local stockmarket or real-estate market — or a combination of the two. It is, perhaps, this aspect above all of Hongkong's role which could be threatened by its future reabsorption within China. That is, of course, unless the volume of China enterprises listing their shares on the Hongkong market grows to the point where international investors feel they must invest in Hongkong as a gateway to China.

As the beginning of trading in company shares in Hongkong can be traced back to around 1860, it may seem hardly surprising that the market should have grown to its present size by now. The historical perspective is misleading though, because the real growth has come only very recently. Until the first oil-shock in 1973, even the Manila stockmarket was bigger than Hongkong's, at least in terms of turnover. Manila has since declined sadly.

The history of share dealing in Hongkong and how the Colony came to have four stock exchanges (since reduced to one amalgamated exchange) offers insights into how competition to open new markets in China could develop. The Hongkong Stock Exchange (not to be confused with the new Stock Exchange of Hongkong which opened for trading on April 2nd 1986) was founded in 1914. It was an exclusive institution representing mainly the British and international community rather than the local Chinese. A second exchange was started in 1921 called the Hongkong Sharebrokers' Association, though it later merged (1947) with the Hongkong

Table 47

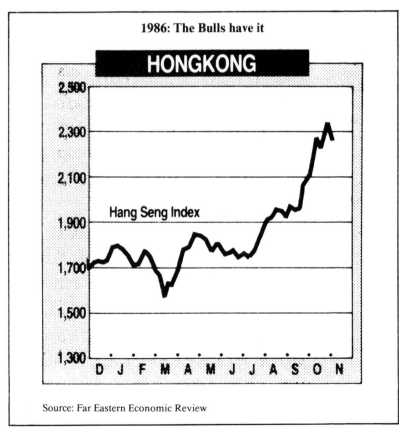

Source: Far Eastern Economic Review

Stock Exchange, which then enjoyed a monopoly for over 20 years (until 1969)

It was in that year that the Far East Exchange was formed by a group of local Chinese brokers who felt that the European brokers dominating the Hongkong Stock Exchange discriminated against them. The Far East exchange went on to become very powerful and one of its leading lights, Dr Ronald Li, became first chairman of the present Stock Exchange of Hongkong.

The new exchange, which occupies the extensive podium of a gleaming modernistic building called Exchange Square on the Central waterfront, has a very Chinese air about it. Telephonists and officials automatically answer the phone in Cantonese rather than English. More important, all members of the governing committee of the exchange are Chinese with no foreign broking houses represented. This is justified on the grounds that a company in Hongkong cannot have corporate directors and none of the foreign brokers trade as individuals. Such things may be understandable in terms of Hongkong's population mix (over 95% Chinese) but they are rather at odds with the stockmarket's pretensions to internationalism.

Until about 15 years ago, relatively few stocks were listed in Hongkong and trading was limited. Things began to change dramatically around 1970, shortly after the Far East exchange came into being. At that time there were no restrictions on sharebroking and virtually anyone could set up his own stock exchange. Once the Far East exchange had proved that the local Cantonese people in Hongkong were interested in stocks — they are archetyal traders in fact — other stock exchanges appeared. First came the Kam Ngan Exchange in 1971 (an offshoot of the long-established Chinese gold and silver market) and then, one year later, the Kowloon Exchange, though both were to remain small relative to the Hongkong and Far East exchanges. A fifth stock exchange was about to be launched in 1973 when, in an uncharacteristic bit of interventionism, the government stepped in and called a halt by banning the creation of any new exchanges.

The beginning of the 1970s was boom time for the new exchanges and for the hordes of brokers. The Hang Seng Index — for long the only barometer of the Hongkong stock exchange, though now running in parallel with a new index run by the stock exchange itself — reached a record high of 1,775 points early in

1973. Then came a sickening crash. By the end of the same year the index was down to around 400 and it touched a nadir of 150 in December 1974. This was not an isolated phenomenon — other markets, including London, were plumbing the depths around this time — but the magnitude and suddenness of the crash caused the government to reflect on how this new South Sea Bubble could have grown to such proportions and then burst so quickly.

The boom of 1972/73 was remarkable not only for the huge amounts of money gambled on the Hongkong stockmarket but also for the bizarre nature of some of the company flotations at the time. One of the more remarkable was the Hongkong Backfire Loop Antenna Company, launched on the Kowloon Stock Exchange in 1972 with its sole asset being the patent on a TV ariel developed by a Taiwan scientist. The shares quickly shot up to 20 times their issue price of HK$1. In the market crash the following year, they fell to just 50 cents. Another prospectus calmly informed potential investors that the proprietors were a group of "Chinese gentlemen" whose habit it was to meet once a week over lunch to discuss investments. They proposed offering the public the benefit of their collective wisdom by selling the portfolio on to them, at a tidy premium to market worth. When the crash came it appears to have been precipitated as much as anything by the appearance of certain forged share certificates in the market.

Times have changed somewhat since the days of 1973 when new issues appeared almost daily and the Hongkong stockmarket acquired what one local broker aptly describes as a "very dodgy" image. The market has "grown up and matured" since then, some say. Certainly it has matured in terms of turnover and the degree of international interest. But much of the speculative flavour remains, helped, no doubt, by the fact that institutional investors account for maybe only 15% of market activity and individuals for nearer 50%. Market capitalisation more than doubled between 1978 and 1983 and turnover again more than doubled from HK$37 billion to HK$76 billion between 1983 and 1985. But in other respects the market has a long way to go. It is still dominated by financial and property (plus construction) stocks and thus very much tied to the fortunes of these sectors.

This became painfully apparent following the collapse of the local real-estate market in 1982 and the subsequent collapse of Carrian, a property-investment, shipping and insurance group launched by a certain George Tan whose business failure embroiled several of Hongkong's leading blue-chip banks and property companies, not to mention Malaysia's leading government-owned bank, Bank Bumiputra, which poured money into Carrian via its Hongkong affiliate, Bumiputra Malaysian Finance (BMF). The Carrian affair hit the stockmarket directly through the listed vehicle Carrian Investments Ltd. (CIL), which went down in 1982 with a HK$1.3 billion deficit, and whose once high-flying shares subsequently became worthless. The market was involved indirectly too, through numerous banks and property companies. These included Hongkong Land — one of the biggest real-estate companies in the world which became involved in various joint ventures with George Tan companies.

No sooner had the dust begun to settle on the Carrian crash than a series of financial collapses were set in train, partly as a result of

Table 48

Market Capitalization

Source: Stock Exchange of Hongkong

the crash in property values. Virtually every local (and many foreign) banks and finance companies had invested heavily in the property market. Fraud also helped sink some of the local banks. The Hang Lung Bank, one of the biggest local Chinese-owned banks, went down in October 1983 and a clutch of quasi-banks or Deposit-Taking Companies failed around the same time. The government took over Hang Lung and then had to do the same thing not long after with the Overseas Trust Bank.

In the following two years, the government had to devise various rescue operation for numerous other local Chinese-owned banks as public confidence (and funds) fled them. The story of inadequate official supervision over these institutions and failure to detect how heavily they were exposed to property and other vulnerable assets, would fill a book. It is mentioned here as a cautionary tale because of the close links which still exist between the worlds of finance and real-estate in Hongkong — and the dominance which both sectors still exercise over the local stockmarket.

The Hongkong Stockmarket is also very "top heavy." As of April 1986, just 20 out of the total 258 companies listed on the Stock Exchange of Hongkong (including 22 foreign companies) accounted for no less than 74% of the total market capitalisation. The Hongkong and Shanghai Bank was the biggest, at just under 10% while Hongkong Land weighed in at something over 5% and two other property-related companies, Hutchison Whampoa and Hongkong and Kowloon Wharf accounted for just under 6% and 4% respectively. Property and construction companies plus finance companies (banks and DTCs) together accounted for a fraction under 72% of total market capitalisation.

Utilities (such as China Light and Hongkong Electric) represented a useful 20% but industrials made up only 5%. This is hardly a picture of the increasingly diversified market which Hongkong likes to present to international investors. Yet, for all their large capitalisations, Hongkong's top 20 companies are by ·no means grossly over-valued on fundamentals. An average price/earnings ratio of around 15 (as of April 1986) for all stocks is not very high in international terms. What is remarkable, in addition to the preemminence which a score of Hongkong stocks enjoy in the local market, is the sheer size of earnings and assets which they have built up in a relatively short space of time.

Things change slowly so far as the composition of listed stocks is concerned. The floating of a 22.5% slice of Hongkong-based international air carrier Cathay Pacific on the local stockmarket early in 1986 — it has subsequently become a component of the Hang Seng Index — helps, but only at the margin. The floating of British-based Cable & Wireless PLC in November 1986, was a further step in the direction of a more broad-based market. Various electronics companies have come to market in recent times. Conic Investments, Evergo Industrial Enterprise, Lambda Technology and Elek and Eltec came to market in 1983 and 1984 but they have not proved to be a stunning success either in terms of trading results or market popularity. Hongkong's manufacturing industry base, with the exception of textiles — only one substantial textile firm (Windsor Industrial) is listed — remains relatively under-represented.

Unlike Taiwan, where the stock exchange is convinced that there are at least 300 large companies eligible to add to the 120 or so already listed, no-one in Hongkong has any real idea of how many more companies might be ready and able to come to market. This reflects the laissez-faire attitude which the government has always adopted toward business and, until quite recently, toward the compilation of meaningful statistics. But it is generally acknowledg-

Table 49

Components of Market Capitalisation

	1986
Finance	21.69%
Utilities	19.15%
Properties	21.86%
Con. Enterprises	28.75%
Industrials	5.27%
Hotels	3.24%
Others	0.04%

Source: Stock Exchange of Hongkong

ed that the stockmarket does not represent anything like the complete profile of the territory's business.

Certain wealthy local Chinese businessmen, such as Sir Yue Kong Pao, head of the Worldwide shipping and property empire; Li Ka-shing, head of conglomerate Cheung Kong (and Hutchison Whampoa), C.K. Tung, head of the Tung shipping group, and the late Fung King Hey, former head of the Sun Hung Kai banking and securities-dealing operation, have brought at least parts of their diverse business empires to the stockmarket. But there are certain other supposedly "immensely wealthy" businessmen who have resolutely declined to bring their companies public. Brokers point to the likes of Sir Fung Ping-fan, head of a very large but private industrial, leisure and travel conglomerate (though one which ran into serious difficulties with bad debts in 1986), K.S. Wong, founder of a construction, retail and catering empire, and others of comparable size.

Meanwhile, despite the fact that wealthy Overseas Chinese entrepreneurs in South East Asia love to punt on the Hongkong stockmarket, relatively few of them have seen fit to list their own companies on the Stock Exchange of Hongkong. This is surprising given the potential for raising large sums of money in the territory. Apart from the fact that there are many super-wealthy individual investors in Hongkong (though just how many is impossible to judge even from counting the numbers of Rolls Royces cruising the streets) there is a huge captive fund-management industry. (As of June 1986, there were fewer than 185 authorised money funds in Hongkong — unit trusts and mutual funds — estimated to be handling around US$20 billion of funds. Over a hundred of these were overseas-based offshore funds operating out of Hongkong for tax reasons, and managing portfolios spread throughout Asia. Around 70 are locally-based and all of them are free to buy Hongkong stocks if they see fit.) The conclusion is that Chinese and other Asian businessmen outside Hongkong find even the territory's relatively lax disclosure laws onerous by comparison with their own.

For a while during 1972 it looked as though things were going to change. The very wealthy but ultra low-profile Indonesian Chinese businessman Liem Sioe Liong, together with his immediate business associates, were revealed to be the buyers of a long-forgotten little shell company called Shanghai Land. (There had been a series of these "Shanghai" companies formed in earlier years to hold assets belonging to emigrant Chinese businessmen. They lay dormant because China froze the assets for about 30 years, though some were unfrozen once the open door policy was introduced in 1980). There was speculation that Liem was about to inject Indonesian assets into a new Hongkong holding company and fund managers from as far away as London and Sydney flocked to talk to First Pacific, hoping to get a slice of the action. Foreign investment in Jakarta's fledgling stockmarket is still not permitted, so this seemed like a chance to get in by the back door. They were to be disappointed. The assets Liem put into his first Pacific group turned out to be nothing nearer to Indonesia than a California bank (Hibernia) and a Dutch trading company (Hagermayer) plus various other activities.

The equally wealthy Kwek family of Singapore and Malaysia,

Table 50

Turnover on the Hongkong stock exchanges

Year	Far East Exchange Turnover (HK$ million)	Turnover as % of total	Hongkong Exchange Turnover (HK$ million)	Turnover as % of total
1981	50,804.39	47.94	17,450.84	16.47
1982	21,109.52	45.67	9,852.92	21.32
1983	15,658.14	42.13	7,238.17	19.48
1984	19,882.08	40.73	11,214.46	22.98
1985*	23,784.63	40.16	16,069.51	27.13

Year	Kam Ngan Stock Exchange Turnover (HK$ million)	Turnover as % of total	Kowloon Stock Exchange Turnover (HK$ million)	Turnover as % of total	Total Turnover (HK$ million)
1981	37,545.42	35.43	170.25	0.16	105,970.90
1982	15,191.75	32.87	67.06	0.14	46,221.25
1983	14,207.93	38.23	62.02	0.16	37,166.26
1984	17,634.70	36.13	77.46	0.16	48,808.70
1985*	19,277.69	32.55	91.78	0.16	59,223.61

* To end-September 1985

Source: All exchanges

also bought a Hongkong shell company but again used it to inject Hongkong-based assets (a bank) rather than use it as a vehicle for quoting investments located elsewhere in the region. Shell-company trading continues to be a profitable business for proprietors (and merchant banks) in Hongkong but nowadays it is mainly the likes of Australian businessmen who buy them and keep them dormant awaiting the injection of assets held in various parts of the world. The name of the game is tax avoidance.

There are a score of foreign companies listed on the Hongkong stock exchange, including one or two well known South East Asian companies such as (Malaysia-based) Sime Darby, (Singapore-based) Jack Chia International, (Malaysia-based) Mulpha and so on. But this does not make the Hongkong market a true regional venue for Asian regional company listings and it is questionable whether it will become one given the increasing preoccupation with China. It is conceivable that the Singapore market could take over this role in time. The local Securities Commission has resisted attempts by various overseas entrepreneurs to bring to market in Hongkong vehicles for more exotic overseas assets such as oil in Canada and minerals in Guatemala. A few did slip through the net in former years. One is Sir James Goldsmith's General Oriental (formed in 1976 out of the shell of Oriental Financial consultants and Promoters Ltd — one of the go-go stocks of the early 1970s boom). Oriental holds a portfolio of assets ranging from a stage in Goldsmith's French flagship Generale Occidentale to a stake in a London gaming club as well as a US timber company — none of which can be said to be exactly Hongkong-relevant assets. Goldsmith, however, de-listed his company from the Stock Exchange of Hongkong in 1986, preferring a listing in Vancouver and legal domicile in the Cayman Islands.

Hongkong had implemented tighter monitoring and adherence to stock exchange listing rules a few months earlier. New Zealand entrepreneur Ron Brierley's Industrial Equity Pacific (formed in 1975 out of another of the long line of Shanghai shell companies) likewise holds a portfolio of international equities plus a stake in a US department store but little closer to home (Hongkong). What is remarkable is that both of these companies ranked for a time among the 20 biggest listed companies in Hongkong in terms of market capitalisation.

Ronald Li, a stockbroker himself, sees the increasing pressure for corporate disclosure as a factor discouraging more businesses from going public in Hongkong. There is no doubt that the tighter laws on corporate disclosure and compliance with listing laws which were introduced in September 1986, are making life a good deal tougher for merchant bankers as well as their corporate clients. Proposed deals are scrutinised a good deal more closely nowadays. It will probably be recorded as one of the ironies of history that Hongkong, ruled for more than a century by the British, began tightening up the laws governing its stockmarket only when the end of colonial rule was imminent. In what was seen as a test case, a locally listed firm, Crusader Investments, was told by the securities commission that approval could not be given for a plan to acquire gold-mining leases in Brazil. The deal would change the whole nature of the company (compared with its listing prospectus) and render it susceptible to control by the vendors of the Brazillian gold leases (who received shares as payment) it was argued. This indicated a tougher official line in future on what proprietors in the public domain can do with their companies.

Brokers who have known the local market and its operators for a long time agree with Ronald Li. "With the Securities Commission (Hongkong's version of an SEC) getting tougher all the time, people are asking what's the point of going public," noted one. The Standing Committee on Company Law Reform in Hongkong declared at the end of 1985 that it was "strongly inclined" to think that the time for more disclosure had come. Yet, that committee first debated the need for greater disclosure 15 years earlier. The committee proposed that every director of a listed company should be required to give notice to the company of his interest (or his immediate family's interests) in that company or in its associates.

The information would be available through a register open to public inspection. Similar obligations would be imposed upon "substantial shareholders" of a company (which could mean anything between 5 and 10%). Any change of interest — in other words, dealings — should also be notified. All this applied only to publicly listed companies. Some of these reforms have since been implemented. As from late 1985, Hongkong demanded compulsory disclosure of directors' shareholdings — though not then of dealings nor of substantial interests by outside shareholders. Disclosure of substantial shareholdings above 10% may come some time in 1987. The power to look behind Hongkong nominee companies to see who the beneficial owners of shares are looks a remoter prospect, especially with the 1997 changeover looming and businessmen highly anxious to avoid letting Peking know precisely just who owns what in Hongkong.

How will the stockmarket react to such changes? Badly, according to stock exchange chairman Li. "On the one hand we have to be international, we have to show the whole outside world that we have fair play for all. But on the other hand Hongkong has a unique market," Li commented to the author. According to him, shares in around 200 of the 260 or so listed companies in Hongkong are "dormant." In other words, they are scarcely ever traded. From time to time the majority (family) shareholders of such companies (who typically would own around 80% or more of the shares with only a fraction in public hands) will go into the market and buy or sell the company's shares simply so that there is a market in them rather than just a listing on the stock exchange. That way, the small investor can deal when he wants to and the owners of the company "save face" and avoid the displeasure of small shareholders who might otherwise find themselves locked in.

The local Securities Commission accepts this, up to a point. It acknowledges the fact that brokers may often have to go to the proprietors of a smaller listed company simply in order to do a deal in that company's shares. There is no regular trading and price quote available in such situations. A typical example might be where a fund has accidentally breached its trust deed and gone over its limit in any one company's shares. Then it has to find a way of doing an off-market deal.

Li claims that once directors and their families have to start declaring all their stock dealings they will lose face in front of their business rivals. It will become transparently obvious that a proprietor has had to make a market in his own shares. The consequence might well be that numerous smaller companies decide to go private again, thus reducing the nominal size of the Hongkong stockmarket. Commissioner for Securities Ray Astin, on the other hand argues that the objective must be to disabuse some people of the notion that a listed company in Hongkong is a "private plaything in the public domain." The Hongkong Government has shown its increasing concern over the prevalence of insider dealing in the stockmarket. An official tribunal was set up to deal with incidents and in 1986 came out with its first public censure of a leading local businessman (Li Ka-shing). It is also debating the possibility of making insider dealing a criminal offence.

The argument over whether fuller disclosure will discourage more companies from coming to market in Hongkong (or even encourage some to buy out their minority shareholders and go back to the private domain) is only one side of the story. There are various reasons why many Hongkong companies do not bother going public in the first place. A public listing is one way of avoiding penal death duties in many countries but in Hongkong such duties are levied at the rate of only a few per cent. This may change of course, if taxes rise appreciably in the run-up to 1997, which seems quite possible.

Another factor is that bank finance has traditionally been the preferred method of financing business for the majority of company

Table 51

Leading Companies in Market Capitalization (as of April 1986)

Rank	Company	Price ($)	Market Capitalization (HK$)	% Of Total
1	Hongkong Bank	7.20	27,180,178,056	9.74
2	Hong Kong Telephone	11.20	17,894,594,211	6.41
3	Hutchison Whampoa	30.75	16,732,794,361	5.99
4	China Light	17.20		
5	Swire Pacific	13.30	16,182,311,069	5.80
6	Hang Seng Bank	40.25	14,765,989,179	5.29
7	Hong Kong Land	6.25	14,538,208,528	5.21
8	Hong Kong Electric	9.00	12,316,641,687	4.42
9	HK & Kln Wharf	7.15	11,131,267,819	3.99
10	Cheung Kong	21.40	8,440,067,552	3.03
11	Industrial Equity	53.00	7,632,000,000	2.74
12	New World Dev.	6.25	6,749,910,838	2.42
13	Sun Hung Kai Prop.	12.50	6,726,789,183	2.41
14	Jardine Holdings	13.60	5,610,510,721	2.01
15	General Oriental	43.00	4,676,293,000	1.68
16	HK & China Gas	14.20	4,605,400,800	1.65
17	World Int'l	2.475	4,124,532,956	1.48
18	Hang Lung	6.45	3,690,045,000	1.32
19	Hong Kong Hotels	35.75	3,526,791,840	1.26
20	Henderson Land	2.10	2,769,900,000	0.99
	Total		205,806,226,800	73.76
	Market Total Capitalisation		278,998,775,781	100.00

Source: Stock exchange

proprietors. Having to go to the public for funds, either by way of an initial company floation or through a subsequent rights issue to shareholders, is seen in the eyes of many Chinese as a sign of weakness. And there is also the fact that corporate takeovers in Hongkong are rarely financed through shares — Chinese shareholders prefer cash. So, the incentive for listing scrip as a takeover currency is limited.

One way of getting more companies to come to market might be to change the listing criteria. When the new amalgamated stock exchange was in the making it was felt by some that a "big board" and "little board" (or first and second section) structure would be appropriate, with different listing requirements in each category. In the event, the idea was dropped. (Listing requirements on the stock exchange proper are in any case rather lax, stipulating only that a newly listed company should have an initial aggregate market value of HK$50 million and a track record of five years. Even then, the stock exchange committee has discretion to vary these rules, as well as the requirement that at least 25% of a company's stock should be sold to the public. The rules have been circumvented too, on numerous occasions through "back-door" listings whereby new assets are injected into old shell companies).

Li and others would like to see a formal Over-the-Counter (OTC) share market in Hongkong, along the lines of London's highly successful Unlisted Securities Market (USM). The stock exchange was expected to submit a formal proposal for an OTC market in Hongkong to the Securities Commission by the end of 1986 and the idea seemed likely to get a sympathetic response. Li maintains that "there is something wrong with our present listing philosophy. We are now only catering for enterprises that have already made good, that have proved themselves. What we need is a sector in the market that caters for budding business."

Li instances a typical company in Hongkong with a net worth (paid-up capital plus reserves) of around HK$25 million and a track record of around three years. In its early phase it might well need additional financing of around HK$10 million for expansion. No bank would look at such a proposition — and neither would the stock exchange, says Li. An OTC market could provide the answer. Li declines to put a figure on the number of companies which could be brought to market in this way but he claims it is very substantial. Such companies could in time graduate to the stockmarket proper, he adds.

There is another reason why the stock exchange is pushing the idea of an OTC market so hard just now. It is a matter of survival for the broking industry as it now stands. As of the end of May 1986, there were 888 brokers in membership of the Stock Exchange of Hongkong and 1,302 registered dealers. (This was in addition to the 112 brokers and 283 dealers transacting business on the separately-incorporated Hongkong Futures Exchange). This is an awful lot of brokers and dealers for a town the size of Hongkong and unless something happens pretty soon to boost stockmarket activity there simply isn't going to be enough business to go round.

Hongkong has a way of overdoing everything and the glut of stockbrokers is a legacy of the past, just as the presence of nearly 500 banks and deposit-taking companies in the territory is a legacy of the booming 1970s when the government disdained to control the influx. (There isn't enough business to keep all the banks and finance companies happy or even solvent either). The great broking boom dates back to the same time as the great stockmarket boom — in other words to the period between 1971 and 1973 when membership of one or other of the four stock exchanges was seen as a licence to print money. Individuals found that, for a relatively modest outlay, they could punt in stocks without having to pay brokerage. Many still do, using their knowledge of what major shareholding families among the local Chinese community are likely to do — and dealing appropriately.

When the stockmarket crash came in 1973 it did not result in a shakeout among brokers. The number stayed at around 1,000. One reason was because so many businessmen had treated broking as little more than a profitable sideline and were able to leave their broking firms dormant and carry on with other business until the market rallied. What is surprising is that so many seat-holders elected to stay on when the four old exchanges were liquidated and the new single exchange came into being. Now they may be regretting it. Business is shifting increasingly to the 20 or so really big brokerages among the welter of smaller fry. Small brokers have been increasingly "pushed aside" since the new exchange opened. As one smaller operator lamented, "people only want to deal with the big boys." The big boys are international operators such as James Capel (now a subsidiary of the Hongkong and Shanghai Banking Corporation), Vickers da Costa (now under the roof of

Asian Stockmarkets

Citicorp) and others of that size.

To an increasing extent, institutional and individual investment business is going to the big brokerages owned by leading investment banks and commercial banks. There are some 25-30 bank-related members of the Stock Exchange of Hongkong and it seems inevitable that these corporate brokerages will take an ever-increasing slice of total business. One worry that has arisen since the introduction of the semi-automated electronic trading system in the new stock exchange is that it might actually encourage cartelised trading and price fixing. With a limited number of big brokers able to deal in huge lines of stock and the new trading system allowing a client to satisfy his order from one or more big brokers (instead of having to work his way down a ladder of offeree brokers as under the told system) the potential is certainly there.

Table 52

Most Active Stocks (In Shares) (April 1986)			
Rank	Name of Stocks	Turnover (Sh.)	% of Market Total
1	Hysan Development	209,920,000	9.87
2	Hongkong Bank	145,009,274	6.81
3	Regal Hotels	120,424,625	5.66
4	Henderson Land	78,838,000	3.70
5	Century City	76,342,600	3.59
6	Evergo	67,893,706	3.19
7	Hong Kong Land	65,370,769	3.07
8	Sino Land	64,637,000	3.04
9	E. Asia Navigation	60,234,330	2.83
10	Hong Kong Electric	48,494,496	2.28
11	Elec & Eltek	47,566,000	2.24
12	HK & Kln Wharf	44,782,623	2.10
13	Swire Pacific 'B'	43,787,798	2.06
14	Crusader War. 89	41,914,000	1.97
15	Cheung Kong	40,638,364	1.91
16	Great Eagle	39,378,353	1.85
17	New World Dev.	37,965,018	1.78
18	Hutchison Whampoa	37,857,165	1.78
19	Swire Pacific 'A'	32,882,146	1.55
20	Shaw Brothers	32,396,500	1.52
	Total	1,336,332,767	62.80
	Market Total	2,127,892,146	100.00

Source: Stock exchange

Compared to other regional markets (including Tokyo, which until recently maintained a closed-shop as far as foreign brokers were concerned) Hongkong has for long been an open market. The first London overseas member was admitted to the (former) Hongkong Stock Exchange as early as 1969. Other London firms followed suit, though also on the understanding that they would pay brokerage to full members who actually transacted business for them. In 1974, the newly promulgated Securities Ordinance — the first official attempt to regulate securities dealing following the chaos of 1973 — allowed corporate membership of the exchanges and the London overseas brokers applied for full membership. They were not to get it, however, until six years later.

Subsequent events were to further internationalise the Hongkong broking industry. One of them, the rise of a local Chinese broking concern, Sun Hung Kai, provides an interesting illustration of how foreigners can misjudge the Hongkong business scene. Sun Hung Kai — the empire of Fung King Hey, a classic rags-to-riches Chinese entrepreneur — built up a formidable position as broker to the local Chinese community. None other than the "Thundering Herd" from New York (Merrill Lynch) became interested in the brokerage and in 1982 took a 25% stake in SHK, joining the French bank Paribas as a substantial shareholder. SHK's securities and banking businesses were to undergo several structural meta-morphses thereafter as the securities side suffered a severe decline in business. Merrill Lynch wound up taking a majority stake in the securities business and banking interests were disposed of. What had appeared to Merrill Lynch to be a pot of gold, turned to dross, partly no doubt because of the depression suffered by the Hong-kong stockmarket in the run-up to the signing of the Sino-British accord on the territory's future in 1984 — but partly too, because neither side had really understood each other's basic business philosophy.

One of the reasons why some Hongkong brokerages are having a hard time surviving is that broking commissions are narrow. The minimum commission rate is 0.25%. Because of this, brokers see little need to introduce negotiated commissions in Hongkong. "They are low enough already" says Ronald Li bluntly. Rumours began circulating in the autumn of 1986 to the effect that some brokers were securing extra business by actually bribing fund managers to place orders with them. This appeared to go beyond

Table 53

**Average P/E Ratio and Average Yield of HKI Stocks
(As at March 1986)**

Year/Month	All HKI Stocks		Finance		Utilities		Properties		Con. Enterprises		Industrials		Hotels	
	P/E	Yield (%)	P/E	Yield (%)	P/E	Yield (%)	P/E	Yield (%)	P/E	Yield (%)	P/E	Yield (%)	P/E	Yield (%)
1985 Jan	11.40	5.32	12.00	4.37	9.96	4.17	16.79	3.27	8.90	9.85	8.40	6.65	23.44	3.32
Feb	12.31	5.30	11.86	4.43	12.46	4.29	19.81	3.12	9.04	9.60	7.97	7.34	22.63	3.44
	13.98	3.94	10.47	4.23	14.07	3.83	19.41	3.78	14.81	3.51	9.79	5.72	17.06	5.25

Source: Stock exchange

the common practice of "rebating" part of a broker's commission. Inquiries were put in hand but it seemed likely that the local Securities Commission would not intervene unless the abuses became too blatant.

The fact that broking commissions are low, probably explains why seats on the exchange are available at only around HK$100,000 — a fraction of the price in places like Tokyo. If any brokers should go down with a crash, there is a slight consolation of a stock exchange compensation fund which pays up a maximum of HK$2 million per defaulting broker. Defaulting brokers in the past have not gone down with liabilities very much bigger than this, but there are fears that competition could squeeze some medium-size as well as smaller brokers out of business in future. In late 1986, the stock exchange (at the prompting of the Securities Commission) introduced a system of quarterly reporting of brokers' liquidity and positions, backed up by random spot checks to see that the rules of the exchange are being complied with. This was perhaps a portent of problems to come.

With the rising influence of foreign brokers and fund managers in the Hongkong stockmarket has come the decline of the local "syndicates" which were able to manipulate the market. It became local folklore that the Hang Seng Index was the plaything of a group of wealthy Chinese businessmen who met every day in the Lok Yew tea house in Hongkong's central business district to decide which shares they would push. Share ramping, or "dealing on both sides of the quotation," is rarer nowadays, especially since banks stopped lending simultaneously against the real estate a company owned and the scrip of that company. It was very much in the interest of such companies to ramp their own shares in order to maintain the value of collateral. (Short selling too, is technically outlawed in Hongkong though it has long been possible via the London Stock Exchange where shares of leading Hongkong blue-chips are quoted. A number of major securities houses such as Merrill Lynch nowadays make a London market in leading Hongkong stocks so as to ensure liquidity. Shorting the Hongkong market is possible now indirectly through the stock index futures contract traded on the Hongkong Futures Exchange.)

The power to move the market appears to reside nowadays with two or three big players, rather than with more scattered and ad-hoc syndicates. In the week that the new Stock Exchange of Hongkong was formally declared open on October 6th, 1986 (by none other than the president of the Bank of China, Wang Deyan) the market suddenly took off like a rocket. Everyone had expected a little window-dressing for the occasion with brokers dutifully doing their bit to get the market looking good for the opening jamboree. But the 25% rise in the market which followed in the following five weeks was well beyond the normal call of duty. The market began consolidating again toward the end of the year but the rise had nevertheless been remarkable. It was helped, no doubt, by an influx of money out of the Tokyo stockmarket, which at the time was undergoing a consolidation after an unrelieved bull-run. And Hongkong's exports were doing well in 1986, boosting hopes for corporate earnings growth in 1987. But there was a suspicion that the market was being given a friendly push by a few helping (big) hands. This needs a bit of explanation.

. Though Hongkong does not publish official figures for net capital outflows, there is little doubt that net capital outflows persisted from around the time of the Sino-British agreement on Hongkong's future in 1984 right up to the time of writing, toward the end of 1986. In turn, there is every reason to believe that these outflows reflected the financial hedging tactics of the more wealthy local Chinese in Hongkong as they acquired overseas assets not vulnerable to whatever happens to Hongkong in 1997.

But for these outflows, there is little doubt that the Hang Seng Index would indeed have broken through the 3,000 barrier (and

Table 54

New issues on the Hongkong exchanges, 1981-85					
	Primary equity issues				Total
	New flotations		Rights issues		
Year	No of issues	Value (HK$ million)	No of issues	Value (HK$ million)	No of issues	Value (HK$ million)
1981	13	3,226.1	23	5,877.7	36	9,103.8
1982	—	—	7	1,157.2	7	1,157.2
1983	4	419.5	4	1,094.1	8	1,513.6
1984	8	1,049.4	3	656.0	11	1,705.4
1985	3	395.5	16	3,173.0	19	3,568.5

Source: Vickers da Costa

possibly even gone on to breach 4,000) as many foreign analysts were suggesting that it should (on fundamentals) in 1985. So, when the market soared toward the end of 1986 it may well have reflected a change of tactic by some of the locals who had long been selling into foreign buying. The question is, which locals and why?

One possible explanation was that big names such as Sir Yue Kong Pao and Li Ka Shing of Cheung Kong were preparing the ground for a series of major acquisitions of assets in Hongkong. The most obvious candidates for their attention were the Hongkong Land company and its sister company, Jardine Matheson. The controlling Keswick family is known to be more than willing to divest itself of fixed assets in Hongkong. A subsequent major asset reshuffle by the Jardine camp, which spun off some of the most profitable bits out of Land, did little to dispel this impression.

It seemed likely that if either or both Sir Y.K. Pao or "K.S." Li were going to bid for Jardine's or Land's assets they would prefer to do so in shares rather than in hard cash. Hence, there was an incentive for them to support the market during the run up period to a bid. Even if this was not a major factor behind the 1986 bull market, it represents a likely scenario for the future as the big Chinese players prepare to square up to the expatriate business

Table 55

Debt Securities listed in Hongkong	
Name	**Description**
Hongkong Electric Holdings Ltd	Loan Stock
Hong Kong & Kowloon Wharf Godown Co. Ltd., The	Loan Stock
Hong Kong Land Co. Ltd., The	Loan Stock
Hutchison Whampoa Ltd.	Loan Stock
Jardine Matheson (Finance) Ltd.	Guaranteed Unsecured Loan Stock
Mass Transit Railway Corporation	Bonds
Mathesons Investments Ltd.	Convertible Loan Stock
Venture Finance (Bermuda) Ltd.	Guaranteed Unsecured Loan Stock

houses or "hongs" for a final round in the corporate power struggle before 1997 gets too close.

Even if local big hands revert to selling, there is no shortage of buyers in the Hongkong market, whether wealthy local individuals and fund managers or regional Overseas Chinese investors and foreign institutions. Two new categories have recently been added.

Tokyo-based securities companies acting on behalf of institutional clients in Japan were piling quite heavily into the Hongkong market during 1986, especially into new issues such as Cathay Pacific and were showing strong interest in the prospective launch of other new issues. Such is the Japanese interest in diversifying their equity portfolios outside of a few well tried and tested markets such as New York and London, that Hongkong seems bound to enjoy a continuing influx of Japanese money.

The other category is interest from China in the Hongkong market. A number of the major broking houses in Hongkong now have direct links with People's Republic of China (PRC) banks in Canton, on whose behalf they deal in Hongkong stocks. The brokers are expecting these links to extend to other Chinese cities such as Amoy and Shanghai before long.

Ronald Li has talked to various enterprises in China (mainly in

Table 56

Year	Listed Company	Listed Securities	Unit Trust	Debt Securities
1976	295	302	1	14
1977	284	291	1	19
1978	265	273	3	20
1979	262	270	3	22
1980	262	270	8	24
1981	269	279	14	23
1982	273	283	15	23
1983	277	288	21	21
1984	278	289	24	18
1985	279	291	31	18
1986*	252	285	31	15

* Up to June 1986

Source: Stock Exchange of Hong Kong

neighbouring Guangdong province) suggesting that they incorporate holding companies in Hongkong and list these on the local exchange as vehicles for holding stakes in various China businesses. This way, the China enterprises would not be directly owned by outsiders and, in turn, outside investors in Hongkong could hold a diversified portfolio of China interests. The idea is imaginative and appears to have aroused interest among their Chinese. Towards the end of 1986, it was disclosed in Peking that four Chinese banks operating in Hongkong and the state-owned China Resources (Holdings) Co., were looking at the possibility of listing on the stock exchange of Hongkong. China Resources also has operations in Hongkong. Peking government sources cautioned that it might take some time before Chinese firms in general could emulate the example of these few based in Hongkong. But they added that, as China continues to open up to the outside world, its enterprises could consider using overseas stockmarkets in order to raise capital.

So far, the only way Hongkong or other outside portfolio investors can get access to China is indirectly, through Hongkong or Tokyo-listed companies which trade heavily with China. Various special funds have been formed to invest in the stocks of just such companies, one being Thornton Management's "Gateway Fund" in Hongkong and another, China & Eastern Investment Company, formed in London by merchant bankers Baring Brothers. This one also takes (limited) direct stakes in China ventures. It seems quite probable that PRC entities like the Guangdong International Trust and Investment Corp (GITIC) along with its Shanghai counterpart, SITIC, and possibly the Peking-based equivalent CITIC, may in time begin issuing stocks in China enterprises, through Hongkong.

Whether these will be listed on the Stock Exchange of Hongkong is another matter. Certain politically-rehabiliated businessmen in Shanghai managed to get a stockmarket of sorts restarted in September of 1986 and Guangzhou (capital of Canton province) is showing equal interest in starting its own exchange. (The Shanghai market is so far a very restricted affair, however, having potential buyers but few sellers — and prices are strictly controlled). A host of other Chinese cities, mainly in the South of the country, are also interested in opening markets.

Shares have made their reappearance in many parts of China

over the past few years. There have been a profusion of issues by
various types of enterprise and even the venerable Dr Sun Yat Sen
(founder of the first republic in China in 1911) and the man who
introduced stock dealing to China might have been bemused by the
variety of issues being made now. They are strange animals by
Western standards, some being redeemable and having characteristics of both fixed-interest and equity instruments. Some offer
interest payments as well as dividends, the automatic right to a seat
on the board to bigger investors — and even the chance to
participate in a lottery and win a TV set or similar prize.

Issuers have come from scores of collective and state-owned
enterprises in China, some with such exotic names as the Heaven
Bridge department store in Shanghai and the Happiness Accoustics
Equipment Company in Guangdong. A few issues, such as those
from Heaven Bridge and the Faoshan Trust and Investment
Company in Guangdong, and the Sanhe Food Company in
Shenzhen special zone near Hongkong, have been technically
available to foreigners but have been snapped up quickly by
Chinese and Overseas Chinese buyers before foreigners could get a
look in. Until the Shanghai exchange reopened, all trading was
carried on through the Bank of China and the Industrial and
Commercial Bank of China — at prices these two institutions
thought fit to fix. At the end of 1986, Peking announced plans to
open a stock exchange early in 1987 to list securities in "large, state-
owned enterprises." Most trading is still done this way, in fact.
Where China ultimately decides its stocks and shares will be traded
is crucial to Hongkong because in this, as in all things, the story of
Hongkong starts and ends in China.

Table 57

Estimated breakdown by investor type	
Locally managed institutions	15%
Foreign managed institutions (US/USA/Europe/Asia)	30%
Local syndicates and individuals	30%
South East Asian investors (variable)	15%
China related organisations	10%
Total	100%

Source: WI Carr, Sons & Co (Overseas) Ltd

Basic Data:

Exchange Square, home of the Stock Exchange of Hongkong

Taxation

Dividends are regarded as having been paid out of taxed profits and are thus not subject to further taxation. There are no Hongkong taxes imposed on foreign shareholders receiving Hongkong dividends and there are no withholding taxes on dividends paid by Hongkong companies. There is no tax on capital gains either.

Exchange Control and Repatriation of Funds

There are no exchange control regulations operating in Hongkong and investors have total flexibility in the movement of capital and repatriation of profits. Funds invested in Hongkong can be repatriated at will; dividends and interest are freely remittable.

Non-Resident Bank Accounts

There are no regulations restricting overseas companies or individuals from maintaining bank accounts in Hongkong.

Takeovers

The Hongkong Code on Takeovers and Mergers (revised 1981, supplement 3 March 1983) provides guidelines for companies and their advisers contemplating, or becoming involved in, takeovers and mergers. It does not have the force of law. As with the City Code on Takeovers and mergers in the United Kingdom, the spirit as well as the precise wording is important. The Code requires a person who acquires at least 35% of a company voting rights to extend an offer to all other holders of shares.

Insider Trading

The Securities Ordinance (Part VII) establishes a tribunal with powers to investigate and deal with insider trading. Section 141B(1) defines the substantive act of insider dealing. Insider trading is not a criminal offence, however.

Compensation Fund

The interests of clients are protected by the operation of the Stock

Exchange Compensation Fund. Each stock exchange has deposited with the Securities Commission a sum of HK$250,000 and a guarantee of HK$25,000 in respect of each stockbroker. The fund is estimated to be in excess of HK$50 million. Any client who has sustained pecuniary losses in respect of a default can claim compensation from the fund up to a limit of HK$1 million.

Trading System

Trading is conducted by the post trading method, with buyers and sellers having to be matched by open outcry. In practice, certain of the larger brokers undertake a market making function, especially in the more popular stocks. All securities are traded in board lots. For most companies, a board lot is 1,000 shares. Odd lots are traded separately, usually at a small discount on the board lot prices.

Early Days

Left: the old City Hall; right: the old Beaconsfield House — where stocks and shares were traded in the early 1900s.

Source: Hongkong Museum of History

Settlement and Transfer

Settlement is made on a 24 hour basis. Share certificates in board lots, together with attached transfer deeds, must be delivered on the day following the transaction. Payment is due against delivery.

Commissions and Other Costs

Buyers and sellers of shares and bonds are charged a brokerage fee of not more than 1%, the minimum fee being HK$25. An ad valorem stamp duty is also payable by both the purchaser and the vendor at the rate of HK$3 per HK$1,000. In addition, instruments of transfer must bear a HK$5 embossed stamp before being signed. Overseas institutions are advised to maintain a Securities Account with a local bank for safe custody.

Nominee Company

A 0.5% commission is deducted from each dividend paid on scrip registered in the name of the nominee company, with a minimum charge of HK$10 and a maximum of HK$2,500.

Market Indices and their Constituents

The Hang Seng Index is the most widely observed indicator of stock market performance in Hongkong. Starting from a base of 100 on 31 July 1964, the nadir of the Index was 558.61 in August 1967. It went through 500 for the first time on 26 July 1972 and 1,000 on 2 February 1973. The Index is computed on an arithmetic basis, weighted by market capitalisation, and is thus strongly influenced by large capitalisation stocks such as Hongkong Bank, Hang Seng Bank, Hong Kong Land and Cheung Kong. The Hang Seng Index is made up to 32 companies, broken down by industry.

From the time that trading started at the Unified Exchange, there have been two market indicators: the Hang Seng Index and the Hongkong Index. The Hongkong Index is calculated every 15 minutes and at the close of each trading session. There are 45 constituent stocks and April 2nd, 1986 was designated the base day with the Index set at 1,000. The total daily turnover of the 45 stocks accounts for more than 79% of total market turnover and their networth exceeds 72% of the total market capitalisation.

Singapore/Malaysia: Funny Money

Throughout 1984 and most of the following year, when Singapore was sliding into one of the worst economic recessions in its history as an independent state, the local stockmarket remained remarkably buoyant. The market fell but nowhere near so far as lead economic indicators suggested it should. This was even more true of neighbouring Malaysia where the stockmarket appeared blithely unaware of a collapse in prices of the commodities the country is dependent upon, and oblivious of gathering problems in the economy as a whole. When queried at the time about this curious gravity-defying phenomenon, local brokers attributed it to foreign buying — from New York, Hongkong or London.

This idea seemed just about credible. US pension funds and other institutions were known to be anxious to diversify their portfolios into selected overseas markets at that time, and Hongkong's stockmarket had suffered its own severe shakeout. Outside of Tokyo and Hongkong, the stockmarkets of Singapore and Malaysia are by far the best equipped in Asia to absorb foreign investment. Whereas in many other countries of the region, stockmarket capitalisation is equivalent to only around 10% of GNP, in Malaysia's case the figure has averaged nearer 100% and, in Singapore's case has been over 200% (depending on whether both markets happened to be in a bull or bear phase).

It seemed odd, admittedly, that even the most concerted foreign buying could absorb what normally would have been a severe bout of local selling at a time of such economic squeeze in both Singapore and Malaysia. But there was no denying the continuing weight of money in the market. Then, a few weeks before Christmas of 1985, came a rude awakening and a realisation of where all this money was really coming from.

At first, the crisis which was to bring about a severe and protracted crash in the two linked markets, to bring nearly a score of broking firms to their knees, to embroil major local and foreign banks and to culminate in the imprisonment of a leading political and business figure, looked like a little local difficulty. A relatively obscure Singapore company called Pan-Electric Industries default-ed on repayment of debt to a syndicate of local and foreign banks. The bankers searched for a solution to the problems of "Pan-E1" and its S$400 million of debt. They wanted to avoid liquidating the company because it had enjoyed a sound reputation in the past and was a not insignificant provider of employment in a recession-afflicted Singapore. The man who controlled Pan-E1, businessman Tan Koon Swan (president of the Malaysian Chinese Association, one of the political parties making up the ruling coalition in Malaysia) was naturally anxious to keep Pan-E1 alive too, for the sake of his own reputation.

But when the bankers discovered that Pan-E1 had been made a repository for a raft of so-called "forward contracts" and share buy-back deals financed by local brokers and banks, and that neither Pan-E1 nor Tan Koon Swan were going to be able to honour them all, they had no alternative but to put the company into receiver-ship. It was not that event per se which triggered the subsequent crash but the awful realisation that the extent of forward contracts outstanding in both Singapore and Malaysia might be well in excess

Table 58

of S$1 billion and that the lion's share of them, associated with the Pan-Electric group, were not likely to be repaid.

It became obvious that what had been underpinning the stock-markets on both ides of the causeway linking Singapore and Malaysia was not foreign investment funds after all, but a mass of money drawn out of the local banking and broking sector by the device of forward contracts. A huge and complex money game had been set in motion in which ever-increasing sums of money were chasing a given amount of scrip. This inverted pyramid of credit had been built on the ingenuity of local financiers/entrepreneurs, the "greed" of foreign as well as local stockbrokers and on the herd-like behaviour of local and foreign banks anxious to acquire assets without asking too many questions.

The whole edifice was ultimately unstable and when it crashed it brought the stockmarkets down with it. Both the Stock Exchange of Singapore (SES) and the Kuala Lumpur Stock Exchange (KLSE) made the unprecedented move of closing their markets for three full trading days, from December 2 to December 5, in an attempt to prevent total collapse. When the markets eventually reopened, they saw more than 10% wiped off their capitalisation on the first trading day alone. They were to fall much further after that and to remain on the floor for nearly six months.

As with many such traumatic events, the Pan-El affair as it came to be called, proved to be salutory for both Singapore and Malaysia. The crash revealed fundamental weaknesses in both markets, not least in the structure of the broking establishment and in the way business was done on the stockmarket. A year after the crash, when both stockmarkets were showing definite signs of recovery from the shock and stigma of Pan-El, various reforms had been implement-ed and the signs were that others would soon follow.

Such is the complex nature of business in Malaysia, however, and so labyrinthine are the business connections of the Chinese communities in both Malaysia and Singapore, that investors in either market would be unwise to assume that the factors underly-ing the Pan-El crisis have completely disappeared. In both Malay-sia and Singapore, politics influence the stockmarket too to a considerable extent, though for different reasons in each case.

Even before the Crash of '85, the Singapore and Malaysian stockmarkets had been reputed to be a theatre of operations for "syndicate" operators whose size or identity was always difficult to

establish but who were reckoned to be significant market movers.
In fact, much of the time they were said to be the principal force
driving the market up or down in both countries. Small investors
played the game of second-guessing what the syndicates would do
— whether they would go long or short on a particular stock — and
hoped to make a profit riding on the coat tails of the big operators.

Institutional investment, in the sense that it is known in
developed countries, by private investment and unit trusts, insurance companies, pension funds and the like was largely absent from
both markets. There were some big players, such as the state-run
Central Provident Fund (CPF) in Singapore and its counterpart in
Malaysia, the Employers' Provident Fund (EPF). And there were
various special funds for the Bumiputra community (meaning
Malays and other indigenous non-Chinese groups), which put some
of their funds into the stockmarket. But by and large the stockmarkets of both Singapore and Malaysia were dominated by individuals and the mysterious syndicates. What foreign investment there
was in both markets tended to concentrate largely on the traditional
Malaysian plantation-sector stocks (often marketed through Singapore) which British investment institutions in particular liked

Table 59

because of the colonial connection with Malaysia/Singapore.

The latter part of 1986 saw the beginnings of what promised to be a fundamental change in the pattern of share ownership in both markets. Traditional big market operators — wealthy Chinese businessmen who had graduated from syndicate operations to the more sophisticated game of forward contracts — were indulging in a massive disposal of stocks to foreigners in order to raise cash which they needed to unwind previous positions. Malaysian state institutions were selling heavily to foreign interests in order to raise cash for the national coffers, and even the once hallowed political principle of buying back the Malaysian plantations from foreign (British) ownership, appeared likely to be compromised. Singapore's various state corporations and funds were meanwhile buying. In short, both Singapore and Malaysian stockmarkets appeared to be graduating toward the model of institutional rather than individual-dominated markets, though with foreign institutions much more predominant in Malaysia's case.

In order to understand the interlocking nature of the Singapore and Malaysia markets and why both suffered from similar weaknesses which led to the post Pan-E1 crash it is necessary to look at their origins and subsequent development. The rapid economic development of Singapore after its founding as a trading outpost of the (British) East India Company in 1819 was accompanied by the formation of various joint-stock companies and share transactions were taking place among local brokers in the 19th century. After the rubber boom of 1910 — rubber is an important plantation crop in neighbouring Malaysia — sharebroking became a major activity in Singapore, while the growth of tin mining in Malaysia resulted in the flotation of a number of tin-dredging companies.

But it was not until the 1930s that stockbrokers in both Singapore and Malaysia formed proper associations for regulated trading and it was only in 1964 that the stock trading rooms in both places were reconstituted to form a joint stock exchange under the name of the Stock Exchange of Malaysia. This was later renamed the Stock Exchange of Malaysia and Singapore (SEMS). SEMS was to have a life of less than ten years, however, because in 1973 after an unsuccessful attempt to integrate Singapore into the federation of Malaysia, (following both countries' full independence from Britain) Malaysia terminated interchangeability of the two countries' currencies. Singapore deemed it necessary at this juncture to have a separate exchange and in May 1973 the Stock Exchange of Singapore (SES) was born. The present Kuala Lumpur Stock Exchange (KLSE) was formally incorporated in 1976 (though it had existed since 1973, under a slightly different designation) and remains to this day the only stock exchange in Malaysia.

Though the two exchanges were thus separated, many of their Siamese-twin characteristics persisted. Most notable was the cross listing of companies on both exchanges. When the two exchanges split in 1973, both continued to list all stocks at that time quoted. They were to all intents and purposes mirror images of each other and the regulatory systems and the legislative framework in which they operated were broadly similar. The difference was that Singapore had a reputation both locally and overseas for being a more developed and efficient financial centre. As a result, a good deal of the orders for Malaysian stocks graduated to Singapore. The Malaysian authorities to some extent compounded this natural advantage of Singapore by declining to list further foreign-incorporated stocks on the KLSE, whereas Singapore has allowed most newly-listed Malaysian-incorporated companies to have a quote on the SES, subject to a prospectus being issued in Singapore and minimal other formalities.

Malaysia's attitude towards foreign company listings has been dictated by the country's New Economic Policy (NEP), which aims at redistributing the country's wealth more in favour of the indigenous Malay community (which makes up just over a half of the population) and to some extent out of the hands of immigrant Chinese (who make up nearly another half) and of foreign investors. What redistribution there has been to date reflects mainly such forced divestment rather than through growth of the economy. In other words, Malays have taken a bigger share of the existing cake. Businesses wishing to list their shares on the KLSE have to vest their activities in Malaysian-incorporated companies which must comply with the requirements of the NEP, at least in terms of 30% Bumiputra ownership. (There was some noticeable softening of the official dedication to NEP goals evident in 1986 as recession bit deep into the Malaysian economy and this could have implications for future listings of foreign companies on the KLSE.)

By the end of 1985 there were considerably more Malaysian incorporated companies (183 of them) listed on the Stock Exchange of Singapore than companies incorporated in the island republic itself (122). Overseas incorporated companies (11) made up the remainder of the total 316 companies listed on the SES at that time. This compared with only 56 Singapore companies listed on the KLSE — roughly one quarter of the number of locally incorporated companies (222). Six United Kingdom-incorporated companies make up the remainder of the total 284 companies listed on the KLSE. Around the same time (November 1985) out of the total capitalisation of S$74 billion for all ordinary shares listed on the SES, no less than 47% (S$35 billion) was accounted for by Malaysian-incorporated companies. These companies accounted for 52% of the total volume of share trading on the SES in 1985. On the other hand, Singapore-incorporated companies represented only 31% (or M$23 billion) of the total capitalisation of the KLSE and a proportionately lower ratio of total trades done on the Malaysian exchange.

An even more telling statistic is the fact that the actual number of shares issued by Malaysian companies listed on the SES is double that of Singapore companies — some 20 billion compared

Table 60

	Stock Exchange of Singapore			Kuala Lumpur Stock Exchange		
		Turnover			Turnover	
	No. of Companies	Volume (shares m)	Value (S$m)	No. of Companies	Volume (shares m)	Value (M$m)
1974	263	534	1,140	264	391	723
1975	269	810	1,840	268	617	1,306
1976	269	715	1,941	264	432	1,011
1977	258	644	1,162	256	598	1,048
1978	266	1,492	3,387	253	1,107	2,539
1979	264	965	2,312	253	638	1,641
1980	261	2,222	7,825	250	1,482	5,600
1981	270	2,778	13,472	253	1,636	8,059
1982	288	1,666	5,177	261	1,066	3,253
1983	301	3,605	11,807	271	2,276	7,934
1984	308	3,043	8,211	281	1,852	5,714
1985	316	3,025	6,319	284	2,869	6,174
1986 (Jan-Jun)	317	1,467	2,722	287	972	1,379

These figures can be understated since there is no firm requirement that brokers report to the Exchanges crossed trades.

Source: Vickers da Costa

with around 10 billion. It was thus that Singapore came to be a theatre for what began as an essentially Malaysian phenomenon of share buy-back deals and forward contract financing. It is worth devoting some space to the genesis and development of this episode in the markets' history because it casts light on the nature of the capital markets which permitted it to happen — and provides a cautionary tale for investors.

There are various versions of just when and why forward contracts came into existence but they were essentially a device for maintaining share prices at high levels. Ironically, the form in which they were drawn up was based on a standard form of legal contract devised by a British law firm, though for an entirely different purpose. It has never been suggested that this firm had any part in what happened in Malaysia and Singapore.

The origin of the forward-contract affair probably goes back to the 1970s. Faced with a need at that time to restructure their assets (under the NEP) so as to permit bumiputra participation, numerous Chinese companies sought ways of maximising the value of those assets, so as to get the best price upon disposal. Some of the bigger and more inventive Chinese entrepreneurs hit upon an ingenious way of doing this. They bought dormant "shell" companies listed on the KLSE and persuaded other Chinese businessmen to sell their corporate assets to them, in exchange for shares in the shell company. Once these assets were injected into the shell it had real value, in return simply for issuing its own scrip. And when the former shells were restructured in line with the NEP — via the sale of a 30% stake to bumiputra institutions or individuals — the original vendors of assets to the shells were sure of a better price than they could have got by selling out direct.

Because the architects of such schemes — the "control groups" — had agreed to buy back the shares issued, at an agreed time and at a prearranged price (so as not to dilute their control over the shell companies), they had to find ways of supporting the market price if they were to avoid losses. So, the control groups — it is estimated that there were some 30-40 of them at one point, representing some of the biggest names in Malaysian-Chinese business — borrowed heavily from the banks and from stockbrokers in order to buy their own shares.

There were other reasons for such share ramping operations.

When the stock and property markets in both Malaysia and Singapore began to turn down, the instinct of the big individual traders and syndicate operators was to cut and run as usual, leaving less sophisticated souls to play the part of last man out. Many of them were heavily committed to property developments as well as their stockmarket positions, however. The only way they could see to offload greatly devalued real-estate assets was to back them into their public companies in return, ideally, for cash but if not then for scrip which could then be sold in the market. So here again, the name of the game was "support share prices at all costs."

The trick was finding ways to persuade banks to lend more than the 50% or so which they might normally be expected to provide by way of margin financing in return for share collateral — and how to obtain such money at below the margins which banks would normally demand. As it happened, banks in both Malaysia and Singapore were becoming increasingly flush with cash around this time because of the reduced demand for business loans in recession conditions. Bank money had not been tied up in the early 1980s property boom in Singapore and Malaysia to the extent that might have been expected, because local entrepreneurs had put much of their own money into development. It was here that the idea of forward contracts really came into its own.

The modus operandi was for a businessman to approach a stockbroker with a package of shares and a request that these be sold forward for settlement in three months time. The broker would pay the businessman around 95 cents in the dollar cash for the shares and in return he would get commission, interest charges and a guarantee that the vendor would buy the shares back at perhaps S$1.10 for every dollar's worth sold. The businessman would then approach a second and maybe third broker with an instruction to buy shares agressively in the company concerned. If the business-man was known to the brokers (as was usually the case) he would not have to pay immediately for the purchase of such shares and because he usually controlled the (fairly narrow) float of shares in the market, it was easy to get the price up. (As controllers of their own share registers in many cases, Malaysian company directors are able to engineer a shortage of scrip, especially at those times when shareholders have sent their shares to the registry in order to claim dividends).

Brokers in turn were able to approach banks for finance, using the buy-back guarantees as collateral. The supposedly bluest of blue-chip brokers in Malaysia and Singapore put their names to such deals — as did certain leading foreign brokers — and so the banks were happy to accept such collateral. They were in any case very anxious to obtain loan assets. It was, as one Malaysian broker who managed to stay clear of the whole money merry-go-round commented to the author, a case of "sheer greed" on the part of the brokers and the "usual herd instinct" among banks. Those who came off best were the businessmen who obtained bank finance to the extent of 100% of the value of their shares in this way, and managed to keep their share prices up in the meantime. Some were thus able to inject private assets into their companies and sell them off while the going was good. Many too, were able to liquidate their forward contracts before the crash came.

Table 61

The largest listed companies on the Stock Exchange of Singapore, end-1985		
Ranking	Company	Market value (Sing$ million)
1	Overseas Chinese Banking Corp	3,611.9
2	SIA	2,689.0
3	Sime Darby*	1,389.9
4	Singapore Press Holdings	1,374.0
5	Development Bank of Singapore	1,363.9
6	United Overseas Bank	1,277.8
7	Harrisons Malaysia*	1,264.4
8	Malayan Banking*	1,182.6
9	Genting*	990.7
10	Consolidated Plantations*	945.1
11	Overseas Union Enterprises	802.0
12	Fraser & Neave	705.6
13	Kuala Lumpur Kepong*	669.0
14	Malaysian Tobacco*	668.2
15	Highlands and Lowlands	640.4
16	Malayan Breweries*	632.5
17	Esso Malaysia*	621.0
18	Straits Trading	577.8
19	Malayan United Industries*	528.8
20	Goodwood Park	495.0

* Incorporated in Malaysia

Source: Stock Exchange of Singapore

The fact that when it did come it happened in Singapore was partly to do with the fact that Malaysian forward contractors had turned to Singapore banks and brokers for financing once liquidity began to dry up in Malaysia. They found a receptive group of new players there. And, of course, there were plenty of Malaysian counters listed on the stock exchange in Singapore which they could use for their games. When Pan-El went down (under the weight of perhaps more forward contracts than any single company had been committed to before) the mutual recriminations were as bitter as the shock was profound on both sides of the Causeway.

Certain Malaysian brokers refused to honour their obligations, and thus vital links in the forward-contract chain relating to the Pan-El group were broken. Things began to get very nasty with legal suits and counter suits flying between Kuala Lumpur and Singapore. One representative of a British broking house even received a death threat when he tried to collect from a defaulting Malaysian broker.

Singaporeans blamed Malaysians for importing what could at best be called sharp practices into Singapore. Malaysians, meanwhile, blamed Singaporean banks and brokers for playing fast and loose with their stockmarket, through forward-contract deals in Singapore-listed Malaysian stocks. Everyone was afraid that both countries stockmarkets might suffer such a catastrophic fall that many brokers and investors would be ruined. The reason for this was that no-one, least of all it seemed the regulatory authorities in each country, knew exactly how much money was out in forward contracts. The banks and brokers knew individually but they had little idea of their collective exposure.

Figures of S$1 billion and even several billion dollars were bandied around as the financial markets reeled from shock. Even this was feared to be only the tip of the iceberg. If banks began calling in all their loans against shares, brokers' ruin would compound the market crash. It was against this background that the SES and the KLSE made their decision (in retrospect probably a wise one) to close the market for three days while they assessed the damage, rather than let it find its own level. In a letter to the *Far Eastern Economic Review* early in January of 1986, an official of the Monetary Authority of Singapore (the quasi central bank) said in response to an article by the author, that the aggregate value of forward-contract obligations by Singapore stockbrokers was around

S$600 million. These could be met by the S$350 million of shareholders' funds held by the brokers (which were to be augmented to the tune of S$70 million) plus the proceeds of a S$180 million "lifeboat" fund put together with the aid of banks (though to be paid for ultimately by a levy on broking transactions).

This proved to be an over-sanguine view because not only did three broking firms in Singapore subsequently go into liquidation but a group of major foreign banks had to negotiate a ten-year loan to the broking industry in order to keep it afloat. They probably had little option if they hoped ever to recover the money they had loaned to brokers. In some cases it was thought likely that the banks would convert their loans into equity once Singapore altered its rules to enable foreign institutions to take stakes in local brokers.

Bank loans to the entire stockbroking industry in Singapore totalled S$668 million at the end of September 1986, of which around S$340 million was owed by five firms which went under — City Securities, E.G. Tan, Lin Securities, Lyall & Evatt and Associated Asian Securities. This money was thought unlikely to be recoverable. As at that time too, only S$12 million had been drawn from the S$180 million lifeboat by two firms, J. Ballas and Cathay Securities, who would have to continue paying a 0.25% transaction levy until the money was repaid. In addition, the SES paid out S$3 million to members of the public who were hit by the failure of local brokers.

If this chapter has dwelt at length on the forward-contracts affair, it is because it caused such a scandal both in Malaysia and overseas and because so many fundamental reforms to both Singapore and Malaysia's stockmarkets have since flowed from it. The fact that both markets could in effect be "rigged" on such a massive scale left investors and regulators agog. At the time, one reform-minded Malaysian merchant banker recalled for the author the words of former Malaysian Finance Minister Tun Tan Siew Sin after an earlier stockmarket crash in 1973. Tun Tan observed that the stockmarket "should be used as a means of making sound, long-term investments." Any departure from this principle, he cautioned, "can only result in badly burned fingers." So it did some 12 years later — and resulted in red faces at the MAS and at Malaysia's central bank, Bank Negara, which (along nowadays with the Ministry of Finance) are responsible for regulating the securities industry.

The immediate concern of these various supervisory bodies was first to salvage the stockbroking industry and then to improve its structure. This took precedence over the desire to split the two markets so that they would not be subject to joint manipulation and to a collective crash again. The first move in Singapore was to allow the four big local banks — Overseas-Chinese Banking Corporation, the Development Bank of Singapore, the Overseas Union Bank and the United Overseas Bank — to acquire seats on the SES. A fifth local bank, Tat Lee, was reportedly negotiating to take over one of the liquidated broking firms, Lyall & Evatt (among the oldest established in Singapore) at the time of writing.

These developments paved the way for corporatisation of the stockbroking profession in Singapore and ultimately for a substantial degree of foreign ownership of what had been very much a closed shop as far as outsiders are concerned. At the time of writing, a firm of British brokers, Hoare Govett, was understood to be in negotiation with a local broking firm, Summit Securities, for what might prove to be the first of the foreign incursions into Singapore broking. Foreigners were to be allowed a maximum 49% stake in any Singapore brokerage initially. But it seems likely that they will be allowed majority control after having held a minority stake for two or three years. Foreigners will not be permitted to buy seats outright on the Singapore exchange, however, as they are nowadays in Tokyo and Hongkong.

In retrospect it seems remarkable that the broking establishment could have remained so small for so long, given the international status of Singapore and the magnitude of trading done on the local stock exchange. There were 25 member companies of the SES and 109 individual stockbroking members of the exchange as at the end of 1985. Their capital and reserves (as was seen during the forward contract scandal) seemed dangerously small in relation to their commitments. Admittedly, Singapore brokers do not act as specialists who take large positions in stocks on their own books. But they seem to have managed to gear themselves up very highly, nevertheless.

It was only with the introduction of the revised Securities Industry Act in August 1985 that the minimum paid-up capital for broking firms was raised from S$5 million to S$10 million. At the time of the Pan-El affair, the biggest of the leading two dozen brokerages probably had shareholders' funds of around S$30 million each against forward contract obligations many times that

Table 62

	The most actively traded shares, Stock Exchange of Singapore, 1985	
Ranking	Company	Trading volume (shares 000)
1	Pahang Investments	142,303
2	Promet*	106,705
3	Pan-Electric Industries	99,501
4	Sime Darby*	82,281
5	Federal Cables & Wires*	82,155
6	Supreme Corporation*	74,521
7	Grand United Holdings*	74,446
8	Raleigh Cycles	68,291
9	Pegi	53,197
10	Malayan United*	51,647
11	United Overseas Bank	51,591
12	Duta Consolidated	50,579
13	Kuala Lumpur Industries*	49,032
14	Development Bank of Singapore	48,460
15	Genting*	48,265
16	Faber Merlin*	47,864
17	Overseas Chinese Banking Corp	47,007
18	Lum Chang	46,012
19	TDM	44,105
20	United Motor Works*	43,419

Source: SES

* Incorporated in Malaysia

size. The amended Securities Industry Act stipulated that brokers' total commitments should not exceed 12 times their capital base. The Stock Exchange of Singapore is likely to be even more cautious and apply a ratio of eight to one. More importantly, limits were introduced in the new Act controlling the extent to which a broker can commit himself to any particular stock or client.

The Malaysian authorities also moved quickly to the rescue of the country's beleagured stockbroking profession at the end of 1985. A M$80 million lifeboat fund was launched by the KLSE to protect innocent third-party clients of brokers hit by the forward contract failures. In Malaysia, as in Singapore, the Pan-Electric collapse embroiled people right at the top of the broking industry. The securities firm of OSK Partners, headed by then KLSE chairman Nik Mohamed Din and the firm of another former KLSE chairman, Noone & Co, were involved in disputes with Singapore brokers over the validity of forward contracts linked with the Tan Koon Swan stable of companies. The refusal by certain Malaysian brokers to honour forward-contracts debts to Singapore brokers helped push the Singapore firms into liquidation. Official receivers continued to pursue the claims however, and the expectation was that out of court settlements would be made in many cases for less than the full amount owed.

Around half a dozen of the 45 or so brokerage firms in Malaysia (having a total of 134 members on the KLSE) were involved in forward contracts, though none of them went into liquidation as in Singapore. The then governor of the Bank Negara, Aziz Taha, admitted that there were "major weaknesses in the structure of the stockmarket." Two which he cited were "under-capitalisation and over-trading" by broking firms and "large operators and syndicates dominating a relatively shallow market." Malaysia's answer, like Singapore's, was to bring in corporatisation of the broking industry and to permit at least partial foreign ownership of brokerages.

The tie-ups under negotiation toward the end of 1986 included Arab Malaysian Bank taking a stake in Kris Securities and an expected link between the government-controlled Bank Bumiputra and G.P. Securities. British broker W.I. Carr was expected to take a 30% stake in Kuala Lumpur broker Seagroatt & Campbell. In Malaysia, foreign institutions can technically own only 30% of a local brokerage, though the finance minister has powers to waive this limit. Such waivers are likely to be numerous.

Foreign brokers would naturally prefer to buy a seat on the KLSE but as that is not yet possible the probability is that they will buy into existing brokerages (so as to avoid commission sharing with local brokers). They will almost certainly insist on a new joint-venture corporate structure which does not get saddled with any of the existing debts from forward contracts. Ditto in the case of Singapore. Broking partnerships will go out in Malaysia as from 1987 and limited company status will come in (though with unlimited guarantees to clients). Seat money will be reintroduced by the KLSE and a seat will be subject to an annually renewable licence. Overall, the aim is to improve the professionalism of a profession which in the past has in the words of one of its own practitioners, ben interested "only in buying and selling."

There is one particular problem which brokers in Malaysia have to contend with and which prevents their growing to a size appropriate to that of the stockmarket. They are not permitted to have branch networks. Consequently, the type of securities houses which have grown up in Japan, for instance, by blanketing the country with branches have not developed in Malaysia. A senior executive of the KLSE told the author that branching was unlikely to be permitted. Instead, brokers would be encouraged to merge. At the same time, the exchange fears that once banks begin buying into brokerages they will quickly come to dominate the whole broking industry by virtue of establishing outlets for the brokers they control via their own extensive branch networks. Malaysian (and Singapore) brokers are not able to list their own shares on the local stockmarket either. So they are also deprived of an important means of boosting their (often inadequate) capital base.

The system of "Remisiers", or dealers' representatives, in both Malaysia and Singapore is yet another factor that militates against size among the securities houses. There are no fewer than 3,000 of these Remisiers in Malaysia (mainly Chinese, though including an increasing number of Bumiputra individuals nowadays) whose job is to collect share-trading business from friends, acquaintances or other contacts and to take it to the brokers. The Remisier keeps 40% of the commission on any deal he takes to a broker. Remisiers sit a KLSE examination and have to pay a deposit to the broker (probably as much as M$100,000 if they are Chinese and as little as M$30,000 if they are Bumiputras) but it cannot be said that they add to the overall degree of professionalism in the broking industry.

The brokers are highly dependent upon these people and their contacts for business. As a result, they often fail to build up their own sales teams and are not directly responsible for monitoring their client base. Neither is the deposit paid by the Remisier really big enough to cover the risks involved in dealing with unknown clients.

Despite such limitations, the forward-contracts debacle will result in the emergence of a stronger brokerage industry in Malaysia and Singapore. Even so, most investors will probably feel safest dealing with the bigger corporatised firms, especially where there is a big foreign partner involved. The forward-contract affair will also result in closer official supervision of the securities industry in both places.

In Singapore, administration of the Securities Industry Act was transferred to the MAS in 1985 and in November of the following year the MAS installed a new committee at the Stock Exchange of Singapore. Instead of being an all-broker affair as in the past, it now consists of four elected brokers and their five nominees — four bankers and a lawyer. The executive chairman of the committee (one of the five nominees) is an MAS governor (Tan Chok Kian) who is also chief executive of the government's Central Provident Fund (CPF). At the time these appointments were announced,

Table 63

Criteria for listing		
	Stock Exchange of Singapore	Kuala Lumpur Stock Exchange
Paid-up Capital	S$4 million minimum	M$5 million minimum
Proportion of Paid-up Capital to be held by Public	S$1.5 million or 25% of paid-up capital, (whichever is greater)	M$1.25 million or 25% of paid-up capital, (whichever is greater)
Profit Record	5 years	3 years
Net Tangible Assets Per Share	Not less than the par value of the share	—
Pricing of New Issue	Should justify projected prospective P/E indicated in prospectus	Prospective gross P/E of 3.5 times to 8 times

Source: Vickers da Costa

MAS managing director Joseph Pillay declared that having a non-broker as chairman of the SES committee would "inspire greater confidence in the investment community . . . a new era in the SES has now dawned." In other words, brokers, like bankers, will now be very much subject to MAS rule in Singapore.

The new Securities Industry Act in Singapore also stipulates that in margin-finance transactions, clients must put up 30% of the value of the contract and the financier can provide 50%. But here again, the SES will apply a more stringent 70:30% ratio to its members. (Forward contracts of course represented 100% financing). The "Settlement" system of allowing one month for share delivery (as distinct from the alternative "Ready" system of one week) was scrapped in 1986. Many brokers favour bringing in a 24-hour delivery system eventually, as in Hongkong.

In Malaysia, the finance minister has taken powers to appoint members to the KLSE and has brought control of the market more under the wing of his own ministry. The official Capital Issues Committee (CIC) which monitors securities transactions, has been brought under the chairmanship of the Secretary General of the Treasury instead of that of the Bank Negara governor. (The CIC is not to be confused with the Foreign Investment Committee or FIC, which decides matters relating to restructuring of equity ownership and corporate acquisitions and which comes directly under the Prime Minister's Department).

The next big question to be addressed, and one which again flows from the Pan-El affair indirectly, is when and how the stockmarkets of Singapore and Kuala Lumpur will be formally split. Immediately after the Pan-El affair there were plenty of people advocating such a move. Singapore brokers, hurt by defaulted forward-contract deals, declared the whole thing to be a result of "huge amounts of junk paper" issued by Malaysian companies. They argued that as soon as Malaysia, in its "rather lax" way, allowed such paper to be listed on the KLSE, more or less automatic listing was permitted on the SES. Singapore was more thorough vetting new companies before initial listing, they argued.

Malaysian brokers for their part noted the ease with which big operators had been able to raise finance in Singapore and use it to punt on Malaysian stocks via the SES. It did not escape their attention either that two of the leading companies in the Pan-El stable (Growth Industrial Holdings and Sigma International which were heavily involved in bad forward contracts) were Singapore incorporated entities. More sombre voices noted, however, that it could be a retrograde step to sever links between the two stockmarkets at a time when markets in other countries were doing all they could to encourage cross-listing of foreign companies.

Throughout most of 1986, no market split materialised and it appeared that the issue had been forgotten about. But then in November an Opposition member raised a question on the issue in the Malaysian parliament and there was immediately speculation that the split would be formally announced during the Malaysian budget a week or so later. In the event, no such announcement came, though this was almost certainly because the governments of both Malaysia and Singapore wanted to get stockbroking reforms through before proceeding with significant structural changes in their markets. Some form of split appears inevitable before long.

It seems very unlikely that this will take the form of a delisting of Malaysian stocks in Singapore and vice-versa. More likely, it will involve, initially at least, the establishing of separate share registries in each country. The implications of such a move go well beyond the purely technical. The decision by the SES and the KLSE to permit common registration of shares after the exchanges split has often led to inordinate delays in registration, in scrip loss, in theft and in forgery. It has also permitted companies which operate their own registries to manipulate the market in their own stocks.

Ordinary shares in both Singapore and Malaysia are normally registered rather than bearer instruments, though many speculators do not bother to register before selling again. They register their stock only when they need to qualify for dividends. One problem is that scrip takes generally at least four weeks to register in Malaysia. There is a tremendous amount of scrip shuffled around the country as well as back and forward between Malaysia and Singapore. It is not unknown for the scrip to be hijacked en-route or for a printer to borrow it from a Remisier in order to do a forging job and then sell the fake scrip for a nice profit. A central depository in each country, with a system of depository receipts being issued in lieu of scrip, would put an end to all these movements and dramatically reduce the scope for theft and fraud, advocates claim. It would also prevent the engineering of scrip shortages by individual companies.

The implications go even deeper. Singapore has traditionally been the preferred centre for dealing even in Malaysian stocks

because brokers there could produce large lines of stock when
required — or conversly absorb relatively large lines. In Malaysia,
by contrast, brokers as a rule find it very hard to lay hands on big
lines. Any attempt to unload even 100,000 shares or so can push
their price down sharply. It is a shallow market where deals are
done in lots of 10 or so rather than in lots of 50. Because Singapore
brokers tend to have better international connections than do their
Malaysian counterparts, companies and investors are more willing
to make scrip available to them. Thus, the situation feeds upon
itself, aided by the fact that Malaysian companies' scrip can just as
easily be registered in Singapore as in Malaysia itself. This is
probably about to change. As one Malaysian broker put it to the
author: "After the split, there will still be dual listing of stocks but
separate registration. So London and other foreign brokers will

Table 64

The largest listed companies on the Kuala Lumpur Stock Exchange, end-1985

Ranking	Company	Market value (Malay$ million)
1	Overseas-Chinese Banking Corporation (OCBC)*	4,143.2
2	Sime Darby Bhd	1,853.2
3	Development Bank of Singapore Ltd*	1,828.8
4	Harrisons Malaysian Plants Bhd	1,692.0
5	United Overseas Bank Ltd*	1,443.8
6	Malayan Banking Bhd	1,431.4
7	Genting Bhd	1,175.5
8	Consolidated Plantations Bhd	1,105.1
9	Highlands and Lowlands Bhd	906.5
10	Malaysian Breweries Ltd*	898.6
11	Malaysian Tobacco Co Bhd	789.8
12	Malayan Airlines System Bhd	784.0
13	Kuala Lumpur Kepong Bhd	782.5
14	Fraser & Neave Ltd*	774.9
15	Esso Malaysia Bhd	718.2
16	Straits Trading Co Ltd*	677.7
17	Malayan United Industries Bhd	631.4
18	Shangri-La Hotel Ltd*	530.0
19	Multi-Purpose Holdings Bhd	518.2
20	Rothmans (M) Bhd	508.1

Source: KLSE

* Incorporated in Malaysia

have to come to Malaysia for stock. This will help to cut capital outflows."

Malaysian brokers realise that this in turn means that they must offer better service to foreign investors, especially institutional investors. Haji Ahmad bin Kadis, managing director of Seagroatt & Campbell, commented that, "any stockbroker in Malaysia who wants to be in the forefront in future will have to improve his capacity to handle large lines of stock and to provide clients with research." Seagroatt has teamed up with British brokers W.I. Carr on Malaysian research in order to learn how it is done. Other Malaysian brokers will almost certainly follow suit. Corporatisation will enhance brokers' ability to handle large lines of stock but they will still have to work harder to persuade institutions to make such lines available to them.

The Chinese broking firms in Malaysia fear, meanwhile, that they may have an especially difficult time in future because of the increasing amount of wealth passing into Bumiputra hands via agencies such as the "national" (meaning Bumiputra) equity corporation Permodolan Nasional Berhad and its associated unit trust Amanah Sahan Nasional. A partner in the Chinese-dominated firm of Charles Bradburne & Co in Kuala Lumpur expressed the fear that agencies such as these and the Tabung Haji (Pilgrim's Fund) would increasingly put their broking business the way of bumiputra brokers in future. Others are more sanguine. Jock Chua (himself a Chinese) of Halim Securities claims that it is a question of "who you know rather than whether you are Chinese or Malay." The solution for most Chinese broking firms (in what has tradition- ally been very much a Chinese-dominated industry) will be, as in Halim Securities' case, to get a bumiputra partner or principal.

If much has been said thus far about likely (and needed) reforms in the Malaysian and Singapore stockmarkets, more needs to be said now about the basic structure of these markets. As noted above, both markets are large in relation to the economies in which they exist, at least in terms of total capitalisation. But this is in a sense misleading. In Singapore's case, a very large part of the capitalisation is attributable to Malaysian companies and in both countries the large capitalisations are partly a function of the high rating put on shares. In Singapore for instance, even at the nadir of the bear market which followed the Pan-El affair, stocks in the local Straits Times 800 share index were selling at around 35 times historic earnings and 25 times prospective earnings. Similar ratios applied in Malaysia.

The 122 local companies listed on the SES are fewer than in Taiwan (130) and much smaller than the 342 listed in South Korea, both of which are nominally much smaller markets. Admittedly, both of these latter countries have considerably larger economies than Singapore's but nevertheless the stockmarket board in Singapore excludes many areas of the republic's economic activity and the same is becoming true of Malaysia too.

A look at the top 20 stocks by capitalisation on the SES reveals the presence of two foreign companies (Hongkong Land and ABN) and a clutch of Malaysian companies — mainly plantations plus a casino operator. Various banks and property companies are listed too, along with some big traders. But there are few indications among this list of the industrial and hi-tech economy which Singapore aspires to be. Manufacturing companies do not figure on the SES in equal proportion to the 20% of GNP which the manufacturing sector is responsible for. There are various reasons for this. One is that foreign multinational corporations account for the lion's share of activities such as electronics and computers, and scientific instruments which Singapore has assiduously promoted. Another is that the government holding company "Tamasek" has a stable of industrial share holdings which are thus not available to investors at large. National Iron and Steel is also a state-owned company.

Few foreign multinationals, with the exception of those such as Shell and Esso, have yet shown any inclination to list their shares locally in Singapore. But the government does have it in its power to privatise more of the state companies and thereby expand the stockmarket menu. There is clearly an investor appetite for such issues. When Singapore Airlines (SIA) offered around 16% of its stock to the public (Tamasek retaining the lion's share of the remainder) even in the middle of the Pan-El crisis in December 1985, the shares were quickly snapped up. The issue was made at S$5 a share and subsequently sank to S$3.80, though in 1986 it reached S$10 at one stage.

Foreign institutional and individual investors were especially keen on the issue and within a short space of time they appeared to have acquired just about all the shares issued. This posed a dilemma for the Singapore government which, like its Malaysian counterpart, has a 20% limit on foreign holdings of "sensitive" stocks such as airlines, banks and so on. Any holdings acquired in excess of this limit cannot be registered, so a premium market quickly developed in SIA stock with foreign investors clamouring to buy from other existing foreign holders.

It remains to be seen whether Singapore will allow the 20% ceiling to be breached eventually. Malaysia seems likely to do so in respect of its own national carrier, Malaysian Airline System (MAS). Thirty per cent of MAS shares were floated in 1986 (following the SIA float) and in October of that year the government announced its intention of offering a further 15% of MAS to European and American investors. This would certainly take their aggregate holdings above 20% but in Malaysia's case the need for the government to raise money appeared to have taken precedence over other policy considerations. Two state-owned Singapore shipping companies, Neptune Orient Lines and Keppel Shipyard,

Table 65

The most actively traded shares on the KLSE in 1985		
Ranking	Company	Turnover (000)
1	Metroplex Bhd	124,820
2	Raleigh Bhd	104,409
3	Norsechem Bhd	78,690
4	MBF Holdings Bhd	77,289
5	Malaysian Resources Corporation Bhd	63,551
6	Johan Holdings Bhd	60,140
7	Federal Cables, Wires & Metal Mfg Bhd	59,539
8	Emtex Corporation Bhd	58,643
9	Innovest Bhd	51,941
10	Chocolate Products (Malaysia) Bhd	51,386
11	Pahang Investments plc	49,382
12	Grand United Holdings Bhd	46,450
13	Duta Consolidated Bhd	46,182
14	Malayan United Manufacturing	43,630
15	Kian Joo Can Factory Bhd	40,475
16	Supreme Corporation Bhd	37,409
17	Kumpulan Emas Bhd	35,746
18	Hong Kong Tin Corp (Malaysia) Bhd	35,105
19	Malaysian Mosaics Bhd	34,982
20	Bedford Bhd	33,987

Source: Kuala Lumpur Stock Exchange

have also offered stock to the public (with mixed success) but what investors would really like is a bite of Singapore's profitable utilities. They are unlikely to get it, at least in the short term. "The big state companies are all profitable but the pace of privatisation will be slow," one Singapore broker noted. "Getting new companies to list now is like finding gold," adds a local merchant banker.

One reason is that Prime Minister Lee Kuan Yew reputedly views his civil servants as being too valuable to assign them completely to the private sector, and does not believe there are enough good people in the local private sector to take over the running of state companies. It might be added too that Lee has the reputation of believing in socialism or at least state capitalism, rather than undiluted private capitalism. His government's numerous clashes with prominent big businessmen (some of whom have ended up in jail on various charges) is also a salutory reminder of Singapore's ambivalent attitude towards capitalism.

A somewhat similar situation applies in Malaysia with regard to the potential future expansion of the stockmarket through new listings. Only in this case, it is a question of new economic development taking place outside the domain of the private sector. The number of indigenous companies listed on the KLSE is large in relation to the size of the economy, albeit increasingly unrepresentative of a fast-growing section of that economy. Plantation and financial stocks dominate the upper end of the market, with a sprinking of industrials such as Fraser & Neave and Tasek Cement.

What is missing is the clutch of major industries in the stable of the government-owned conglomerate Hicom. Established in 1981, to further the ideal of Prime Minister Mahathir Mohamad that Malaysia graduate from a plantation economy to industrialised-country status, Hicom holds four cement factories, petrochemical and methane complexes, a sponge iron plant and the company which manufactures the "Malaysian" car (actually a joint venture with the Japanese), the Proton Saga. A listing for Hicom "would give respectability to the Malaysian stockmarket," Haji Ahmad bin Kadis of brokers Seagroatt & Campbell noted. So too would the proposed listing of the national shipping company, Malaysian International Shipping Corporation (MISC) and of the national telecommunications network or even the national railways. In Malaysia's case, this may well happen quicker than in Singapore's given the current exigencies of the national finances.

Singapore, meanwhile, is addressing the problem of getting new company listings, not from the top down but from the bottom up. An official economic reform committee set up to find ways of pulling Singapore out of its protracted recession in 1984 and headed by Lee Kwan Yew's son (and heir apparent) Brigadier General Lee Hsien Loong, included among its recommendations one that an Unlisted Securities Market (USM) be established to "help expand the stock market and promote the development of the fund-management industry." The idea is that small companies which are unable to go to the big board — either the first or second section — for a listing should turn to the USM instead.

Singapore's USM will be known as Sesdaq, or Stock Exchange of Singapore Automated Quotations. An earlier proposal to call it Semaq (Stock Exchange Market for Automated Quotations) had to be dropped when it was discovered that the acronym sounded too much like the word for "sudden death" in one of the local Chinese dialects. Singapore would not want to risk having another sudden or lingering death on its hands following the failure of the local market in traded share options which was set up in the late 1970s. Such symbols matter a lot in Chinese societies.

Sesdaq will be a market-making system run by the SES and with brokers, banks and merchant banks participating. It is expected to get off the ground some time in 1987. Admission standards would be less demanding than those for the big boards. For instance, a company may well be admitted with a three-years' track record instead of five years and the minimum paid up capital requirement may be S$1 million instead of S$3 million. The idea is a good one, provided the new exchange takes a liberal view (as London has done with its own USM) of what stocks are elligible for listing and does not insist on pure venture-capital situations or high-tech companies only.

One former chairman of the SES told the author in a conversation before the Sesdaq was launched that he feared this was precisely what would happen. According to this well-informed source, as much as 80% of the companies in Singapore are unable to meet the full SES requirements and are thus "squeezed by the banks" when they need finance. But the majority of them are rather mundane component manufacturers, service establishments, commercial firms and so on which would not look very exciting on a new issue prospectus, even if they are vital to the economy. The SES claimed in response, however, that "we will not close our eyes to any company on the USM."

An interesting sidelight on the nature of the Singapore market as a whole comes from the USM. Some local brokers fear that the "still active" local shareholding syndicates and other would-be market manipulators will seize eagerly upon the USM as a new theatre of operations. Because the float of USM companies' shares will be relatively small and the market in them comparitively narrow, syndicates will find it easy to corner the market and to squeeze the market makers, say some brokers. "This could lead to a thousand small Pan-El-type situations," warned one. For the record, similar fears apply in Malaysia as a result of amendments that were proposed to the National Land Code at the end of 1986. These would permit agricultural (including plantation) land to be pledged as security to foreign banks. This prompted a local broker to comment to the author that a whole new raft of forward-contract deals might well be predicated upon such security in future instead of upon share collateral.

The idea of an unlisted securities market or over-the-counter market for shares does not appear to have received serious consideration in Malaysia yet, apart from privately by a few

Table 66

Number of listed companies, market value overall and by sector, Kuala Lumpur Stock Exchange, end-1985

Sector	No of listed companies Domestic	Foreign	Total	No of securities (million)	Market value (Malay$ million)
Industrials	134	32	166	15,582.9	28,193.0
Finance	14	8	22	4,420.0	12,894.1
Hotels	2	9	11	881.8	2,356.2
Properties	13	7	20	2,687.6	3,536.2
Palm Oils	12	0	12	1,471.8	4,357.6
Tins	19	4	23	812.6	1,297.8
US$ Rubbers	29	0	29	2,448.6	4,792.4
£ Rubbers	0	1	1	4.1	82.5
Total	223	61	284	28,309.4	57,510.3

Source: Kuala Lumpur Stock Exchange

forward-thinking individuals such as Dato Malek Merican, managing director of Arab-Malaysian Merchant Bank. Dato Merican has also advocated a one-stop capital markets agency in Malaysia to both develop and monitor capital markets instead of the plethora of agencies which currently exist. But factional interests within government and government agencies seem too strong to permit such an elegant solution at present.

Malaysia is, in any case, too preoccupied with redividing its equity cake between Chinese and Bumiputras to consider anything so straight-forward as a USM. For many years, the KLSE was preoccupied with the establishment of a special Bumiputra stock exchange. Ultimately it was established but few would claim that it has been a great success. The special exchange, where it was envisaged that the unsophisticated small Bumiputra investors would be free to trade their shares free of the machinations of the bigger (mainly Chinese) market operators, was originally set up under the auspices of MARA (the Council of Trust for Indigenous People). It was later transferred to Komplek Kawangan (Financial Complex Berhad) with current deputy Prime Minister Ghafar Baba as its chairman. It has only nine companies listed (with a minimum paid up capital of M$250,000) and because it has no marketing network small farmers and other Bumputras in rural areas need to come to Kuala Lumpur if they wish to trade shares. There is no trading floor. The KLSE has proposed that the Bumi market move into the exchange proper to assist the marketability of its stocks. But this would presumably mean that it would be subject to the provisions of the Securities Industry Act and the market is not big enough or sophisticated enough for that.

Neither is it likely to become so because the Malaysian government's preferred vehicle nowadays for getting a stake in the nation's manufacturing and business enterprises into the hands of Bumiputras is the national unit trust Amanah Sahan. In the several years that it has been in existence, this trust has acquired over 2 million unit holders or around 40% of the eligible Bumiputra population and at the time of writing money was flowing in at the rate of around M$70 million a month. This is hardly surprising given the attractive inducements to invest. For a minimum investment of M$10, a Bumiputra investor has 100 units of M$1 each earmarked for him and which accrue to him in full by 1990. This particular bit of legerdemain is achieved through the device of having assets bought by the government in the first place (often at a premium) and then transferred at well below book value to Amanah Sahan. Amanah Sahan units are marketed via banks rather than brokers.

Malaysia perhaps does not need a USM in the same way that Singapore does because the number of new listings (both in terms of companies and shares) has grown quite briskly over the years despite rather cumbersome and restrictive listing procedures. It is these new listings in Malaysia that have in turn helped boost the size of the Singapore market and it is probable that Singapore's plans for a USM are in part an insurance against the day when it will decline to list all but blue-chip Malaysian stocks.

The number of companies listed on the KLSE grew by 33 between 1980 and 1985, which is reasonably good. What is remarkable is the number of shares in issue more than tripled over this period, from 8.7 billion to over 27 billion. Much of this increase, however, derives from the popularity of bonus issues with local investors and the numerous shares issued in pursuit of takeover bids. It also reflects the large numbers of new shares that companies have had to issue to Bumiputras in pursuance of the NEP. (Underwriting of new share issues is not approved until 30% is firmly committed by Bumiputra investors, including government agencies, pension funds and social welfare organisations).

The Malaysian new-issue market is unfree in other respects too.

Table 67

	New issues in Malaysia, 1984-85[1]			
	1984		1985	
	No. of companies	Value (Malay$ million)	No. of companies	Value (Malay$ million)
Rights issues	29	1,284.5	8	348.2
Special issues	16	372.4	6	66.5
New listings	14	160.3	5	199.6
Total	59	1,817.2	19	614.3

[1]The table relates only to companies incorporated in Malaysia and does not include companies which are incorporated in Singapore and which have a dual listing on the KLSE.

Source: Rashid Hussain Securities Sdn Bhd

Companies are allowed to issue or list shares at prices ranging from only 4 to 8 times their pre-tax earnings for instance. This "systematic underpricing of shares," as Dato Merican refers to it, is typical of many countries in the region and often results in massive over-subscriptions of new issues and consequently in heavy short-term profits for those lucky enough to be allocated shares. It encourages the casino mentality. Hopes that companies would be free to issue shares on the basis purely of net worth and earnings capacity have so far proved unfounded.

This applies as much to Singapore as it does to Malaysia. For example, forced divestment of interests to the public by local newspaper companies have been made at net asset value with nothing allowed for the (usually heavy) goodwill element that such a company would normally command in its balance sheet. The local bus company was forced to go to market too, at a considerable discount to its true worth. This is yet another example of the guided capitalism practised in both countries and official distrust of the market mechanism. Yet, at the same time, this rather paternalistic attitude toward the development of the primary capital markets sits uneasily with the rampant speculation and often manipulation which goes on in the secondary markets.

So far the Malaysian government's attempts to intervene in the secondary market have been rather arbitrary and ill-adept — though it must in fairness be said that they have not been so heavy handed as in places such as South Korea and Taiwan. The current Finance Minister in Malaysia (Daim Zainuddin) has especially laid himself open to charges of interference with the market. In February 1985, for instance, his ministry announced a freeze on new share listings, to allow the stockmarket to "consolidate." This was widely regarded as an unwarranted intervention in the market.

Daim also exhorted banks and other institutional investors to buy shares because they were fundamentally "cheap." This provoked the comment by one Hongkong fund manager (at an Asian Development Bank seminar on capital market development) that if any minister feels free to declare that a market is cheap he has a moral duty to point out to investors when the market is dear. Better still, ministers should maintain a safe distance from such things.

Many people in Malaysia felt that Daim had not distanced himself sufficiently from his own business connections and dealings upon assuming office. In September of 1986, Prime Minister

Mahathir finally announced that cabinet ministers and their immediate families were to reduce their holdings in listed companies. Days after this announcement, the finance minister went ahead with a sale of his controlling interest in United Malayan Banking Corp. (UMBC) to the Malaysian state-owned Perbadanan Nasional Bhd (Pernas) on terms which were generally reckoned to be favourable to the vendor. Deputy Prime Minister Ghafar Baba also disposed of share stakes.

It was not only government ministers who were selling heavily around this time. A massive disposal of Malaysian shares to foreigners was taking place — one which promised to alter the fundamental structure of share ownership. First, a large block of shares worth M$120 million in Malaysian conglomerate Sime Darby was placed in London, Hongkong and Singapore. The seller was initially thought to be Daim, though he subsequently denied it and the vendor was disclosed to be a semi-state agency Peremba. Shortly after this, the government placed a big block of Malaysian Airline System (MAS) shares (15% in fact) with foreign investors for a total of M$236 million. (Given that foreign buyers had already acquired a substantial part of the 30% of MAS which the government had earlier floated, this almost inevitably meant that the 20% limit on overseas holdings had been breached). Sime Darby, in turn (which is effectively government controlled since it was "bought

Table 68

Nominal Value of Listed Bonds, Debentures, Loan Stocks and Notes				
As At		28.6.85	30.12.85 (In Millions)	30.6.86
Malaysian	Bonds	M$18.96 (US$7.61)	M$18.96 (US$7.78)	M$18.96 (US$7.89)
	Debentures	M$2.81 (US$1.13)	M$2.81 (US$1.15)	M$2.81 (US$1.17)
	Loan Stocks	M$133.85 (US$53.72)	M$133.28 (US$54.69)	M$133.28 (US$55.45)
	Notes	M$392.12 (US$157.38)	M$388.09 (US$159.25)	M$387.55 (US$161.24)
Singapore	Loan Stock	M$308.48 (US$123.81)	M$261.87 (US$107.46)	M$271.86 (US$113.11)

KLSE

back" from British interests via Malaysian state agencies at the end of the 1970s) disposed of a 10% stake in its subsidiary Consolidated Plantations. A local publisher, the Fleet Group, was also looking to place 20% of its stock with foreigners, though in the event had to place them with Singapore interests. City Developments in Singapore placed 30 million shares overseas too.

The significance of all these, and reportedly many more, disposals of stock to foreigners seemed potentially far reaching.

Table 69

Kuala Lumpur Stock Exchange	
Turnover & Value	Jan-June 1986
Local Companies	
Bonds	
Turnover	381,000 Units
Value	M$358,000
	(US$148,949)
Average Daily	
Turnover	3,149 Units
Value	M$2,959
	(US$1,231)
Loan Stocks	
Turnover (Mln units)	4.17
Value (Mln)	M$3.39
	(US$1.41)
Average Daily	
Turnover (Mln units)	0.03
Value (Mln)	M$0.03
	(US$0.01)
Shares	
Turnover (Mln units)	1,105.50
Value(Mln)	M$1,545.59
	(US$643.06)
Average Daily	
Turnover (Mln units)	9.14
Value (Mln)	M$12.77
	(US$5.31)
Foreign Companies Shares	
Turnover (Mln units)	30.62
Value (Mln)	M$91.36
	(US$38.01)
Average Daily	
Turnover (Mln units)	0.25
Value (Mln)	M$0.76
	(US$0.31)

Overseas investors who had long complained that they were unable to lay hands on large lines of Malaysian stocks found the situation reversed almost overnight. Coming at the same time as a severe austerity budget announced in October 1986 by minister Daim, the sales added credence to the view that the Malaysian government was being compelled to raise funds in any way it could, especially as its burden of foreign debt was mounting rapidly.

This view was reinforced by concurrent moves to amend the land code (referred to above) in a way which enables foreigners to purchase agricultural land. The irony of this was that it appears to herald a reversal of the Malaysian government's policy of buying back its plantations from foreign (mainly British) ownership — again presumably in the interests of raising money. There were numerous large share placements going into foreign hands from private sources in Malaysia and Singapore at the same time. These almost certainly reflected attempts by big market operators in both countries to unwind their positions in the wake of the forward-contract affair as banks, especially foreign ones, intensified their efforts to recover loans made to individuals and brokers.

Indeed, the sharp rise in the Singapore stockmarket during the latter part of 1986 — accompanied by a somewhat more modest rise on the KLSE — appeared to owe more to financial engineering than to fundamental economic factors. The Singapore government, which had already amended the rules affecting the national provident fund (CPF) in May to allow members to use 20% of their investible savings to buy shares, unit trusts and gold, permitted them in October to use a further 20% for this purpose. These moves promised to bring S$4 billion or more into the market eventually, if CPF holders so chose.

As a good deal of the early releases from the CPF, in fact, went to refinancing existing positions rather than financing new investments, the moves seemed designed to help improve market liquidity in general and the position of hard-pressed brokers and individuals in particular. Numerous Singapore government companies and agencies, as well as the army pension fund, were reported to be heavy buyers of shares at this time too, reinforcing the idea that an officially-orchestrated bale out was in progress.

Brokers and merchant banks in Singapore estimated around this time that as much as 60% of the hectic share buying in the local market was being done by foreigners and a further 20% by state institutions. One foreign broker estimated that the level of foreign ownership in many Singapore (and Malaysian) stock could have risen from around 10% in the middle of 1986 to nearer 30% by the year end as a result of the buying spree. "There has been a tremendous shift of ownership from locals," he commented to the author. "Syndicates, brokers and banks have all been liquidating shares, and individuals in Singapore and Malaysia have been massive sellers. All the stocks are going overseas." Singaporean analysts took a more conservative view. In the view of one working for Merrill Lynch, the foreign component in total share ownership in Singapore doubled from around 5% to over 10% during 1986. Probably the truth lay somewhere between the two estimates.

It was too early at the time of writing to assess what overall impact this would have on share ownership in both countries but it seemed likely to be significant. For Malaysia, history seemed to be repeating itself because traditionally the majority of shareholders in most quoted companies there were domiciled outside the region (principally in the U.K.) until the government began buying back

Table 70

Listing and Trading on the KLSE and SES				
	KLSE (M$ billion)	%	SES (S$ billion)	%
Number of companies listed (As at November 1985)	283	100.0%	315	100.0%
of which: Malaysian incorporated	222	78.4%	183	58.1%
Singaporean incorporated	) 61	) 21.6%	121	38.4%
Other foreign incorporated	)	)	11	3.5%
Total market value (As at November 1985)	64.2	100.0%	73.9	100.0%
of which: Malaysian incorporated	43.6	67.9%	34.9	47.2%
Singaporean incorporated	) 20.6	) 32.1%	23.0	31.1%
Other foreign incorporated	)	)	16.1	21.8%
Turnover by value (Jan-Nov 1985)	5.9	100.0%	6.0	100.0%
of which: Malaysian incorporated	NA		3.1	51.7%
Singaporean incorporated	NA		2.8	46.7%
Other foreign incorporated	NA		0.1	1.7%

Source: KLSE Investors' Digest & SES Journal

plantations, tin companies and other interests under the NEP. The result of this exercise was a remarkable shift of shares into the hands of domestic institutions.

A little-publicised survey by the KLSE revealed that by the beginning of 1985 institutional holdings of Malaysian shares had reached just under a half (47.8%) of total holdings, while individual holdings represented another 25% or so and nominee holdings (held mainly on behalf of individuals) a further 25%. This high institutional concentration surprised even the KLSE. Traditionally, private holders had accounted for as much as 60 or 65% of total holdings. Previous estimates had suggested that only 20% of total holdings were in the hands of investment companies such as the the state-run Permodolan Nasional Berhad (National Equity Corporation), pension funds such as the EPF and state economic development corporations. Merchant banks and insurance companies were thought to hold a further 10-15% and foreign investors around 5%. These figures are certainly history now.

The SES does not publish a breakdown of shareholders by institutional and individual holdings. This is curious for a market which purports to be so open. Even the relatively closed markets of South Korea and Taiwan publish detailed breakdowns. It is possibly because the authorities in Singapore do not wish to publicise too much the position of institutions such as the CPF as shareholders, or the large holdings by government corporations such as Tamasek, Intraco and others. The size of some of these stakes in listed companies is thought to range from 20 to 70%. OCBC is also a major holder of stakes in many listed companies. One foreign broker estimated that if these various holdings are taken out of the equation, then the proporation of "free" stock available for trading in Singapore is only 30-40%. This may also help explain why stockmarket turnover in both Singapore and Malaysia is low as a proportion of market capitalisation — sometimes as low as one tenth in a year — though the inveterate market traders in Taiwan manage to achieve remarkable levels of turnover on a relatively low proportion of free stock.

The dominant position of the CPF in Singapore as an absorber of savings has limited the growth of investments institutions dramatically. Insurance companies and private pension funds do not show up to anything like the extent they would elsewhere as forces in the stockmarket. And mutual funds do not exist, though

Table 71

Ownership of a representative sample of 128 Malaysian companies as at December 31st, 1984

		Industrial	Finance	Hotels	Property	Rubber	Oil Palm	Tin	Total Commercial
Individual Shareholdings	No. Of Companies	79	8	6	9	13	8	5	128
	Shares Issued (Units)	1,924,360,979	520,240,499	31,214,310	198,103,408	208,002,629	146,916,960	12,112,465	3,040,951,250
	% Of Total Sector Shares	27.29	26.67	9.72	21.16	23.08	23.02	22.05	—
	% Of Total Market Shares	15.47	4.18	0.25	1.59	1.67	11.98	0.10	24.44
	Paid-Up Capital ($)	1,655,832,488	432,183,745	35,457,357	179,954,928	198,257,926	112,456,087	11,245,328	2,625,387,859
	% Of Total Sector Paid-Up Capital	27.61	26.86	9.75	22.36	22.77	11.44	23.96	—
	% Of Total Market Paid-Up Capital	15.51	4.05	0.33	1.69	1.86	1.05	0.11	24.60
	No. Of Shareholders	361,517	90,685	6,545	62,894	36,891	24,651	4,281	587,464
	% Of Total Sector Shareholders	96.00	96.43	93.84	97.17	94.29	92.31	91.28	—
	% Of Total Market Shareholders	58.99	14.80	1.07	10.26	6.02	4.02	0.70	95.86
Institutional Shareholdings	No. Of Companies	79	8	6	9	13	8	5	128
	Shares Issued (Units)	3,082,815,741	808,706,944	171,136,464	512,264,773	507,091,829	827,158,591	37,332,471	5,946,506,813
	% Of Total Sector Shares	43.72	41.45	53.30	54.71	56.27	67.46	67.95	—
	% Of Total Market Shares	24.78	6.50	1.38	4.12	4.08	6.65	0.30	47.79
	Paid-Up Capital ($)	2,642,955,135	776,889,474	188,158,800	429,872,685	501,102,428	684,996,389	32,220,451	5,256,195,362
	% Of Total Sector Paid-Up Capital	44.08	48.29	51.76	53.41	57.56	69.69	68.64	—
	% Of Total Market Paid-Up Capital	24.76	7.28	1.76	4.03	4.69	6.42	0.30	49.24
	No. Of Shareholders	10,953	2,108	349	1,166	1,480	1,388	232	17,676
	% Of Total Sector Shareholders	2.91	2.24	5.00	1.80	3.78	5.20	4.95	—
	% Of Total Market Shareholders	1.79	0.34	0.06	0.19	0.24	0.23	0.04	2.88
Nominees Shareholdings	No. Of Companies	78	8	6	9	13	8	5	127
	Shares Issued (Units)	1,833,261,771	622,053,108	118,725,288	225,896,250	186,008,181	252,057,934	5,496,101	3,243,498,633
	% Of Total Sector Shares	26.00	31.88	36.98	24.13	20.64	20.56	10.00	—
	% Of Total Market Shares	14.73	5.00	0.95	1.82	1.50	2.03	0.04	26.07
	Paid-Up Capital ($)	1,592,218,082	399,693,735	139,939,356	194,986,818	171,211,525	185,471,229	3,477,440	2,686,998,185
	% Of Total Sector Paid-Up Capital	26.55	24.84	38.49	24.23	19.67	18.87	7.41	—
	% Of Total Market Paid-Up Capital	14.92	3.74	1.31	1.83	1.60	1.74	0.03	25.17
	No. Of Shareholders	5,327	1,255	213	644	751	674	172	9,036
	% Of Total Sector Shareholders	1.41	1.33	3.05	1.00	1.92	2.52	3.67	—
	% Of Total Market Shareholders	0.87	0.20	0.03	0.11	0.12	0.11	0.03	1.47

there are a number of specialised unit trusts nowadays. If unit trusts are formed to channel CPF savings into the market, as seems possible, this could help transform the position in future, however. Neither has an active private mutual fund or unit trust industry been encouraged in Malaysia. There are a few private funds, such as the Asia Unit Trust and the Kuala Lumpur Mutual Fund, but so far the government-owned PNB and Amanah Sahan have been all powerful (along with special funds allied to Chinese guilds and companies such as Multi-Purpose Holdings of which Tan Koon Swan was a controller). This again seems destined to change, though as the government's finances decline and thus its overall hold on the economy.

Another relatively undeveloped area in both countries is the bond market. Although there are a number of government stocks in both Malaysia and Singapore, marketability is very thin and only Singapore issues are quoted. Bond trading in Malaysia is done at the Bank Negara (central bank). There is a government securities section on the KLSE but a manager at the exchange noted somewhat ruefully to the author that "we have had only one quote in ten years." In Singapore, the CPF is by far and away the biggest force in the government bond market but its tradition has been to take bonds at issue and sit on them until maturity. There are some corporate bond issues on the SES but the offshore "Asiadollar" bond market (the local equivalent of the Eurobond market) is much more active. Domestic Singapore bonds are unattractive to foreigners because of withholding taxes.

At the end of 1986 the government had plans for promoting a full-fledged bond market in Singapore but as there is no budget deficit in the republic this was seen by outsiders as a rather artificial move — another example of market making to enhance Singapore's role as a regional financial centre. As the population ages, however, and as CPF contributions decline and payments to members increase, the government may well find itself developing a budget deficit which it will need to finance through bond issues.

The bond market would probably be incorporated within the SES, which might help it recover some of the status it has lost to the Singapore International Monetary Exchange (SIMEX) in terms of trading more sophisticated instruments such as currency and interest-rate futures and, as from 1986, a future contract on the Japanese Nikke Stock Average. A contract on one of the Singapore equity indices was expected to follow too.

The SES is due to move from its present location in the Hong Leong Building to the shiny new 70-storey OUB Centre (also located adjacent to the business district waterfront) sometime in 1987. This will enhance its physical appearance and allow physical space for more seats to be created. The open-outcry trading system will probably be maintained, though with electronic backup. With new premises, new regulations and a better capitialised broking industry, the SES should be better positioned to stave off the increasing threat of trading shifting away from the market. Increasingly the big US investment banks are making markets in New York and elsewhere in Singapore stocks and the Pan-El scandal has no doubt increased this desire to deal off the Singapore market. The SES plans, meanwhile, to make it obligatory for all deals done in Singapore to be done on the stock exchange floor, though big block deals and crossed deals will be identified as such and not form part of the input for share price date.

The KLSE, situated in remarkably pleasant and semirural surroundings just off Kuala Lumpur's Damansara Heights, is

Table 72

Malaysian Securities Market Statistics:		
	1980	November 1985
Number of listed companies	250	283
No. of shares listed (Million)	8,741	27,227
Total market capitalisation (M$ million)	$42,930	$64,231
Annual volume turnover of shares (Mn)	1,482	2,709
Annual turnover value of shares (M$ million)	5,600	5,898
Turnover/market capitalisation	13.0%	9.2%
KLSE Industrial Index	535.15	436.02
Average price-earnings ratio	22.6	35.4
Average dividend yield	4.8%	4.7%
New issues (M$ million)	2.1	164.2
Rights issues (M$ million)	103.2	357.5
Special issues (M$ million)	31.8	81.8
Total corporate funds raised from equities (M$ million)	105.3	521.7
Market capitalisation as a % of GNP	83.2%	83.6%

Source: KLSE Investor Digest
       Bank Negara Quarterly Bulletin

considerably more backward than the SES. It is an open outcry
system of trading without electronic backup. A press of trading
clerks from brokers offices struggle to be heard calling out their
orders to the board writers who chalk up prices second by second.
The clerks in turn communicate by telephone with dealers' representatives in the brokers' offices. There is no real-time system of
indicating prices at which deals are done as yet, though the KLSE
hopes to remedy this in 1987 with a computerised system which
will indicate prices both on the trading floor and in brokers offices.
The trading board will be retained for the time being but may
eventually give way to a computersied system of quotations.
Crossing is permitted by the KLSE, though since the Pan-El crisis
it has requested members to report all transactions, including
"marriage" deals and block trading. "There has been so much going
on out there which we did not know about," one KLSE official
acknowledged rather plaintively to the author in 1986.

One final word. London's Big Bang of 27 October 1986 seems to
be having its reverberations in both Singapore and Malaysia too.
Both the SES and the KLSE acknowledge the need to move toward
a system of negotiated commissions before long. The sheer size of
trades nowadays, the increasing importance of foreign investors
and the growing role of foreign institutions, both as shareholders in
local brokerages and as offshore trades of Singapore/Malaysia
stocks, means that that the fixed-commission structure will break
down. "The fixed-commissions structure cannot last for very long
here," commented an SES official. Similar sentiments are voiced in
Malaysia. Probably both will move to a system of fixed commissions up to a certain transaction value (to protect small brokers
offering specialised business) and negotiated rates above that.

Basic Data:

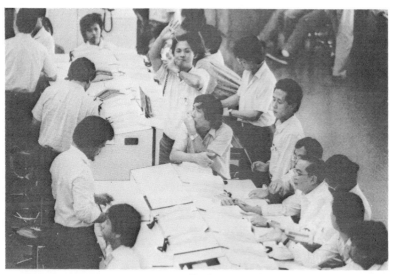

Traders on the Stock Exchange of Singapore

Kuala Lumpur Stock Exchange floor

Basic Data (KLSE)

Number of Stockbrokers	30.6.85	31.12.85	30.6.86
	125	133	134

Chairman	:	**Nik Mohamed Din Bin Datuk Nik Yusoff**
Deputy Chairman	:	**Teh Ghee Kok**

Number of Stock Exchange Staff	30.6.85	31.12.85	30.6.86
	72	75	90

Type of Market
Trading post system — by bids and offers; only highest bid (buyer's price) and lowest offer (seller's price) are recorded on Trading Board.

Cost Relative to Stock Transactions:
Brokerage Rates:
(a)   Stocks, ordinary shares and preference shares
      (i)   Quoted in or converted to to Malaysian dollars

Price	Ready Contracts	Other than Ready Contracts Including Arrival
Less than 50 sen	½ sen	½ sen
At or over 50 sen but less than $1.00	1 sen	1½ sen
$1.00 and above	1%	1½%

      (ii)   Quoted in other currency

	Ready Contract	Other than Ready Contracts Including Arrival
	1%	1½%

Technical Services
Clearing House — Securities Clearing Automated Network Services Sdn. Bhd. an associate company of the Exchange, effects the settlement of all business done through the Trading Floor of the Exchange.
Stock Exchange Library — Literature on a wide range of topics is available.

(b) Government bonds and Municipal debentures

Up to $20,000 nominal value	3/8% on nominal value
On nominal value in excess of $20,000	1/4% on excess over $20,000
Asian Dollar bonds	3/8% on the market value

(c) Other debentures (non-convertible)

Less than $50,000	1%
$50,000 — $100,000	½%
More than $100,000	¼%

(d) Overseas options

Half the above rates applicable to the security

(e) Minimum brokerage payable by both buyer and seller

(i)	on loan transactions	$2.00
(ii)	on any other transactions	$5.00

Clearing Fees: 0.05% of transacted value

Stamp Duty:

Contract notes: $1/ — for $1,000/ — or fractional part of value of shares, stocks or marketable securities.

Share Certificates: $2/ — for every certificate.

Taxation:

In Malaysia, interest and dividend income are subject to income tax. But double taxation on dividend income of an individual is completely eliminated as an amount corresponding to the corporate tax of 40% is treated as tax credit when he files the tax return. Interest and dividend in Malaysia are not subject to the withholding tax system for foreigners. Hence a non resident stockholder will be able to receive the full amount of the divident less corporate tax.

There is no tax on capital gains derived from transaction of securities in Malaysia.

Norms Regulating International Investments:
All investments exceeding M'$1 million must be approved by the Foreign Investment Committee.
There are no restrictions on domestic investors buying foreign securities except for Exchange control.

Capital Issues Committee

The CIC is a five-member agency which vets and approves the issue and listing of all new shares arising from offers for sale, rights, bonus, takeovers, schemes or arrangement, share options and acquisitions by all listed companies. In addition, the CIC formulates policies relating to the securities industry.

Foreign Investment Committee

The FIC is a seven-member agency whose principal function is to ensure that all takeovers, mergers and acquisitions comply with the objectives of the NEP. FIC also rules over all acquisitions of assets valued in excess of M$1 million.

Insider trading

Both the Securities Industry Act of 1983 and the Companies (Amendment) Act of 1985 address the issue of insider trading. Under these laws, officers, agents and employees of a company and officers of the KLSE have a duty not to make improper use of information acquired by virtue of their positions to gain advantage for themselves or others, or to damage the company. There are severe criminal penalties for violating these provisions.

Compensation fund

Each member of the KLSE is required to contribute to a fidelity fund held in trust by the KLSE, upon becoming a member and annually thereafter. The fund is intended to be used to compensate victims of default or fraud by a member of the exchange.

Basic Data: (SES)

The Singapore/Malaysian ADR programme contains the following stocks:-

Bandar Raya Developments Bhd
Boustead Holdings Bhd
City Developments Ltd
Cycle & Carriage Ltd
Development Bank of Singapore Ltd
Genting Bhd
Inchcape Bhd
Keppel Corporation Ltd
Kualal Lumpur Kepong Bhd
Malayan Credit Ltd

Malaya United Industries Bhd
Overseas Union Bank Ltd
Perlis Pantantions Bhd
Selangor Properties Bhd
Sembawang Shipyard Ltd
Sime Darby Bhd
Singapore Land Ltd
Supreme Corporation Bhd
United Overseas Bank Ltd
United Overseas Land Ltd

Indices:

The most commonly quoted index is the one published by the "Straits Times". The Straits Times Industrial Index has 30 constituents and is computed twice daily on an unweighted basis, and its base date is December 1964. The OCBC Index has 55 constituents including bank shares and is weighted by market capitalisation. The Stock Exchange compiles the SES All-Share Index, which covers all the companies listed on the Singapore market.

In Malaysia, the most popular index is the 30 constituent New Straits Times Industrial Index while the KLSE recently introduced the KLSE Composite Index comprising 83 counters weighted by market capitalisation.

Trading System (Singapore)

The call-over system is used. Trading is carried out by dealers calling out bids and offers. The highest and lowest bids for each share are recorded on a scoreboard. For all stocks, trading is in lots of 1,000 shares. For some of the stocks which have market prices per share above S$10, however, trading may also take place in lots of 500 or 100 shares.

Settlement and Transfer

Shares traded on a cash or ready basis must be delivered on the second business day following the transaction. Those traded on a settlement basis must be delivered at the end of each calendar month. All shares listed on the second section must be traded on a ready basis. Since 1979 all trading transactions have been registered and cleared through a central clearing house operated by the SES.

Commissions

Commission rates on share transactions in Singapore vary between 1% and 1.5%. For shares denominated in foreign currencies the rate of brokerage is 1% for both ready and forward contracts.

Brokerage rates		
Share price	Ready contracts	Forward contracts
Under 50 c	0.5%/share	0.75 c/share
50 c and over	1.0%/share	1.0 c/share
S$1.00 and over	1.0%/of value	1.0% of value

Source: Stock Exchange of Singapore

Stamp duty

Stamp duty on share transfer deeds was standardised at 0.2% of the contract price as from 1 April 1980.

Taxation and regulations affecting foreign investors

Dividends are taxed at source at a rate of 40% and there is no additional withholding tax payable on dividends by non-residents. There is no double taxation relief for dividends and no tax levied on capital gains in Singapore, so long as stock is held for more than three months. Non-residents may freely purchase or sell any Singapore securities without limit and in any currency. Proceeds from investments may be repatriated freely or credited to any account. There is no capital gains tax on securities in either Malaysia or Singapore.

Shareholder Protection Codes

Insider trading is banned by the Companies Act. Local companies must maintain a share register and disclose changes in the holdings of directors and those holding 5% or more of the shares. The Securities Industry Council was established in January 1978 as an advisory body to provide guidance to the stock exchange and to co-ordinate its activities with the needs of the investment public, business community and also with the policies of the government.

Thailand, Philippines & Indonesia: Take-off aborted.

One title aptly describes the condition of all three stockmarkets covered in this chapter. They have all failed so far to fulfil earlier hopes (certainly those of foreign investors) and really get off the ground. Admittedly the Bangkok and Manila markets performed remarkably well during 1986 but if anything that simply served to disguise certain structural weaknesses in each, and possibly helped stave off pressures for reform. Except perhaps in the case of the Philippines, the markets occupy a disproportionately small place in the economy and thus need to grow much more rapidly if they are to serve future investment needs.

The Securities Exchange of Thailand (SET) launched a promotional conference in December 1984 under the banner "Take-off Time for the Thai Capital Market" — but that time has not yet come. Likewise, Manila, which has had a stock exchange since 1927, soared for a number of years but then became grounded again. Indonesia (where organised securities trading began as early as 1912) has a real fear of flying so far as its capital markets are concerned and has not even begun to open its stockmarket to outsiders in the way that Thailand and the Philippines have.

Thailand, though the youngest by far of the three stockmarkets — it was founded only in 1962 — is nowadays the biggest, in terms of capitalisation and turnover. Yet, even there development has been disappointing. An Asian Development Bank (ADB) study on regional capital markets published early in 1986 summed up the situation succinctly. "There are still only 93 (now 95) companies listed on the SET with a [total] market value of US$1.75 billion. This is equivalent to less than 1% of Thailand's GNP. Of the 97 listed securities, only 20 are actively traded and some 30-40 are almost dormant." A rise of 25% or so in the Book Club Index (measuring the SET's performance) during 1986 altered this situation only marginally, though the rise was good news for investors.

Just five companies account for more than 50% of the turnover on the SET, demonstrating further just what a narrow market it is. A couple of those companies are banks — which is ironic given that it is largely the influence of banks in Thailand that has prevented the stockmarket growing faster. The same thing applies if the market capitalisation yardstick is used, except that banks loom even larger then. The next five biggest companies in market capitalisation terms are all banks too.

The Thai financial system is dominated by 16 privately-owned domestic banks — among which the biggest are Bangkok Bank, Krung Thai Bank, Thai Farmers Bank, Siam Commercial Bank and the Bank of Ayudhya — and by 14 foreign banks. Some measure of this domination is given by the fact that the commercial banks accounted for nearly 75% of total credit extended in Thailand in 1983.

An even better measure, perhaps, is the size of funds raised in

Table 73

SET: statistics	1985	1986 (Jan-Aug)
Corporate Securities		
Turnover Volume (million units)	99.34	62.81
Turnover Value (billion baht)	15.33	9.69
Monthly Average (million baht)	1,277.83	1,211.36
Daily Average (million baht)	62.59	59.45
(Turnover value divided by types of securities)		
Ordinary and Preferred Stocks (billion baht)	14.99	9.57
Unit Trusts (million baht)	346.39	121.39
Debentures (million baht)	+	2.67
SET Index	134.95	149.84
Average Dividend Yield (%)	8.15	5.89
Average Price Earning Ratio	9.59	11.07
Capital Mobilisation (million baht)	4,143.32	801.59
Number of Listed and Authorised Companies	97	96
Listed Companies	95	94
Authorised Companies	2	2
Number of Listed and Authorised Stocks	100	101
Listed Stocks	97	98
Authorised Stocks (Value of Listed & Authorised Stocks)	3	3
At Face Value (billion baht)	24.58	24.76
Market Value (billion baht)	49.46	55.03
Government Securities		
Turnover Volume (million units)	7.04	2.68
Turnover Value (million baht)	1,148.87	1,902.17
Number of Listed Securities	134	137
Face Value (billion baht)	180.46	190.21

Source: SET

the stockmarket compared with total commercial bank assets (of which a large proportion represents loans to industry). The figure of slightly less than Baht 10.5 billion raised in the stockmarket over the entire five-year period to the end of 1984 is less than one fiftieth of the size of bank assets, and even then the bulk of the funds from the market represented new listings rather than capital raising by existing companies. As the ADB noted: "Securities markets in Thailand have not been a major source of funds for the corporate sector." The natural corollary of this is a high degree of loan financing by Thai companies and highly geared balance sheets.

The Thai authorities have made laudable attempts to develop the country's capital markets in general and the stockmarket in particular during recent years. And, like Singapore and Malaysia, Thailand has been brave enough to open its stockmarket to direct foreign investment. Yet, the market still suffers from many of the classical defects of a bank-dominated economy: shortage of stocks, lack of liquidity, absence of institutional investors and domination by individuals and speculators. Individuals and domestic institutions, in fact, account for around 95% of total turnover. ("Institutions" means, in the Thai context, banks and commercial corporations who maintain large invesment portfolios as well as securities companies and finance companies.)

These defects are being addressed to some extent. Provident funds, mutual funds and insurance companies are coming into the market. There are four managed funds in Thailand, all formed and managed by the Mutual Fund Company (MFC) which is the only securities company licensed to manage locally-established mutual funds. Its shareholders include the IFC (a World Bank affiliate) as well as a partly government-owned development finance institution — the Industrial Finance Corporation of Thailand (IFCT). But the pace of reform is slow and cautious.

The experience of the SET in its relatively short history to date illustrates its defects clearly — and what needs to be done in the future. A private group set up the first organised stock exchange in Thailand in 1962. This was shortly afterwards converted into a limited company called the Bangkok Stock Exchange Company (BSE), though trading on the BSE was largely inactive. The public knew little about stockmarket investment and the government did little by way of market promotion or supervision. It was only in 1975, when the present SET was established that the government

Table 74

Thailand Securities Market Data		
	1980	1984
Equities		
No. of Companies Listed	77	96
No. of Multinational or Joint Venture Companies	23	32
No. of Shares Listed (million shares)	165.5	290.3
Market Value of Shares Listed (million B)	25,522	43,573
No. of Shareholders	70,350	185,106
Share Ownership		
Individuals (%)	32	37
Institutions (%)	68	63
Foreigners (%)	12	14
Annual Turnover Volume of Shares (million shares)	58.2	83.3
Annual Turnover Value of Shares (million B)	6,549.2	10,595.2
SET Index (30/4/75 = 100.00)	124.67	142.29
Market Dividend Yield (%)	9.4	9.1
Market P/E Ratio (x)	6.4	7.2
New Issues		
Number (million shares)	0.3	15.2
Amount Offered (million B)	65.6	3,881.3
Amount Subscribed (million B)	65.6	3,881.3
Rights Issues		
Number (million shares)	3.0	16.5
Value (million B in nominal)	298.2	767.7
Total Corporate Funds Raised from Equities (million B)	696.5	4,944.3
Debt Securities		
Listed Government or Public Bonds		
Issues Listed (Cumulative)	71	124
Listed Amount (million B)	78,048	152,742
Annual Turnover Volume (000)	10	1,850
Annual Turnover Value (million B)	10.0	276.0
Listed Corporate Bonds		
Number of Issues (cumulative)	3	1
Annual Turnover Volume (000)	58,244	83,268
Annual Turnover Value (million B)	6,549	10,595

Source: ADB

began to take an active interest. (The SET is a quasi-official entity, governed by government appointees as well as brokers and others, and it fulfils the function of both securities market and securities commission).

The SET, which is the only stock exchange in Thailand, did not get off to an exactly dazzling start. At the outset it had only 14 securities listed and neither individual nor institutional investors were confident about long-term investments, given the political instability and conflict in neighbouring Indo-China. The end of the Vietnam war and renewed political stability in Thailand brought flight capital back from abroad after a while however, and toward the end of 1978 turnover on the SET was hitting record levels of around Baht 15 billion a month while the SET Index reached a record level of 266 in November of that year. This was to be the beginning of the market's real troubles.

As the ADB report rather blandly expressed it: "Massive speculation by inexperienced investors with inadequate access to information eventually led to an overbought market in which prices no longer reflected underlying share values. A lack of legislation dealing with manipulation and inside trading made things worse." This greatly understates the speculative euphoria which swept the market at the time. Because the concept of share trading was new to Thailand, investors came to believe that prices were ordained to keep rising indefinitely. They had never experienced a bear market.

Share syndicates, often in league with local finance companies and securities houses, capitalised on this financial naivety with all sorts of schemes. Their main target was the relatively affluent middle classes, especially professional people whose assets had previously been deposited with banks. Before the bull market had run its course, a great many people who had never before even thought about share speculation, but who came to regard it as a one-way ticket to a fortune, had been drawn into the market.

Their dream was to be rudely shattered at the beginning of 1979. The collapse of one company, Raja Finance, precipitated a crash on the SET — rather as the collapse of Pan-Electric Industries was to bring about the downfall of both Singapore and Kuala Lumpur stockmarkets some five or six years later. Raja Finance had been one of the stars of the 1977-78 bull market in Bangkok and its shares were among the most actively traded on the market. It was also one of the principal providers of margin finance for stockmarket investors. The company's auditors were subsequently discovered to have given false reports to shareholders. When Raja failed at the end of 1978, the Bangkok bubble burst.

The bubble had, indeed, grown very big. From a level of around 80 throughout 1976, the market (as measured by the SET Index) took off at the beginning of 1977 and had breached the 200 mark by the end of the year — a rise of around 150%. Toward the end of 1978, it had scaled the peaks of 260 — a rise of well over 200% in two years. Half-way through 1979 it was back down to around 160 and bottomed out at around 120 by the end of that year. It was to languish between there and around 160 for several years.

The government could not stand idly by after the collapse of Raja Finance and the subsequent market crash. So many ordinary people had been drawn into the market boom of 1977-78 that simply to have allowed them to endure the bust would have invited

Table 75

	The largest listed companies on the SET, end-1985	
Ranking	*Company*	*Market value (Baht million)*
1	Bangkok Bank	8,080
2	Siam Cement	5,460
3	Thai Farmers Bank	3,920
4	Siam City Cement	3,072
5	Siam Commercial Bank	2,402
6	Thai Military Bank	2,020
7	IFCT	2,002
8	Laem Thong Bank	1,764
9	Bank of Ayudhya	1,404
10	Union Bank	804
11	Bangkok Metropolitan Bank	777
12	Singer Thailand	690
13	Bank of Asia	606
14	Asia Credit	600
15	Bangkok Insurance	597
16	Mah Boonkrong	586
17	Thai Danu Bank	554
18	Jalaprathan Cement	536
19	Dusit Thani	487
20	United Flour Mills	440

Source: T. C. Coombs & Co

social unrest in a country which has not been a stranger to political instability. Two special funds, the Krung Thai Fund (KTF) and the Capital Markets Development Fund (CMDF) were set up with funds provided through the banking sector and by the government to buy up huge quantities of stock and thereby support the market. Had it not been for this massive intervention, the SET Index would no doubt have plumbed levels very much below the 120 level and many people would have been financially ruined rather than just having their fingers badly burned.

When the public dumped stock onto the two rescue funds they were given an option to buy back at a later date but in fact only around 12% of sellers did so, leaving a massive amount of stock overhanging the market. Some of the stocks were good ones — blue-chips which had been indiscriminately savaged in the market collapse — but some of its was devalued or virtually worthless scrip

Table 76

	The most actively traded shares, SET, 1985	
Ranking	*Company*	*Trading volume (Baht million)*
1	Siam Cement	2,074.0
2	Bangkok Bank	1,798.2
3	Siam City Cement	1,786.0
4	Thai Farmers Bank	1,625.0
5	Jalaprathan Cement	769.4
6	Mah Boonkrong	692.9
7	Siam Commercial Bank	638.0
8	Bank of Ayudhya	599.9
9	IFCT	461.2
10	Bangkok Metropolitan Bank	387.1
11	Siam Citizens Corp	315.4
12	Union Bank	301.5
13	Bangkok Agro-Industrial Products	245.8
14	Post Publishing	229.3
15	Laem Thong Bank	220.8
16	Siam Food Products	217.3
17	Ayudhya Investment and Trust	216.9
18	Thai-German Ceramic Industry	199.0
19	Dusit Thani	179.2
20	Dhana Siam	176.1

Source: T. C. Coombs & Co

which had been ramped up purely for the purposes of speculation during the great boom. The state-run Krung Thai Bank bought about Baht 1.7 billion worth of stock through the Krung Thai Fund and the CMDF bought another Baht 700 million worth. Much of this stock is still in the hands of the two funds, though proposals have been made recently for selling part of it to the various specialist funds for foreign investment which are being set up in Thailand.

Various regulatory changes were made in the wake of the 1978-79 stockmarket crash in Thailand. The SET raised loan margin requirements — the 1977-78 boom was financed largely on margin money and readily available bank credit — and stricter corporate auditing and reporting requirements were introduced. Market surveillance was stepped up and insider-dealing was clamped down on. In place of an emergency ban on new public share offerings introduced in 1979, at the height of the crisis, came new securities

Table 77

SET turnover of corporate securities by sector, 1984			
Securities by industry	*Units*	*Baht million*	*Percentage*
Financial institutions	18,842,799	3,895.05	36.76
Banking	15,742,335	3,570.94	33.70
Finance and securities	3,031,142	383.85	2.67
Insurance	69,322	41.26	0.39
Commerce	9,834,509	619.19	5.84
Services	4,972,976	458.79	4.33
Industrials	15,051,948	4,305.32	40.64
Others	15,193,894	945.31	8.92
Total	63,896,126	10,223.66	96.49
Preferred shares	64,890	35.00	0.33
Unit trust	19,306,788	336.53	3.18
Grand total	83,267,804	10,595.19	100.00

Source: Securities Exchange of Thailand

legislation in 1984.

To quote the ADB report on the Thai capital market once more: "Despite improvements in the regulatory and legislative framework of the SET, suspicion remains on the part of the general public concerning the high degree of uncertainty and risk associated with investment in shares." This is hardly surprising, given the series of crises which have impacted on the stockmarket in recent years.

One such was the rather obscure sounding but in fact crucial issue of stock "fungibility" or transferability which occured in the immediate aftermath of the 1979 crash. Speculators who placed purchase orders with brokers during the market boom refused to take delivery of the stock after the market collapsed. In some cases of course, they could not afford to, but in others they resorted to the legal device of claiming that the stock which they had bought was not the same as that subsequently offered to them. It seems inconceivable that such a claim could be entertained — one share certificate normally being as fungible (or transferable) as one banknote is with another. But it led to a mountain of legal claims and counter-claims in Thailand.

The amended Securities Exchange of Thailand Act which was enacted in 1984 — ten years after the original act was passed — clearly defined the transferability of stocks, as well as introducing penalties for stock manipulation and insider trading. The amended SET Act also authorised listed companies to make public offerings of ordinary shares and debentures again after a five-year moratorium.

If Thai investors felt the stockmarket to be no longer safe after the Crash of '79, they were in for another rude awakening several years later. Though not directly connected with the stockmarket, this episode is worth mentioning because it helps illustrate the kind of forces which act upon the market and which will continue to do so until Thailand's capital market becomes fully mature. Thailand has for many years had an active kerb (or underground) money market centering on the so-called "chit funds." The biggest of these grew to be the pool operated by Mrs. Chamoy Thipyaso (Mae Chamoy), wife of a prominent Royal Thai Air Force officer. At its peak, this chit fund was reported to have reached between Baht 3-5 billion in size, through offering incredibly high returns of up to 6.5% per month on funds deposited. Unfortunately these astronomic interest rates were paid not out of earnings but out of cash flow. In other words, new money coming in was used to pay interest to existing members (as well as to the proprietors). This game of musical chairs could continue only so long as new money kept pouring in — rather like the great stockmarket boom. It can hardly have been coincidence that the chit funds boomed after the stockmarket collapse.

Both the Bank of Thailand (BoT) — the central bank — and the Ministry of Finance (MoF) became concerned over the rapid growth of these funds in 1983 and sought to intervene. The following year, a royal decree was issued in Thailand banning them. By this time, one small pool had collapsed and Mae Chamoy had run into a liquidity squeeze and was having to postpone interest payments. An official order was made confiscating Chamoy's assets but in the event the chit fund became subject to a slow run-down rather than a rapid break-up. As with South Korea, kerb-market operators in Thailand tend to have powerful connections in high places and in this sense there are political as well as economic difficulties in putting a curb on kerb practices.

The moral of both the story of the stockmarket collapse in 1979 and the subsequent chit-fund scandal was that Thailand lacked properly run savings institutions, such as pension funds, insurance companies, mutual funds and so on, into which investors could put their money and which in turn would invest in the stockmarket, helping to give it breadth and depth. Various proposals have been made to encourage the establishment of corporate provident funds

Table 78

Newly listed companies and capital raised, 1981-85		
Year	No of companies	Market value (Baht million)
1981	10	1,084.36
1982	16	2,163.88
1983	16	1,456.65
1984	26	6,495.30
1985	3	295.00

Source: Securities Exchange of Thailand

and to list some state enterprises which have been earmarked for privatisation. But progress has not been rapid.

The other side of the coin is what the ADB termed the "distinct lack of interest by Thai companies in equity financing." This, said the bank, "remains an important factor in the low level of securities market activity. Information and disclosure requirements deter many family-dominated firms from going public. Altough the corporate tax levied on listed companies is 10 percentage points lower than that levied on unlisted companies, this differential may still not be great enough to lure tax evaders to the market." (Listed companies pay 30% corporate tax compared with 40% for unlisted companies).

Both demand-side and supply-side problems afflict the SET. The crux of the matter on the supply (of securities) side is the fact that so many companies in Thailand have been nurtured on a diet of bank-overdraft financing. That financing has in turn been available because the banks were so well established compared with other (non-debt) capital-market institutions. The public too, has preferred bank deposits on which interest is taxed at a flat rate of only 12.5% rather than dividends on shares which are subject to full income tax above a level of only Baht 5,000 annually. And banks, being in many cases owned by powerful Chinese banking families, did not demand that borrowers (often other Chinese entrepreneurs) should disclose their financial affairs beyond the confines of the bank manager's office.

Table 79

Foreign Investment in SET					
Year	Purchase Value	Sale Value	Net Purchase	Total Trading of Foreigners	Foreigners' Trading/Total Trading (%)
1982	168.33	70.02	+98.31	238.35	2.05
1983	166.25	172.66	−6.41	338.91	1.83
1984	1,023.21	162.06	+861.15	1,185.27	5.51
1985 (Jan.-Sept.)	962.89	305.35	+657.54	1,268.24	4.51
Source: Vickers da Costa					

With the appointment in August 1982 of Mrs Siriluck Ratana-korn as president of the SET, a new chapter appeared to have opened in the market's history, one that would see its role enhanced considerably. She launched a series of promotional campaigns, aimed especially at getting more overseas investment into the SET. But if her popularity was high with foreigners, the same was not always true at home. A strict regulator who gave high priority to protecting investors' interests and who acted against brokerage houses involved in dubious deals, Mrs Siriluck was not always a favourite of local brokers. Their resentment of her increased over what they saw as the unreasonably strict provisions of the 1984 SET Amendment Act.

Siriluck resigned half way through 1985, claiming insufficient government support for her efforts to promote the SET and was replaced by (this time Mr) Maruay Phadungsit. But though Siriluck is no longer its head, the philosophy of development for the SET which she propounded remains valid. Thai companies, she said, like the country as a whole, are "over-borrowed." While most government agencies and the commercial banks pay-lip service to

Table 80

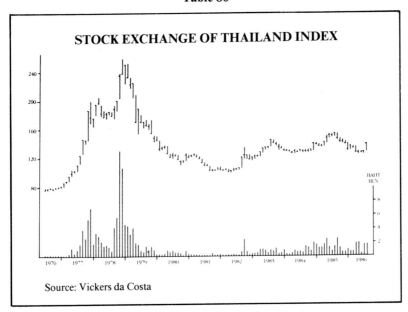

Source: Vickers da Costa

the concept of developing a mature capital market in Thailand (with the stockmarket at its centre) they are in fact "obsessed" with the concept of borrowed funds. In this context it is worth noting that the rather half-hearted attempts made by the Thai government to reduce the degree of family control within the banking sector (and thereby dilute the power of the banks) through mandatory disposals of shares to the general public have met with little success. Siriluck tried hard to promote the concept of equity financing among Thai firms. Evidently she had some success. In 1983 there was only one new company listing but in 1984 there were 15. In 1985 the number of new listings on the SET fell back to just three and Siriluck's resignation half way through that year, even though it did not take effect until September, was seen as a contributory factor.

Listing requirements on the SET are not unduly onerous. A company must have a minimum number of 300 shareholders (who individually must not own more than 0.5% of its equity) and at least 25% must be in public hands. (Some companies are affected by a 1978 law which stipulates a minimum 100 shareholders with no single one owning more than 10%). The minimum capital for listing is only Baht 20 million. Listing requirements are likely to become even less demanding for some companies when the SET implements a plan announced in mid-1986 to open a "second board" on which newly-incorporated Thai firms with a minimum capital of Baht 10 million and at least 100 shareholders will be quoted.

Though the SET boasts a fair sprinkling of industrial, commercial and construction stocks among its 95 listed securities, the market is dominated by banks and finance companies. Unless this situation changes, the stock exchange could become a sideshow to the mainstream development of the economy in coming years. As a senior official at the Bank of Thailand (BoT) pointed out to the author during a conversation in 1985, the requirements for capital to develop Thailand's Eastern Seaboard energy and infrastructural facilities by the early 1990s will be enormous. The programme will require US$1 billion or more over three or four years and part of that will have to come from abroad. But with Thailand's official debt-service ratio (ratio of export earnings to debt service payments) having reached over 20%, what this official termed a "warning light" is flashing. Thailand, he added, does not want to become "another Latin America or Philippines". The answer seems to be more equity financing for the Eastern Seaboard programme, but the equity risk will remain concentrated unless the stockmarket is expanded as a vehicle for wider financing.

The main culprits behind the rising level of foreign debt in Thailand are the country's numerous state enterprises. A lid has been put on the expansion of their borrowing and privatisation is being recommended as a way of reducing their drag on the national budget. Privatisation does not necessarily mean that state enterprises will be listed on the SET. They may be sold direct to private concerns. Nevertheless, it seems likely that some degree of stockmarket participation will be required in order to help finance privatisation.

In the meantime, state corporations are being encouraged to make use of the (embryonic) bond market in Thailand. At present only corporate debentures (though not corporate bonds) are listed on the SET. There are, however, 38 government securities listed. These include bonds issued by the Electricity Generating Authority of Thailand (EGAT) and by the national Telephone Organisation of Thailand. At the time of writing, these seemed likely to be joined by more bond issues from such as the state railways and the metropolitan water authorities. A proposed mass-transit expressway in Bangkok will probably be financed partly through bond issues too. The Washington-based International Finance Corporation (an arm of the World Bank) is encouraging the SET to further develop its bond market as a means of broadening and deepening the stockmarket as a whole. Thailand is also receiving a good deal more support nowadays from foreign investment banks and broking houses (European and American rather than Japanese) for the development of its stockmarket. Such institutions have been actively courting the SET and the Thai government, especially since the days of Khun Siriluck's presidency.

For a while it looked as though a Thailand Fund, to be established jointly by the IFC, British stockbrokers Vickers da Costa (now controlled by Citicorp) and by the Mutual Fund Company — a member of the Industrial Finance Corporation of Thailand (IFCT) group — would be the first major manifestation of this increased foreign interest. This open-ended, unit-trust type vehicle was supposed to take over part of the portfolio of the Capital Market Development Fund and the Krung Thai Fund, mentioned above.

It was beaten to the post, however, by the US$30 million Bangkok Fund announced in London in July 1985 and simultaneously offered to investors in the US, Asia and Australasia. Like the proposed Thailand Fund, the Bangkok Fund is an on-shore unit trust and was established by US brokers Merrill Lynch and British brokers Cazenove and Company. The fund is managed by a Singapore-based entity, First Overseas Bangkok Investments, with Bangkok First Investment and Trust (BFIT) acting as advisor and securities broker to the fund. The Bangkok Fund's launch did not prove to be quite the success that its proprietors hoped for. Initial subscriptions amounted to only around US$10 million instead of the US$30 million targetted. Undeterred, the Bangkok Fund began building up a portfolio of investments on the SET.

The reasons for the fund's rather indifferent reception (and also for the delays in launching the Thailand Fund) are worth noting. The Thai stockmarket has for some years been open directly to foreign investors, subject to certain controls on foreign exchange transactions, such as staggering of outward remittances. In fact by 1984 foreign investors' purchases in the Bangkok market accounted for 5.5% of total turnover on the SET. In value terms, this amounted to some Baht 1.2 billion or four times what foreigners accounted for in 1983. By late 1986, foreign investment was accounting for nearer 10-15% of total market turnover.

Many foreign investors appear to take the view that there is little point in going through an indirect gate such as the Bangkok Fund when they can enter through the front door. The promoters of the special Thai funds believe, however, that they can offer a package deal which will appeal to overseas investors unfamiliar with the Thai market. They also argue that the scale of international marketing they can engage in is likely to attract many more foreign investors than have previously entered the SET. (London brokers T.C. Coombs have made an informal market in Thai shares in London for some time).

The institutions behind the Thailand Fund believe, however, that specialist funds must also be able to offer special concessions, over and above what the ordinary investor enjoys, notably on taxes. Specifically, what the Thailand Fund's promotors (especially the IFC) are pressing for is a reduction in the 20% dividend withholding tax and 25% capital gains tax which Bangkok levies on foreign investors. At present, losses cannot be offset when the tax is computed, a situation which one British broker described as "downright iniquitous." It appeared at the time of writing (toward the end of 1986) that the Thailand Fund would obtain such special concessions when it is finally launched. These were expected to include capital gains and dividend tax at half the normal rates.

Meanwhile, foreign investors were eagerly buying Thai stocks during 1986 as the SET Index surged upwards to levels not seen since before the 1979 collapse. A number of factors were at work behind the new bull market. One was the high degree of domestic liquidity in Thailand and the relatively low interest rates which accompanied it. High interest rates have long been a factor inhibiting the stockmarket. Dividend yields on equities, averaging around 8.6% over the past five years, may look attractive enough compared with some other markets but they still pale against returns averaging around 13% on (one-year) bank deposits and up to 16% paid by finance companies. Another favourable factor helping the market in the latter part of 1986 was the Thai government's decision in September to tax interest on debentures at a flat rate of 15%, thus alleviating some of the bias in the tax system in favour of debt.

By November the SET Index had pushed back up through the 180 level and the floor of the stock exchange — located in the gleaming white Sinthorn Building in Wireless Road, Bangkok — began to reverberate with sounds other than those of the air-conditioners. The 300 or so blue-uniformed authorised representatives of the 30 or so broking firms who trade on the two-board floor, found that they were suddenly active again in market making rather than going through the motions from time to time for the benefit of visitors.

Yet, for all this, the market remained thin. Apart from the lack of institutional investors, individuals are not present in large numbers. It is estimated that only around 165,000 of the six million population of Bangkok alone invest on the stockmarket. The proportion outside is very much smaller still. Former SET president Siriluck tried to persuade the 29 member securities companies on the SET (who act as both brokers and principles) to look outside Bangkok for clients, arguing that the future of the exchange lay in establishing a much wider shareholder base — among farmers for instance. But in this as in other proposed reforms, her efforts met with limited success.

For all the bullish mood of 1986, the Thai stockmarket remains essentially cheap in terms of earnings and dividend yields. Even during 1977/78, average price/earnings ratios on the SET did not climb above 11.5 — later to fall below six — and they had pushed back only to around 10.5 during 1986. Average dividend yields, which have touched 10% in recent years and were at around 6.5% in 1986, are also rewarding by other market's standards. All this is a reflection of the general undervaluation and under-support of the SET — both by local investors and by the Thai government.

Philippines:

The story of the Philippines' stockmarket is one of a remarkable rise in the early days, of subsequent decline and fall — and more recently of revival again. But apart from the very real political risks facing investors and the considerable economic problems facing the country as a whole, there are numerous structural defects in the stockmarket itself which need to be remedied before optimism such as that which swept the market during 1986 can be said to be soundly based.

Manila had a stock exchange as early as 1927 — the Manila Stock Exchange — during the mid-period of American colonial rule and, as one Manila broker recalled wistfully to the author, "for a long time this was the premier stockmarket of the region." It was not until the early 1970s that the Hongkong stock exchanges overtook the Philippines in terms of capitalisation and turnover. But the political and economic strife which was to overtake the country in later years reduced the Manila stockmarket to a minor role compared to burgeoning markets elsewhere in Asia.

By the end of 1985, the total capitalisation of the Philippine market amounted to slightly under 3% of GNP — insignificant compared with Hongkong and Singapore and bigger only than in Indonesia, which has no pretensions to having an international market. This decline was certainly not because the Philippine economy had grown faster than the stockmarket relative to other regional economies. In fact, in terms of absolute and per capita GNP, as well as stockmarket capitalisation, the Philippines is now the poorest nation in the region.

The Philippines stockmarket has an appearance of sophistication and maturity at first sight. (This is deceptive however, as is the impression of a "modern" financial system in the Philippines). Manila boasts two stock exchanges. The Makati Stock Exchange was founded in 1956 by Filipino broker Bernard Gaberman, a partner in the firm of Hagedorn, to compete with what was still the American-dominated Manila Exchange (even though the Philippines had gained formal independence from the US ten years earlier). The Makati exchange has since continued to grow in importance — for a while it lured clients from the Manila exchange

Table 81

Philippine Securities Market Data			
	1975	1980	1984
Equities			
No. of Companies Listed	179	194	154
No. of State-Owned Entities Listed	0	1	1
No. of Multinational Companies	1	1	2
No. of Shares Listed (million shares)	62,155	3,004	n.a.
Market Value of Shares Listed (P million)	10,534	26,432	16,487
No. of Shareholders (million)	137,278	361,460	498,903
Annual Turnover volume of Shares (million)	56,695	61,437	13,823
Annual Turnover value of Shares (Pesos million)	1,612	2,584	1,398
Annual Sales Volume (million shares)	58,401	40,075	8,912
Annual Sales Value (Pesos million)	1,534	2,067	648
General Index of Shares Prices			
Commercial-Industrial			
High	70.76	133.21	149.02
Low	44.91	105.01	127.77
Mining			
High	2,543.18	3,048.53	1,252.42
Low	2,229.21	1,957.37	1,041.22
Average Dividend Yield (%)			
Commercial-Industrial	9.7	7.5	n.a.
Mining	5.0	10.5	n.a.
Average Price Earnings Ratio (x)			
Commercial-Industrial	4.31	9.5	n.a.
Mining	17.8	5.7	n.a.
New Issues			
Number	21	5	1
Amount Offered (Pesos million)	930	220	25
Amount Subscribed or underwritten	194	84	17
Rights Issues			
Number	12	12	—
Value (Pesos million)	138	178	—
Total Corporate Funds Raised from Equities (Pesos million)	31,887	110,134	—
Debt Securities			
Number of Corporate Issues Listed*	n.a.	1	1
Annual Sales Volume	n.a.	n.a.	n.a.
Average Yield of Corporate Bonds (%)			
nominal	n.a.	n.a.	n.a.
current	n.a.	n.a.	n.a.

* n.a. denotes not available

Source: Asian Development Bank

with lower commissions until rates were unified in 1972 — and nowadays the market leader (in turnover terms) varies from year to year. Proposals that the Manila and Makati exchanges should be merged have met with a good deal of opposition among brokers and a merger seems unlikely in the forseeable future.

For a while there were actually four exchanges operating in the Philippines — the Manila and Makati exchanges, the Cebu provincial exchange set up in 1971 to serve the southern cities but which had a life of only a few months and the Metropolitan Stock Exchange set in in Manila during 1974. This exchange too had a very short life.

The 135 companies listed on the Manila and Makati exchanges — a uniform listing agreement between the two exchanges automatically allows companies admitted to one to be listed on the other — is somewhat bigger than the number quoted in Taiwan, 50% greater than in Thailand, around seven times the number in

Table 82

	Most actively traded stocks, Makati Stock Exchange, 1985	
Ranking	*Company*	*Turnover value (₱ 000)*
1	Insular Bank of Asia & America	280,371
2	Philex Mining Corp	33,812
3	Globe Mackay Cable & Radio Corp	33,723
4	Ayala Corp	20,053
5	Overseas Drilling & Oil Devpt Corp	14,210
6	Phil Long Distance Telephone Co	13,675
7	San Miguel Corp	12,914
8	Seafront Petroleum & Mineral Resources	12,422
9	Benguet Corp	11,806
10	Concrete Aggregates Inc	10,499
11	Bank of the Philippine Islands	7,150
12	Lepanto Consolidated Mining Co	6,695
13	Liberty Flour Mills Inc	6,615
14	AGP Industrial Corp	5,901
15	Atlas Consolidated Mining & Devpt Co	5,725
16	Manila Broadcasting Co	5,047
17	China Banking Corp	3,639
18	Family Bank & Trust Co (Common)	3,298
19	Ayala Fund Inc	2,659
20	Metropolitan Bank & Trsut Co	2,374

Source: Makati Stock Exchange

Indonesia and bigger even than Singapore if Malaysian-incorporated stocks there were excluded. Manila's two-board system — one for "regular" and the other for "speculative" stocks — plus a mechanism for over-the-counter trading of unlisted securities also gives an impression of a market that is broad and deep. Yet the story of the Manila market has been one of sad decline in recent years.

During 1985, combined turnover on the two exchanges was only some Pesos 2 billion in value terms, less than it was in 1970 and

Table 83

Year	Manila	Turnover Makati (Million Peso)	Total	Market Capitalisation (Million Peso)
1976	3,370.3	3,350.0	6,720.3	12,732.8
1977	1,208.1	1,397.0	2,605.1	12,465.5
1978	3,670.1	2,912.7	5,482.8	18,379.4
1979	2,249.6	2,703.3	4,952.9	17,90083.6
1980	2,067.5	2,584.3	4,651.8	32,057.5
1981	614.1	682.8	1,296.9	18,600.1
1982	724.0	490.7	1,214.7	12,357.6
1983	1,365.8	1,998.5	5,364.3	19,229.7
1984	648.9	1,434.0	2,082.9	16,486.4
1985	1,557.2	509.9	2,067.1	26,111.6

Source: Vickers da Costa

only one third of the level reached in 1976. If the most recent figures were corrected for successive devaluations of the Peso in the intervening years — the currency has depreciated by two thirds since 1978 — they would look even worse. Total market capitalisation stood at around Pesos 26 billion by the end of 1985, well below the peak of Pesos 32 billion reached in 1980. Again, this takes no account of subsequent currency devaluations. During the dark days of 1984 — one year after the assasination of Philippine opposition leader Benigno Aquino and some two years before Aquino's widow was to take over the Philippines presidency from Ferdinand Marcos in a popular revolt — turnover on the Manila exchange slumped to its lowest level in 25 years and on certain days turnover on both exchanges registered practically zero.

All this was a far cry from the picture of booming activity five years previously. The Manila market moved up sharply in 1978 following the discovery of oil in the Palawan area of the southern Philippines. Mining stocks were also riding high in those days and the market enjoyed a boom reminiscent of the gold boom 50 years earlier. (It was, in fact, the gold boom which led to the establishment of the Manila Stock Exchange). In the late 1970s, oil stocks came to dominate the Manila trading boards to a greater extent than mining stocks, which had traditionally been the backbone of the market, reflecting the importance of copper and gold mining in the Philippines. There are three principal indices measuring the Manila markets — Mining, Oils and Commercial and Industrial — plus a Composite Index based on ten shares from each of the three sub-sectors. Which of these indexes is the most important and the most closely watched varies with the condition of the economy at any particular time.

Throughout 1978 and part of the following year the market rode high. Then things began to go wrong with the economy in general and the financial sector in particular. Oil prospects were found to have been exaggerated. A credit squeeze in 1979 led to the failure of several brokerage firms (and the sudden departure of one prominent broker leaving big debts behind him). At least one speculative mining stock was suspended on the stock exchange too. What was

Table 84

Manila Stock Exchange Indices

Year-end Dec	Commercial/ Industrial	Annual Change (±%)	Mining	Annual Change (±%)	Oil	Annual Change (±%)
1976	68.15	+14.4	2,930.45	+ 22.6	1.64	+ 19.7
1977	82.36	+20.9	2,516.73	− 14.1	2.41	+ 47.6
1978	168.86	+86.8	3,158.67	+ 25.5	4.90	+103.0
1979	130.52	−23.2	2,440.84	− 22.7	4.75	− 3.0
1980	105.95	−18.8	1,940.32	− 20.5	2.33	− 51.1
1981	99.24	− 6.3	1,302.47	− 32.9	1.61	− 30.9
1982	90.46	− 8.8	923.30	− 29.1	1.70	+ 5.8
1983	145.63	+60.9	1,247.61	+ 35.0	1.13	− 33.4
1984	106.31	−26.9	727.97	− 41.6	0.59	− 47.7
1985	160.86	+51.3	721.20	− 0.9	0.86	+ 45.1

Source: Vickers da Costa

to prove a much worse blow was struck in 1981 when a well-known
and respected banker, Dewey Dee, fled the Philippines, also leaving
in his wake very large debts. To understand the trauma this caused
— halving the level of the Composite Index by early 1982

Table 85

Five year performance

Year-end share index, US dollar and sterling exchange rates, 1981-85

	1981	1982	1983	1984	1985
Commercial-Industrial Index	99.24	90.46	145.63	106.31	160.86
P/US$	7.97	8.97	13.71	19.06	18.20

Source: GT Guide to World Equity Markets

compared with levels reached in 1980 — it is necessary to
understand certain aspects of the local financial market.

As stockbrokers Vickers da Costa observed: "The Philippine
money market serves as a medium through which banking, quasi-
banking and other financial institutions, business corporations and
individual investors can adjust their liquidity positions. Being one
of the most developed money markets in South East Asia, it serves
as a real competitor to the stockmarket for investible funds." The
Dewey Dee scandal sent severe shock waves through this essentially
short-term market and through the banking and financial system as
a whole. So big had the volumes of commercial paper being
processed through the money market become (both in absolute
terms and relative to corporate financing as a whole) that the
money-market crisis quickly embroiled corporations and banks
too. Government efforts to inject liquidity into the system failed to
restore confidence.

No sooner had the stockmarket recovered from this severe
setback and begun to rise in 1983 (toward levels not seen for four
years) than political crisis overtook the Philippines. Benigno
Aquino was assassinated in August of 1983 on his return from years
of exile in the US. Even if the economy had been sound this would
have had a very severe impact on investor confidence. As it was,
the economy was far from sound. The prices of just about all the

leading export commodities on which the Philippines depends — minerals, sugar, coconuts — were suffering from a collapse owing to international recession. The trade deficit and foreign borrowings were mounting and the country's official reserves were being fast depleted. Inflation was rising on the back of what was suspected to be currency printing by a government desperate to secure legitimacy at the polls by any means it could.

Domestic capital began to flee the country in ever increasing amounts, driven by the mounting level of corruption associated with the martial-law regime of President Ferdinand Marcos and his numerous business "cronies." The Centre for Research and Communications in the Philippines estimated between 1979 and 1984, as much as US$30-40 billion went offshore — a considerably larger sum than the Philippines' total foreign debt, which presently stands at around US$26 billion. The impact on the stockmarket was devastating. By early 1985 it had fallen back toward the nadir reached after the Dewey Dee crisis and it did not really recover until shortly after President Aquino came to power in February 1986.

One of the factors which drove the market down so sharply was that Philippine companies with surplus liquidity to invest have traditionally been big players in the stockmarket. During the depth of the 1984/85 economic recession however, they were forced to sell stocks at whatever price they could get, simply in order to meet wage bills and other overheads. Their sales revenues had all but

Table 86

Average yield, price/earnings ratios

PERs and average dividend yields for the Commercial-Industrial Index, 1981-84

Year-end	PER	Yield%
1981	5.78	16.32
1982	7.57	10.15
1983	5.18	10.98
1984	5.84	—

Source: Stock exchanges

dried up. It is difficult to say precisely what proportion of trading corporate investors account for in Manila, as no detailed figures are available on the type or distribution of investors in the market. Some brokers estimate that individuals account for around 70% of trading but this figure probably understates the influence of corporate players, especially since the government took steps after the Dewey Dee crisis to reduce the lure of the short-term money market — by imposing a 17.5% withholding tax on money-market earnings, for instance.

Table 87

Market value of shares on the Manila and Makati stock exchanges, 1984-85

| | *Market value (P million)* | | | |
| | *1984* | | *1985* | |
	Manila	*Makati*	*Manila*	*Makati*
Commercial & industrial	277.3	1,125.0	1,313.4	421.0
Mining	346.9	291.6	227.0	59.0
Oil	24.5	17.4	16.4	30.0
Total	648.7	1,434.0	1,557.3	510.0

Source: Makati Stock Exchange

Another major factor helping topple the stockmarket was the flight of capital out of Pesos and into US dollars or other foreign currencies. Wealthy Filipinos have always had ways of getting money out of the country despite exchange controls. One is the suitcase method. Another is to go through the (local-Chinese controlled) "Binondo" black market in Manila, where the rate can be penal but where there is always a market at a price. Money poured out in 1983 and 1984 and when it finally began to return it did not head for the stockmarket. In an effort to mop up the liquidity caused by the indiscriminate printing of money (and to conform with IMF demands for an austerity programme) the Philippine government began issuing high-yielding Treasury and Central Bank bills known as "Jobo" bills after the bank governor, "Jobo" Fernandez. These were paying up to 45% interest annually at one stage. In these circumstances, it paid the wealthy to bring their money back onshore, despite the exchange-rate risk. But the rub-off effect on other interest rates had a crippling effect on business generally in the Philippines.

Table 88

Trading on the Makati and Manila stock exchanges, 1984-85				
	Trading volume (shares million)			
	1984		*1985*	
	Makati	*Manila*	*Makati*	*Manila*
Commercial & industrial	30.2	57.2	30.1	38.9
Mining	12,052.4	3,010.0	638.6	3,585.9
Oil	2,620.1	5,845.6	3,978.6	3,367.3
Total	14,702.7	8,912.8	4,647.3	6,992.1

Source: Makati Stock Exchange

Foreign investors too, pulled out of the Philippine stockmarket during the dark days of '84/85. What foreign investment there was in the Manila market — again no reliable figures are available as how much of turnover and capitalisation foreigners accounted for — had traditionally come from London. Many foreign accounts are registered there because Britain has the only double-taxation treaty in force with the Philippines, which helps offset the 15% withholding tax on stock dividends. Investments also came from Hongkong which is able to offer the same tax advantages as London and where many funds keep a nominee office. But investors who got into Manila at an exchange rate of Pesos 8 to the US dollar and then had to get out again a year or so later at a rate of Pesos 14 to 1, were badly disillusioned.

One of the casualties of the market crash was the Luxembourg-based Philippine Investment Company, an investment fund launched in 1976 by ten European investors who each subscribed US$1 million for investment in the Manila stockmarket. Successive Peso devaluations and the market crash finally brought about the liquidation of the fund in 1983. A successor to that venture has been the Jardine Fleming Philippine Trust run out of Hongkong by investment bank Jardine Fleming (JF). This is a happier story.

While its portfolio (in net asset value terms) showed a 38% decline over the five years up to March 1986, it had appreciated by 16% since March 1985. The more recent market revival in Manila boosted those figures appreciably.

Foreign investors have direct access to the Manila market (as well as indirect access via such vehicles as the JF fund), though most Philippine companies allocate so-called "B" shares to foreign holders whereas "A" shares can be sold only to Philippine nationals. By dividing their capital into 60% "A" and 40% "B" shares, companies can thus ensure that foreign ownership is limited to 40% in all. Yet another way in which overseas investors can gain access to Philippine stocks is through the eight Philippine stocks years.

Turnover on the market as a whole during the first seven months of 1986 amounted to Pesos 5.4 billion (US$267 million at prevailing exchange rates) which was nearly one third higher than the total combined turnover for the whole of 1984 and 1985. A cautious revival had begun in mining stocks such as Philex and Lepanto in

Table 89

Source: Vickers da Costa

1985. Dealers were once more to be seen queueing in line at the trading posts specialising in these two companies' stocks on the stock exchange floors. Then, quite suddenly in early 1986 there were queues at other market-makers' post too. What had been cautious and highly selective buying turned into a mad scramble for industrials such as PLDT, San Miguel, Globe Mackay Cable and Radio Corp, Ayala Corp — and Philex. One striking example of the gains made in 1986 was PLDT. A minimum board lot of 50 shares in the company's stock would have cost just over Pesos 2,000 on 21 February, the day before the rebellion which ousted Marcos. By the end of October, that same lot was worth just under Peos 15,000.

Local brokers were predicting confidently toward the end of 1986 that the revival would continue. This seemed entirely possible. However, just as the Philippines economy had still to demonstrate that it was lifting out of the mire of recession — and just as the Aquino government had still to prove that it had the strength and the policies to survive — so the stockmarket needed to prove that it had the structural capacity to deal with new investment flows, and to go on attracting them.

One weakness is the low importance accorded by the Philippine stockmarket to commercial and industrial issues (despite their popularity during 1986). The number of listings of such stocks does not reflect the importance of the industrial and commercial sector in the Philippine economy. To quote Vickers da Costa again: "This is attributable chiefly to the ownership structure of most manufacturing/trading firms in the country. With the exception of a few major companies like San Miguel, Engineering Equipment Inc, and PLDT, most of the commercial/industrial firms are privately owned, family corporations whose shares are traded only within the family. This results in a very thin market for the shares. In a desire to preserve management control, these companies maintain limited expansion programmes and resort to debt rather than equity financing." The mining sector, on the other hand, has a wider equity base and makes frequent calls upon the public to provide capital.

The Philippine government has tried to broaden the equity listed on the New York Stock Exchange or the American Stock Exchange. These are: Atlas Consolidated Mining & Development Corp, Benguet Corp, Lepanto Consolidated Mining, Marinduque Mining, Philippine Long Distance Telephone Company, Philex

Mining Corp, San Carlos Milling and San Miguel Corp.

The withdrawal of both local and foreign investors from the stockmarket in 1984/85 drove price/earnings ratios for even blue-chip Philippine stocks down to record lows and dividend yields up to record highs (even though some mining companies were forced to reduce or waive payouts during the depth of the recession). P/E ratios averaged around 6 from 1981 to 1985 and yields were up in the 11% range on average. But this average disguises some remarkable lows reached during 1984/85, especially in the rating of blue-chips. The Philippine Long Distance Telephone Company (the national telecommunications agency) was selling at little over one year's earnings (net profits) at one point, whereas a more reasonable rating at other times or in other markets might have been at least ten times. The shares of local brewer San Miguel were yielding 25% cash. (One factor which has influenced the yields of Philippine stocks is the presidential decree, issued some years ago, to the effect that a company cannot have retained earnings in excess of its paid in capital. This has encouraged high dividend payouts, arguably at the expense of reserve-building. Resort to paying scrip dividends would help to solve this problem).

One major obstacle to any return of foreign funds was foreigners' virtual inability to get money out of the Philippines again — at least across the official exchanges. In theory, remittances were permitted all along but in practice the central bank was simply not processing permissions for a long time. It was estimated at the end of 1984 that some Pesos 110 million of frozen foreign funds were sitting in Manila (mainly in the custody of the Hongkong and Shanghai Banking Corp) and not earning interest. A few braver souls such as Jardine Fleming opted to reinvest their money in the Manila market. By 1986, the situation was a good deal easier and it was taking only about one week to repatriate investments in the Philippine market, so long as the original investment had been registered with the Central Bank.

Some foreign money was venturing into the Manila market again by 1986. But what spurred the market's revival more than the initial euphoria which greeted President Aquino's bloodless coup in February was the diminishing attraction of central bank securities. Wealthy Filipinos found that when the yield on Central Bank Securities fell to around 15% in 1986 (a third of what they had enjoyed two years earlier) they were no longer assured of a guaranteed high income. They turned instead to the stockmarket. (The high-interest-rate regime which persisted for two years succeeded in stablising the Peso to an extent which hardly seemed possible given the degree of previous capital flight. This in turn created the conditions for an eventual return of both domestic and foreign capital into the stockmarket).

All three market indices began to lift off in February 1986, though the oil index noticeably lagged the other two. In fact, activity in 1986 was centering on commercial and industrial stocks, which accounted for 87% of turnover in the first seven months of the year. The Manila Stock Exchange's Commercial and Industrial index rose nearly 100% between the end of February and the beginning of August, which brokers saw as a welcome trend away from the domination of the market by mining stocks in previous structure of companies in general and to encourage more stock exchange listings. The Board of Investments, for instance, requires that at least 10% of the capital stock of a corporation registered under the Investment Incentives Act should be sold to the public,

Table 90

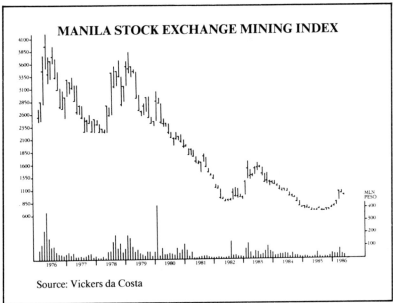

Source: Vickers da Costa

and requires the shares to be listed on one of the stock exchanges within ten years from registration. But such incentives have not proved to be very effective. One reason, no doubt, why the commercial-paper and short-term money market in the Philippines grew so big was that it permitted corporations to borrow liberally without having to reveal their affairs to shareholders and competitors. The Dewey Dee affair revealed the deficiencies of such financing but the corporate sector did not have time to recover from that before more serious economic and political crises hit the Philippines. Corporations have been concerned with survival in the face of such developments and of course equity capital was costly while the stockmarket was so depressed. Now that it is reviving, the financial conditions for attracting more companies to list are better, but the extreme volatility of the market may have scared some companies away.

One potential source of future expansion for the stockmarket is the huge portfolio of companies held by the Development Bank of the Philippines (DBP) and the Philippine National Bank (PNB) — a legacy of the economic and financial disorder which accompanied the final years of Marcos' reign. These, plus the defection of certain presidential cronies, all helped to bring about the downfall of numerous business corporations spread across a very wide range of industries. Many of these companies could be rescued only through being taken under the wing of one or other of the two main national development banks. But funding them in the future is beyond the capability of either DBP or PNB.

The same applies to various major industrial projects which were begun during the Marcos years but never completed. (Some indeed were simply a device through which presidential cronies secured large foreign loans, only to appropriate a big chunk of the proceeds for themselves). Privatising this portfolio of national business (some of it good and some of it bad) is being done partly through a debt: equity conversion programme which the government of President Aquino launched in 1986. Under this programme, holders of Philippine foreign debt can exchange it for equity in various business enterprises held in the portfolios of government institutions such as PNB and DBP. Some of these enterprises might conceivably be sold directly to investors via the stockmarket too.

The market badly needs such strengthening. As the Asian

Development Bank noted in its study of selected Asian capital markets (referred to above): "The Philippines' securities market is not very developed and although quite old [the stockmarket] has been fairly unimportant both in terms of capital mobilisation and listings." At the end of 1983 total capitalisation of the two exchanges amounted to less than 0.5% of Philippine GNP. The corporate bond market is under developed too. The ADB observed that, "although a few corporate bonds are listed, the bond market is dominated by government securities consisting of national govern-· ment issues, government-corporation issues and central bank issues. Of these, treasury and central bank securities have become particularly important in recent years in terms of amount outstanding."

Yet another weaknesses in the Philippine market is official regulation, or rather the comparative lack of it. One long-established and well-known Filipino broker (whom it would be impolitic to name) suggested to the author in Manila during 1985 that 'if the stockmarket really turned round now it would be frightening. We just do not have the infrastructure [to deal with it]. It would be active for a time and then fizzle out." He cited the inadequacies of the local Securities and Exchange commission (SEC) in preventing "fraud and mismanagement" among finance companies and other institutions. One reason for this is that the SEC has a lot of ground to cover with a relatively small staff.

Securities legislation (modelled on US legislation of the day) was passed in the Philippines back in 1936 (the Securities Act) and has not been brought properly up to date since. The rules badly need updating. For instance, there are no specific rules governing cash and margin accounts. Because there is no formal provision for topping up of margins, both brokers and their clients can be left dangerously exposed. "It is pure speculation and gambling," commented the Manila broking source. So-called "cash" transactions can be paid as far down the line as two weeks after a buy or sell order has been placed. Delivery of scrip can take up to one month and registration of shares (though not essential for trading) takes even longer.

A senior official at the SEC itself was remarkably frank too, with the author over the defects in the market. He acknowledged that as recently as the early 1980s share "ramping" by brokers and others was prevelant. "We have practically no institutional investors, so speculation makes the market more volatile," he commented. Mutual Funds (really open-ended unit trusts) were set up in the 1960s (under an Investment Company Law) but when many of them found themselves unable to redeem their investments they became illiquid and eventually failed. Two more were founded later but are highly restricted. The SEC has been encouraging the formation of closed-end funds with no obligation to redeem but so far none have appeared. There is one government-sector fund, the National Development Corp, but it has not been popular among investors. Pension funds too, are not popular and what little business exists is done by trust banks. Pensions funds certainly do not figure as significant investors in the stockmarket.

"Ordinary people in the Philippines don't have much disposable income to invest and the middle classes got burned during previous bull markets," the SEC official noted to the author. "Groups of brokers would build up positions, drawing small investors in on top of them and then get out from under the bottom of the heap." The SEC had been unable to pin the blame for this on anyone in particular — though various brokers had "left the country" after investigations were launched, he claimed. But he added: "We have a gambling streak in us. Everyone likes to get in and having our fingers burned will not change that." That seems to sum up some of the official philosophy toward market regulation in Manila.

Stockbrokers were hard hit in the stockmarket crash of 1984/85. Out of around 50 brokers on each of the Manila and Makati exchanges, only around a half are still operating. Two major brokerages — Anselmo Trinidad & Co (Atco) — one of Manila's "glamorous" firms in its heyday — and Jalandoni, Jayme, Adams & Co Inc (Jajadco) were among the victims of the slump and had to suspend operations. The stock exchanges, seeking desperately to raise money, threatened numerous firms with suspension if they did not pay their dues and more than a dozen were in fact suspended. Sections of the Philippine brokerage industry remain weak and under capitalised and lack technical expertise. (On the other hand, some of the bigger brokers perform functions rather akin to those performed elsewhere by investment banks). It seems likely that there will have to be further consolidation of the brokerage industry in the future, though the 1986 bull market may have staved off rationalisation and reform for a while. Foreign brokers (such as Merrill Lynch, which has an office in Manila mainly to serve the needs of Filipinos wishing to invest in the US market) have shown little interest in acquiring a seat on either of the two Manila stock exchanges.

Late in 1986, officials of both Manila and Makati stock exchanges urged President Aquino to allow foreign brokers to participate directly in the Manila market and were told the government would study the matter. Some local brokers, anxious to recoup their losses of recent years, are not keen on the idea of seeing foreigners eat into their commission income, however. Some of the brokers act on behalf of wealthy Chinese businessmen who bought seats on one or other of the exchanges to avoid having to pay commissions — and can afford to keep their brokerage operations dormant during lean periods of market activity. (The power of the biggest business families in the Philippines extends into the securities business. The Soriano family, for instance, has links with Anscor Capital (a joint venture with Bankers Trust Co); and the Cojuancos are connected with Ventris Securities. The Ayala family is represented through Philsec Securities as well as through a joint venture with Merrill Lynch).

The revival of the Manila market during 1986 and the renewed interest of foreign investors should provide some incentive for the government to take the stockmarket more seriously and to encourage higher professional standards in the market. At the time of writing, however, there was little indication that the government had reached any consensus on even the broadest of economic issues let alone more specific financial reforms. So, it appeared that there was a very real danger that the 1986 boom might once again be followed by a 1983-type bust.

Indonesia

If the Indonesian stock market had merited a separate chapter in this book it would have had to be entitled "The One Least Likely To." Of all the stockmarkets in South East Asia, Indonesia's ranks last and seems the most unlikely — on the basis of past performance at least — to expand significantly. There are only 24 companies listed and their total capitalisation as at the end of 1985 was just Rupiahs 132 billion or roughly US$80 million. This amounts to just 0.007% of the Tokyo market capitalisation and yet Indonesia's economy is approaching one tenth the size of Japan's (in GNP terms). This is one measure of the Jakarta stockmarket's under-development. A more telling one is the fact that market capitalisation in Indonesia amounts to little more than 0.01% of GNP. This is minute compared with other Asian markets, and yet Indonesia's economy is the fourth biggest in Asia after Japan, China and India.

Not only is Indonesia's a tiny market, it is also a closed one as far as outsiders are concerned (except for bond purchases on a limited scale). So, it would appear to be a case of "end of story" as far as this chapter is concerned. It would be wrong to bring down the curtain on Indonesia, however, without at least taking a look at what lies behind it. If nothing else, the sheer size of the economy and of the Indonesian population (at 168 million, the third biggest in Asia after China and India) suggests potential for the future. If there is ground for hoping that Communist China will expand its embryonic stockmarket then there must be ground for believing that (nominally capitalist) Indonesia will one day allow its youthful market to reach maturity.

The term youthful needs some qualifying, as it could obviously be argued that a stockmarket which was founded in 1912 is hardly in its first flush of youth. The market established in Jakarta some 65 years ago — the Vereeniging voor den Effecten Handel (Securities Brokers Association) — was, however, very much a Dutch affair, serving the needs of the (colonial) Dutch business community in Indonesia and dealing mainly in Dutch stocks, including those of Dutch plantations in Indonesia. There were also exchanges in Surabaya and Semarang. All three were closed during World War II.

The market reopened in 1952 (three years after the transfer of sovereignty from the Dutch government to the Republic of

Table 91

Indonesia Securities Market Data		
	1980	1984
Equities		
No. of Companies Listed	6	24
No. of State-Owned Entities Listed	0	0
No. of Multinational or Joint Venture Companies	6	18
No. of Shares Listed (000 shares)	14,588	57,650
Market Value of Shares Listed (million rupiah, Dec. 10, 1984)	39,520	94,946
No. of Shareholders	9,845	31,217
Share Ownership		
Individuals (%)	6	12
Institutions	16	27
Government (%)	0	0
Foreigners (%)	78	61
Annual Volume Turnover of Shares (%)	11	2
Annual Value Turnover of Shares (%)	14	2
Annual Sales Volume (# shares)	1,656,290	1,218,833
Annual Sales Value (million rupiah)	5,733	2,139
Average Sales Value (million rupiah)	22.8	8.7
Composite Share Price Index	103.5	63.5
Average Dividend Yield (%)	15.0	n.a.
Average Price Earning Ratio (x)	6.5	5.4
New Issues		
Number of companies	3	1
Amount Offered (million rupiah)	8,528	897
Total Corporate Funds Raised from Equities (million rupiah)	8,528	897
Average Annual Return from Stocks (%)	39.2	n.a.
Debt Securities		
Number of Bonds Listed	—	3
Annual Nominal Value (million rupiah)	—	100,718
Average Bond Yield (%)	—	16.5
Total Corporate Funds Raised from Bonds (million rupiah)	—	100,000

Source: Asian Development Bank

Indonesia) to cater for the issue of government bonds and pre-war listed securities. It was to remain open only for six years. Former Indonesian President Soekarno's policy of "Confrontation" against the Netherlands, a ban on trading Dutch securities in Indonesia and finally the expropriation of Dutch business in the country led to the effective demise of the stock exchange once again in 1958. The country was then without a stockmarket for nearly 20 years and it was only in 1977 that the "New Order" government of Sukarno's successor President Soeharto opened the present Indonesian Stock Exchange, which is situated in Jalan Medan Merdeka Salatan, Jakarta.

Foreign companies operating in Indonesia were persuaded to sell up to 51% of their shares (via the stockmarket) to Indonesian nationals over a period of ten years from the market's reopening. In addition, numerous tax incentives were given to persuade companies to go public. The disappointing response to these moves (though nine concerns, mainly joint ventures, rushed to go public in 1983) led to their being waived in 1984. From then on the strategy for mobilising funds was switched to the banks, whose

Table 92

The largest listed companies on the Indonesian Stock Exchange, end-1985		
Ranking	*Company*	*Turnover value (R million)*
1	Unilever Indonesia	29,210
2	Pan Indonesia Bank	16,917
3	BAT Indonesia	16,500
4	Jakarta International Hotel	9,928
5	Tificorp	7,975
6	Goodyear Indonesia	7,688
7	Semen Cibinong	7,022
8	Multi Bintang Indonesia	5,526
9	Sucaco	5,280
10	Centex	3,558
11	Merck Indonesia	3,192
12	Bayer Indonesia	3,079
13	Panin Putra	3,009
14	Sepatu Bata	1,897
15	Sari Husada	1,850

Source: BAPEPAM

deposits are free of withholding tax, while dividends and capital gains from shares are taxable.

At the time of the stockmarket's reopening in 1977, a Capital Markets Executive Agency, the Badan Pelaksana Pasar Modal (BAPEPAM for short) was set up to manage the stockmarket as well as to act as a kind of SEC for the monitoring of listed companies. The fact that all these tasks were alloted to a government agency is hardly surprising in a country where government dominates finance and business to an extent more befitting a socialist economy. It would be wrong to see the Indonesian economy as being simply capitalist or socialist however: it is a curious and possibly unique mixture of state and private enterprise, a military/business alliance in which an (essentially Chinese) business community coexists with a "pribumi" (indigenous Javanese and other races) ruling elite. Malaysia's system is somewhat similar but there the environment and certainly the stockmarket is more open.

To quote once more the Asian Development Bank report on selected Asian capital markets, "an important characteristic of Indonesia's financial structure is the extent of government ownership of financial institutions. When the assets of the central bank (Bank Indonesia), the state-owned commercial banks plus (also state-owned) development banks and insurance companies are considered, these alone account for some 87% of financial institutional assets." The money market, like the stockmarket, is "thin." The only part of the non-bank capital market which can be said to

Table 93

The most actively traded shares, 1985		
Ranking	Company	Turnover value (R million)
1	Unilever Indonesia	204.8
2	Semen Cibinong	188.4
3	Jakarta International Hotel	154.7
4	Sucaco	148.6
5	Centex	126.7
6	Bayer Indonesia	124.2

Source: BAPEPAM

be thriving is that which is euphemistically called the "informal" market — in other words, the kerb market.

One reason for all this is the fact that the Indonesian government has for long collected huge oil revenues and used the financial system as a conduit for redistributing these revenues rather than as a means of collecting and investing people's savings. The enormous wealth disparities in Indonesia also mean that private capital is located in relatively few hands — and operates hand in glove with government financing. In fact, the two are often synonomous with much wealth (and thus economic power as well as business muscle) residing in the hands of the ruling military elite.

Statistics on the size of the state financial institutions in Indonesia tell only half the story of why the stockmarket is so under-developed. It caters largely still (as in the Dutch colonial days) for foreign multinational companies as well as Indonesian-foreign joint-venture companies and a few local "blue chips." In the top one dozen companies (by market value) listed on the Jakarta exchange, figure such un-Indonesian names as Unilever, British American Tobacco (BAT), Goodyear, Merck and Bayer. This seems odd in an economy which BAPEPAM chairman Barli Halim admits needs a "huge amount of investment" for rehabilitation and modernisation of its industries and a good deal of long-term capital, including equity.

True, there are a sprinkling of big Indonesian enterprises listed on the stock exchange — including a bank, a hotel corporation and a cement company among others — but there is little sign of the

Table 94

Share trading volume and value, and average daily value, 1981-85

Year	Sales volume (shares 000)	Sales value (R million)	Average daily sales value (R million)
1981	2,891	7,651.7	30.1
1982	5,019	12,624.8	50.7
1983	3,508	10,107.6	40.4
1984	1,219	2,139.0	8.7
1985	1,822	3,076.0	12.3

Source: BAPEPAM

enormous business empire, for instance, of presidential-associate Liem Sioe Liong, or indeed of other Chinese-Indonesian "towkays'" (big businessmen's) empires. The nearest that foreign investors have come so far to getting even a whiff of the investment action in the Liem empire was when he and a group of investment associates launched a quoted vehicle on the Hongkong stockmarket in the early 1980s (see chapter on Hongkong). There are many other big Indonesian business concerns which foreign investors (and no doubt Indonesian ones too) would dearly like to participate via the stockmarket.

Why are such companies not listed? No doubt the answer lies partly in the general reluctance by Chinese businessmen to reveal their financial affairs beyond the immediate family circle (and sometimes not even within that), and the dominance of the (mainly state-owned) banks in Indonesia. But there is a special factor. Most Chinese business tycoons in Indonesia are supremely sensitive to the resentment and envy of their wealth among the pribumi population. They thus deem it prudent to keep an ultra-low public profile — even if accounting, auditing and financial disclosure standards in Indonesia are still very rudimentary.

The performance record of the stockmarket in its short history to date has not been exactly dazzling. To quote Barli Halim again: "(From 1977) up to 1983 there was an increase in companies going public while the volume and value of transactions and daily averages reached a peak in 1982. The year 1984 (saw) only one company going public and transactions at the stock exchange showed a declining trend. The index figure of 100 in 1982 declined to 63.5 in 1984 but recovered (somewhat) in February 1985 and

Table 95

Year-end share index, US dollar and sterling exchange rates, 1981-85					
	1981	*1982*	*1983*	*1984*	*1985*
Share price index	100.26	95.00	80.37	63.53	66.50
R/US$	623.73	691.22	996.53	1,074.00	1,120.72

Source: GT Guide to World Equity Markets

came to 68.5 in October (1986)." This development (or lack of it) he added, "has obviously been much influenced by the world recession and the macro-economic policies of the government."

Micro-economic policies, such as those affecting interest rates in Indonesia, have also played a part, as indeed they have in the relatively slow growth of other South East Asian stockmarkets. Indonesia's bond market has thrived on the back of interest-rate and tax incentives compared with the equity market. The first bond issue took place in 1983 by PT (meaning limited private company) Jasa Marga, with a value of Rs 23.7 billion followed by an issue by (state agency) Bapindo of Rs 25 billion and PT Papan Sejahtera of Rs 6 billion. Two additional issues by PT Jasa Marga in 1985 brought the total to Rs 225 billion by March of that year.

By the end of 1985, the total nominal value of issues (by these same entities) came to Rs 295 billion or well over twice the secondary market value of the 24 equity-share issues quoted on the stock exchange. As Barli Halim noted, "this indicates that, in the short run, bonds have a more significant role than shares." This is not altogether surprising, given that bonds yield (at the time of writing late in 1986) over 16% and bank time deposits nearly as much.

What has kept the equity market going through all these vicissitudes is the National Investment Trust or "Danareksa" which was established (also as a state agency) along with BAPE-PAM to promote equity ownership among Indonesians. Danareksa is no ordinary unit trust. Probably its nearest equivalent in South East Asia is the Amanah Sahan Nasional in Malaysia (see previous chapter) though Danareksa is not aimed quite so overtly at indigenous (meaning non-Chinese) individuals in Indonesia as Amanah Sahan is in Malaysia.

Danareksa, to quote its President Director, J.A. Sereh, is "charged with the task of purchasing shares through the capital market for subsequent sale to the public in the form of small-denomination, back-to-back bearer certificates. (The purpose of these is to enable Danareksa to hold the original shares "in trust" while passing back dividends to the certificate holders. It is thus the price of these certificates, rather than the underlying shares, which Danareksa controls). It also manages a number of mutual funds.

Danareksa has the unenviable task of ensuring too, that share prices on the stock exchange "do not fluctuate too violently" as

Sereh put it. This involves both buying and selling and the agency has been criticised for preventing investors from enjoying what they regard as rightful capital gains (though not presumably for safeguarding them from heavy losses). This enforced price stability means that the Indonesian stockmarket is very much a "dividend-driven" one rather than being based on capital gains. But, in order to compete with the high yields (and favourable tax treatment) on bonds, companies need to offer a dividend yield of over 20% in order to attract the investor. Few of them can afford to. In fact, average dividend payments tend to be somewhat under 10% annually on the nominal value of shares, though the fact that some share price have fallen below par on occasions has raised the yield above this.

In October 1983, the Indonesian government flirted with real risk/ reward on the stock exchange and told Danareksa that it need no longer prevent share prices falling below their nominal (par) value. The experiment was short-lived. Prices plummetted and, in order to "protect the small investor," Danareksa once more had to

Table 96

PT (Persero) Danareksa	
	1984
Results (million rupiah)	
— Revenue	15,013
— Profit before tax*	14,049
— Profit after tax	13,544
Position at the year end (million rupiah)	
— Total Assets (excluding Dana)	145,577
— Authorized capital	50,000
— Paid up capital	35,192
— Working capital	116,367
— Investment in securities	118,960
— Dividends paid to the sharesholders	2,188
— Dividends paid to The Unit	
Certificate's holders	11,003
— Retained earning	15,575
Per Share (thousand rupiah)	
(1 share = 1 million rupiah)	
— Net Profit	385
— Dividends paid to the shareholder	62.2
— Assets	4,137

Source: Danareksa

resume its market propping role. As a result, it now accounts for around 60% of total share holdings by value, according to Sereh. (This is considerably higher than the estimate of 40% or so put on Danareksa's market holding by other official sources. These sources also suggest that a further 20% of shareholdings are in the hands of insurance companies, 10% in bank hands and nearly 30% in individual hands).

"We don't want to see private investors frightened away," says Sereh in defence of Danareksa's market-support role. His philosophy on this point underscores the government's ambigious attitude towards markets. "Market manipulation by a small number of participants to exploit a mass of inexperienced, uneducated and uninformed small investors must be prohibited," he noted. "This is why the capital Market Police Council (yet another government agency) forbids speculation in the capital markets." Danareksa itself is also charged with "eliminating speculation" not only by means of intervening in the market but through encouraging disclosure of dealings — there are no formal rules covering insider dealing in Indonesia — spreading share ownership as widely as possible and generally "educating" the public.

That is not the end of Danareksa's powers and duties. A presidential decree says that any company going public in Indonesia must offer at least 50% of its shares to the state-owned mutual fund. According to Sereh, there is no "obligation" upon Danareksa to take this proportion, or indeed any shares at all. Much depends upon the level of funds available to Danareksa at the time. Despite its obligations to buy shares, to prop up the market and the poor performance of the equity market in recent years, Danareksa has somehow managed to go on increasing its revenues and profits handsomely since 1981. Bond dealing may account for part of this but the assumption must be that funding from the state budget underlies much of its revenue.

Until quite recently, Danareksa (plus ten non-bank financial institutions) was the sole underwriter of stocks and bonds in Indonesia. Banks, as members of the stock exchange, were able to operate as stockbrokers but not as underwriters. (Of the 40 broking firms operating in Indonesia, 27 are banks or other financial institutions and the remainder are investment or quasi-financial companies). Nowadays they do have underwriting ability, though in practice only the biggest, state-owned banks are expected to have the financial muscle to be able to take advantage of this privilege. Even so, extending underwriting powers to banks is one step toward spreading risk in the primary issue market. And if the Indonesian state banks are able to make use of their 2,000 branches (in aggregate) to market stocks, this might have the effect of widening share ownership too, over a period of time.

Nevertheless, the problem is obviously as much on the supply side (number of listed companies and stocks) as on the demand side (number of investors), as far as future growth of the Indonesian stockmarket is concerned. This too is being addressed, though in a perhaps rather arbitrary fashion. According to Sereh, there are around 200 foreign companies in Indonesia which were established between 1967 and 1974 and which are supposed to reduce their degree of foreign ownership to a maximum of 49% within ten years of 1974. Technically, that deadline is now past but according to Sereh (in early 1986) around 40 of them are "undergoing Indonesi-anisation at present." They are, he noted, "potential companies for placing shares in the stock market in the next few years." On the other hand, he feels that "only very few of them can meet the listing requirements of the exchange."

At present, any company wishing to go public in Indonesia must have a fully paid up capital of Rs 200 million and (much more onerous) must have "registered a return on equity of at least 10% for the last two consecutive years." By contrast, the additional requirements that the company's financial statements must have been audited by a Certified Public Accountant for the two previous years only and that the "last" audit report must not be qualified, seem almost ludicrously lax and incongruous. It is the minimum return on capital criterion that is likely to discourage many companies wanting to go public.

At the time of writing, Indonesia was studying the possibility of launching an Over-the-Counter (OTC) market to augment the present market. The idea is that it would appeal to companies who cannot meet normal listing requirements and would permit local investors to acquire "more risky" stocks, as Sereh puts it. In addition to the proposed OTC market, a "second-section" is being considered for the stock exchange proper, according to Barli Halim of BAPEPAM. A wider range of investment trusts is considered another option for expanding the stockmarket and, on the regulatory front, a new law on the capital market is being drafted. This may include establishment of a "Bureau for Securities Administration."

The Indonesian government seems loathe to commit itself, however, on when and to what extent the stockmarket is likely to be opened up to foreign investment in the future. (Over-the-Counter bond purchases are currently the only Indonesian instruments available to foreign investors). Danareksa chief Sereh told the author early in 1986 that an initial move could be to sell foreign investors stakes in foreign companies already listed on the Jakarta exchange. This, he suggested, would provide a "reference price" when local companies' shares were eventually made available to foreign investment. Sereh also suggested that Indonesian companies might be permitted to offer convertible bonds (CBs) — convertible into ordinary shares — to foreigners. These would be along the lines of those issued by South Korean companies. He also hinted at the possibility of an "Indonesia Fund" — again along the lines of the Korea Fund. But none of these suggestions had materialised at the time of writing. In any event, a limit of 5% is likely to apply to foreign portfolio holdings in any (indigenous) Indonesian company.

The question is whether foreign investors will be all that keen to buy Indonesian equities given the successive and steep series of devaluations of the Rupiah over the past five or six years. These slashing devaluations played havoc with the assets of direct investors (foreign multinational concerns) in Indonesia. They also raised the foreign debt-service burden of Indonesian companies considerably, gearing up their balance sheets and presumably providing a ground for even more caution on the part of foreign investors.

Thailand: Basic Data

Bangkok Stock Exchange

Stockmarket Indices

There are three different indices calculated for Thailand's stockmarket:- the Book Club Index, the SET Index and the TISCO Index.

Book Club Index — calculated daily by the broker, "The Book Club Finance and Securities Co. Ltd", this Index retains its popularity among local investors. Its base date is April 30, 1975 (the day the SET commenced) and includes all listed and authorised securities weighted for market capitalisation and adjusted for capital changes in the number of components.

SET Index — almost indentical to the Book Club Index, the SET Index includes all issues and is weighted and calculated daily by the SET. While both indices use closing prices to calculate the current market value, the SET Index uses the last transacted price when no transaction occurs whereas the Book Club Index uses an average of the bid/offer quotation, or if there is no quotation, the last traded price. The formula for calculating capital changes varies somewhat as well.

TISCO Index — calculated by the broker "Thai Securities Company, Limited", the TISCO Index is unweighted and unadjusted for capital changes. It is calculated daily using closing prices.

Dealing Procedures

Dealing

Trading is conducted on two separate boards:- the main board for regular trading and the special board for big lots, special lots and bonds.

SET regulations decree that opening prices on each day must not vary more than four spreads from closing prices of the previous trading day. Price spreads of securities vary in accordance with their market price and prices are not permitted to fluctuate more than 10% either side of the previous day's closing price.

Except when approved by the Exchange, members cannot trade listed securities outside the market.

Board Lots

When a security is first listed, a board lot on the main board is the number of shares amounting to approximately Baht 10,000 in terms of market value and which is in multiples of 25 shares, with 25 shares as the minimum unit.

When a transaction in one single lot exceeds Baht 10 million in market value of 10% (whichever is lower), of the registered paid-up capital of the listed company, it is classified as a big lot trade and must be traded on the special board after obtaining approval of the SET.

Commissions & Other Charges

Commission rates are fixed by the SET and are the same for both purchases and sales:-

Ordinary/preferred stock and debentures	0.5% of value trades (minimum Baht 50)
Government bonds	0.1% of value traded (minimum Baht 50)

There is no stamp duty on share transfers for which the SET acts a registrar. Otherwise, stamp duty is Baht 1 for every Baht 1,000 or less, calculated on the par value or value of share transfer, whichever is higher. On certain shares (e.g. IFCT), there is a charge of Baht 10 per transfer deed.

Margin Financing

Both SET members companies and non-members provide margin financing and the current minimum requirement is 25% of the stock's value which the investor must provide in cash on the transaction day. (Margin is not available to foreign investors).

Foreign Investors

In general, foreign investment in Thai securities is encouraged, however it is subject to certain limitations and conditions imposed by the authorities.

Under the Alien Business Act and the Finance Securities and Credit Foncier Business Act, foreign shareholdings are limited to a maximum of 49% , (for commercial banks, 25%) however, the Articles of Association of quite a few listed companies are even more restrictive, limiting non-Thai ownership in 10-25%.

Taxation

Corporate

Tax incentive are provided for listed companies and the corporate tax rate is 30% (35% for non-listed companies). Dividends which a listed company receive from Thai incorporated companies are tax free if the sum total does not exceed 15% of the listed firm's total income.

Capital Gains

For individual domestic and foreign investors there is no capital gains tax on securities transactions. For "juristic" foreign investors there is a 25% withholding tax on the capital gain, although resident corporations of countries having tax treaties with Thailand can recover all or some of this tax.

Dividends

For individual investors, both domestic and foreign, a dividend withholding tax at source is levied. On dividends received from unit trusts and shares in the IFCT, the first Baht 10,000 is tax free and between Baht 10,000-400,000, a 30% tax rebate is provided and the balance taxable at personal income tax rates withheld at source. On dividends received from listed and authorised companies, tax at personal rates is withheld.

Disclosure

In general, practices of the International Accounting Standard Committee or the American Institution of Certified Public Accountants apply when an accounting problem is not covered by a Thai auditing standard. Consolidation is required in cases where the investment in another company exceeds 50%.

Source: Vickers da Costa

Philippines: Basic Data

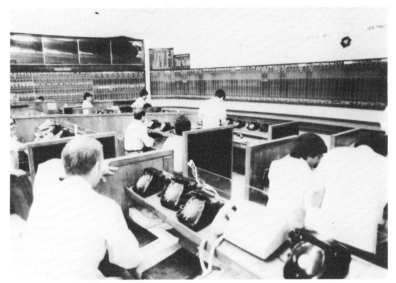

Manila Stock Exchange

Membership

There are 106 broker-members on the two stock exchanges:-

	Brokerage Houses	Registered Broker-Members
Manila Stock Exchange	32	53
Makati Stock Exchange	49	53
	81	106

Generally, brokerage firms are also authorised dealers of securities and are permitted to trade for their own account, apart from buying and selling for client accounts. They handle transactions in debt and equity securities and often exercise investment banking functions, such as the underwriting and public distribution of new issues. However, they cannot engage in money market operations or the borrowing and lending of funds from the public, without authority from the Central Bank of the Philippines, which imposes minimum paid-up capital requirements.

Listed Securities

There are presently 135 companies whose securities are listed on both the Manila and Makati Stock Exchanges. Under a uniform listing agreement, any application filed and approved in one of the exchanges automatically qualifies the company to list its shares in the other exchange. Basically, there are two types of issues traded on the exchanges:-

Big Board	More popularly known as "blue chips", these are stocks of the more established corporations which are engaged in full-scale operations and belong to one of the following industries:- banking, insurance and finance, cement, flour, logging, sugar, textiles, fertiliser, construction, food services, and mining. Stocks traded on the Big Board are generally high-prices shares, compared to those listed on the Small Board. To qualify for listing on the Big Board, the company must have paid dividends for at least three years prior to listing and must have at least 300 stockholders with fully paid shares equal to a minimum of 10% of the total paid-up capital.
Small Board	Small Board issues are those stocks of newly-established companies, mostly in mining and oil exploration operations, whose value depends on the success of on-going development work. The criteria for listing on the Small Board are that the company should have at least 300 stockholders with fully paid shares equal to a minimum of 10% of the total paid-up capital.

Unlisted Securities

Shares not listed on the stock exchanges, but registered and licensed by the Securities and Exchange Commission for public offerings, are traded over the counter.

The Stock exchange requires members to report such over-the-counter transactions and monitors the trading of unlisted securities. Over-the-counter trading of unlisted securities by exchange members amounts to only 1% of total volume at most.

Listed shares may be traded in the over-the-counter market as well as on the stock exchange. This market is maintained by the investment banks. All transactions are negotiated through the stockbrokers.

Total over-the-counter turnover value in 1984 equalled Pesos 89.1 million. Roughly two-thirds (Pesos 56.4 million) resulted from Makati Stock Exchange over-the-counter trading, while the remainder (Pesos 32.7 million) was accounted for by Manila.

Stockmarket Indices

Both Stock Exchanges compute various indices, but because of its longer history and more complete price data, the Manila Stock Exchange indices are more commonly followed.

The Manila Stock Exchange produces three indices:- the Mining Index (nine constituents since 1947); the Commercial/Industrial Index (ten constituents since 1958) and the Oil Index (six constituents since 1969). These indices are arithmetic averages of the last transacted prices of the constituents and are weighted not by their market capitalisations, but by their respective par values. All three indices are computed thrice daily.

The Makati Stock Exchange also produces the Mining Index (ten constituents); the Commercial/Industrial Index (eleven constituents) and the Oil Index (twelve constituents) which together form the Composite Index (thirty-three constituents). The Indices are computed once daily at the close of the market.

Dealing

The two stock exchanges use the "post system" which is similar to that used in New York.

Stockbrokers are required to time-stamp all orders upon receipt, and also upon execution, withdrawal or cancellation, so as to assure the investing public that orders are executed on a first-come, first-served basis. Confirmations of transactions are sent to clients before the close of business on the day the transactions are consummated.

In addition to dealing on a ready basis which requires that delivery is made within four trading days, brokers are allowed to carry out "Delayed Delivery" and "Futures" transactions.

Board Lots

Both stock exchanges have board lots, and the prices are lowered or raised according to a scale of minimum fluctuations. Transactions that are beyond the minimum fluctuation of the last traded price are not allowed.

Over a given trading day, share prices are allowed maximum fluctuations:-

Big Board Issues	40% up	30% down
Small Board Issues	100% up	50% down

Commissions & Other Charges

Commission on listed shares is 1.5%. The minimum charge on each transaction with a value of Pesos 3,000 of less is Pesos 45. The commission rate on bond transactions is 0.75%. For selling orders, in addition to the commission which is deducted from the sale proceeds, a sales tax is also imposed which is equivalent to ¼% of 1% of the gross proceeds.

Settlement & Registration

Transactions are usually done on a spot basis, with cross and part sales very common. Block sales negotiated outside the market must be reported to the Exchange.

The two stock exchanges each have a bank which acts as its central clearing and registration house. The Manila Stock Exchange uses the "Far East Bank and Trust Company" while the Makati's is the "Rizal Commercial Banking Corporation".

Foreign Investors

Foreign portfolio investment has been permitted since March 1973 under Central Bank Circular No. 365.

Taxation

Individuals and Coporate

Under Philippine tax regulations, individual citizens and resident citizens are taxed on their income from all sources worldwide. However, non-resident alien individuals are taxed only on income from Philippine sources and tax is withheld at source.

Withholding tax on dividends received by non-residents of the Philippines is currently levied at rates dependent on the status and the tax laws in the country of incorporation of the foreign investor:-

a) Trust and individuals	30%
b) Hongkong incorporated companies	15%
c) Other companies	35%

Transfer and Capital Gains

For securities listed and traded on the stock exchanges, a transfer tax equivalent to ¼ of 1% of the gross proceeds of the stock is imposed on sellers.

For over-the-counter stocks, gains arising from the sale of such stocks are charged as follows:

Up to Pesos 50,000	10%
Over Pesos 50,000	20%

Disclosure

Accounting methods are based on U.S. principles, and the degree of disclosure required is generally in excess of the standards prevailing in other South-east Asian countries.

Source: Vickers da Costa

Indonesia: Basic Data

Indonesian Stock Exchange

Market Indices and their Constituents

The stock exchange in Indonesia has had a composite index since April 1983, using the stock prices on 10 August 1982 as its base. All shares listed on the Indonesian Stock Exchange are taken into account when calculating the index.

Trading system

Transactions on the Indonesian Stock Exchange are effected via two trading systems: a call-out system and a continuous system. Under the call-out system of trading, which is used primarily for the newly listed shares, the call manager, a BAPEPAM official, announces the previous day's closing prices first. Members then call out their orders to the market officials who is turn post them on a board. A transaction is made at the price most quoted in accumulated orders. Pricing via this method is carried out twice a day for each issue.

Continuous, or board, trading is the method used for the more actively traded shares. After five trading days, brokers and dealers are free to trade the newly listed shares through the continuous trading system.

Settlement and Transfer

Settlement and delivery take place within 14 days. Almost all transactions are on a cash basis. Margin loans are a rarity, and short selling is not permitted.

As there is no central clearing corporation, contracts concluded on the stock exchange are settled individually between the parties concerned.

Commissions and other costs

The commission for trading in shares and bonds in Indonesia is 1% of the value of the transaction. In addition to the commission cost, investors are also required to pay a stamp duty of R500.

Taxation and foreign investors

Generally, dividends paid by Indonesian corporations to foreign shareholders in approved projects are subject to a withholding tax of 20%, unless a lesser amount has been established by a tax treaty between Indonesia and the country of the foreign investor.

Prior approval from the Investment Coordinating Board (Badan Koordinasi Penanamam Modal, or BKPM) is required before foreigners can invest, and then they may invest only in foreign capital investment companies (joint ventures). In practice, this means that foreign portfolio investment is not allowed in equities, but foreign investors may purchase bonds in the over-the-counter market.

Reporting requirements for listed companies

Listed companies are subject to various disclosure and reporting requirements. Companies must submit financial statements to

BAPEPAM no later than 120 days after the close of the company's financial year. Furthermore, the company is obligated to notify BAPEPAM within 30 days of any significant event which may materially affect the company's operations. The company must also provide any additional reports that BAPEPAM may request.

The listing documents and financial statements submitted are public records and copies can be obtained through BAPEPAM. Any reports which are deliberately misleading or not submitted to BAPEPAM on time may render the company liable to fines and possible delisting.

India and other Sub-Continental markets

When Indians mention the "great share mania" it might be assumed they are referring to the 1985/86 bull market when many share prices doubled and stock indices reached all-time highs. In fact, the term is used to describe the remarkable market boom of 1860-65 at the time of the American civil war when a cotton famine brought unprecedented demand for Indian stocks and unprecedented inflows of gold and silver into Bombay to pay for it. The Bombay stockmarket, one of the oldest established in India and today still the biggest by far, went wild — until it crashed in 1865. Many more boom and bust periods were to follow. So was 1985/86 simply a case of history repeating itself, of another "share mania," or did it signify a more lasting expansion of the Indian stockmarket?

The most recent bull market was certainly not without its speculative excesses. At the height of the boom, India's business capital of Bombay saw new issues of equities and debentures coming out at the rate of over a score a day. The "equity cult" claimed seemingly countless adherents. Everyone it seemed was clamouring to buy shares. ¬ot simply the wealthy sophisticates of Bombay but also farmers who snapped up stocks from fertiliser companies which acted like investment banks and sold scrip via their own rural outlets.

During 1985/86 there were again scenes reminiscent of that famous boom a century earlier when it was said that "man and woman, master and servant, banker and merchant, rich and poor of all races and creeds were seized by share madness." The Economic Times share price index (the most popular measure of the Indian market) which closed 1984 at around 277 points (1970=100) reached just under 520 by August of 1985, and then closed the year somewhat lower at just under 490 — still for a gain of 76%. The total capitalisation of the Indian market at the end of 1985 stood at close on Rs 200 billion or some US$15 billion — roughly double the level a year previously.

By the end of 1986 the Indian stockmarket boom had retreated considerably from the mid-1985 peaks but it had not quite gone bust. Nor did it appear likely to, saving a catastrophe for Prime Minister Rajiv Gandhi's reformist government (a possibility which has always to be borne in mind after the assasination of his mother Mrs Indira Gandhi). As with elder statesman Deng Xiao Ping in China, the longer Gandhi is in office to promote his economic reforms, the more likely they are to persist in the future and the more open the environment for business, including the stockmarket, is likely to become. India's need for increasing amounts of foreign capital to help finance its ambitious programme of economic expansion over the next five years suggests too that the stockmarket will become a focus for foreign investment.

Despite the fact that stock trading has been carried on in India since the 1830s, the stockmarket — nowadays consisting of a dozen exchanges scattered across the country — has remained closed to outsiders. The exceptions are non-resident Indians (NRIs) and foreign citizens of Indian origin. Maintaining barriers to outside investment reflects a defensive attitude born partly of colonial experience (under the British) and partly of the socialist thinking which has dominated much of India's post-independence economic history. This manifests itself in highly restrictive attitudes toward direct investment in India by foreign multi-national corporations too.

Just as it would be naive to think that the efforts of one man, such as Rajiv Gandhi, could free India of the bureaucratic controls and protection of sectional interests which keep its markets closed to outsiders, so it would be dangerously simplistic to view the Indian stockmarket as an Aladdin's Cave of treasures ripe for plundering by overseas investors. Many of India's biggest industrial empires — acquired in many cases by Indian businessmen from foreign owners after Independence — have become inefficient through lack of competition and near-monopoly privileges. Many more medium-sized business houses are officially classified as "sick." On the other hand, there is an active, but arguably undercapitalised, small-business sector which probably represents the nearest approach to free enterprise which India has to offer.

Rajiv Gandhi's task since he came to power in October 1984 has been to try and cut through this decades-old undergrowth of inefficiency, bureaucracy and corruption. He has made a promising start. Gandhi has begun to reduce controls on the freedom of

Indian companies to expand and diversify, he has cut tariffs on imported high-technology goods and called on the private sector to finance a higher proportion of India's national industrial and infrastructural development. He has also cut taxes, including long-term capital gains tax, which impeded stockmarket investment in the past. In the long run, such policies are likely to be much more beneficial to the stockmarket than those of his mother, the late Indira Gandhi, requiring foreign-owned companies to localise their ownership via the Indian stockmarket.

In addition, a whole range of technical but collectively important reforms relating to the Indian securities market have been implemented by Rajiv Gandhi's government. All of these policies — aimed at reinvigorating the long-supressed private sector of the economy — helped fuel the stockmarket boom in 1985/86. That boom engendered what D.R. Mehta, a former controller of capital issues in the Ministry of Finance's Department of Economic Affairs describes as an "unprecedented upsurge of public interest" in the Indian stockmarket.

The value of equity and bond issues in the market rose from Rupees Rs 3.2 billion in fiscal 1979 to Rs 20 billion in fiscal 1985. The increase in 1984 alone over the previous year was 100%. The amount of money raised in the stockmarket in the financial year up to the end of March 1986 was an estimated Rs30 billion. More significantly, it is forecast that by 1989/90 (the final year of India's current five-year plan) the amount of new money raised is likely to reach Rs50-60 billion annually. This suggests that the role of the stockmarket in the Indian economy is going to become more

Table 97

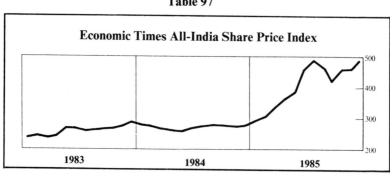

significant in future.

This is important because, despite the recent market boom, the market's role in the overall economy has been declining. Thirty years ago, funds raised in the stockmarket accounted for 13% of net domestic savings in India. Nowadays, that proportion is around 3-4% (though admittedly it was lower still in the late 1970s). And the share of equity in total listed capital instruments on the stockmarket has steadily declined, from around 75% in 1960 to nearer 55% now. In turn, this means that debenture and bond issues have become proportionately much more important in Indian corporate financing in recent years.

Another significant feature of the 1985/86 bull market so far as the future of the stockmarket is concerned, is the fact that during (fiscal) year 1985, 712 companies came to market on the Indian exchanges compared with 408 in the previous year. In the first nine months of fiscal 1986 a further 790 companies sought listings. Such statistics may be of more lasting significance than the fact that the total market capitalisation of all Indian listed companies virtually doubled (from Rs 99 billion to Rs 180 billion) between the end of 1984 and the end of 1985, or indeed the fact that turnover on the Bombay stock exchange rose by some 35% to Rs 61 billion in 1985 compared with the previous year. (Total turnover for all the Indian exchanges during 1985 was Rs 100 billion).

A further factor which probably augurs well for the future growth of the Indian stockmarket is the size and profile of the investor class. Financial institutions and "professional investors" (as Mehta terms them) dominated the primary (new issue) and secondary (trading) markets in the past. The market boom of 1985/86 saw the middle classes getting involved too, including professionals, self-employed people and salaried categories. Such people have traditionally shied away from securities markets because of the risks involved, preferring to keep their money in the bank. The size of India's shareholding community increased after the passing of the 1973 Foreign Exchange Regulation Act (FERA) when owners of foreign companies in India were asked to disinvest or dilute their holdings to not more than 40% of paid-up capital. The enthusiastic response on the part of local investors at that time was only to be expected, seeing that these shareholdings were made available to Indians on favourable terms. What is interesting is that the 1985/86 boom brought in its train an even greater broadening of the shareholding base. Yet shares were not being sold cheap this time. The Reserve Bank of India (central bank) estimates that the total number of shareholders in Indian companies tripled from 6 million to 18 million between 1978 and 1984. Individuals constitute the largest single group of shareholders in the Indian market. According to a survey (of just under 450 companies) made by a leading local development-finance institution, individuals account for 31% of total equity holdings, financial institutions for fractionally under 25%, companies for a further 22% and government for around 20%. The government-owned Unit Trust of India (the only unit trust in the country) is a big player in the market nowadays. It has 1.8 million unit holders and a portfolio spread over some 800 companies. That may sound like very wide portfolio diversification within one country, but it has to be seen against the fact that the number of listed companies on the Indian stock exchange dwarfs even the number in New York, London or Tokyo. Excluding listings common to several exchanges, there were 3,883 companies listed as of January 1985. (These companies had in issue just under 5,500 securities of which some 4,100 were equity issues, 850 were preference shares and the remainder debentures).

The number of stock exchanges in India is also large compared to other countries. (India's only potential rival in this respect would appear to be China where numerous cities are presently clamouring to open or re-open stock exchanges). Bombay is the biggest of the exchanges by far, as well as being the oldest. At the end of 1985, stocks listed on the Bombay exchange represented just over 80% of the total share-market capitalisation of all exchanges in India. Bombay, however, does not boast the biggest number of listings. That honour falls to the Calcutta exchange. The respective figures at the beginning of 1985 were 1,295 and 1,862. Delhi comes next with 952, after which rank Madras and Kanpur (Uttar Pradesh) with around 440 each. The remaining eight exchanges — out of the 14 exchanges currently "recognised" under the Securities Contracts (Regulation) Act of 1956 — range from 265 listings (in the case of Ahmedabad) to just 20 (in the case of Ludhiana exchange). The other exchanges are at: Hyderabad, Bangalore, Indore (Madhya Pradesh), Cochin, Pune, Gauhati and Mangalore (Kanara).

Yet, for all the size of the Indian stockmarket, in terms both of exchanges and companies listed (not to mention the age of the market), it lacks the solidity and maturity of some smaller markets in Asia. A comment by the GT Management group sums up this aspect rather well. "Despite the large number of exchanges and lengthy list of shares, no national market for securities exists and there is no national quotation system. India's market can be highly volatile, due partly to changes in economic conditions and government intervention on corporate profitability, and partly as a result of speculative activity and price manipulation in thin markets. As a result, considerable business volume is conducted by arbitraging between markets." Poor communications in India make arbitraging a lively and profitable business. As from February 1985, trading hours for all recognised stock exchanges were standardised (from 12 noon to 3p.m.) in an attempt to rationalise market operations. But much remains to be done to make the markets · efficient and trustworthy.

Even on the Bombay Stock Exchange (BSE), situated in the business capital's Dalal Street, the atmosphere is one verging on anarchy. The BSE accounts for two thirds of India's total stockmarket trading (though equity traded on the BSE accounted for over

Table 98

(As at 31st December, 1984)

Name of Stock Exchange	Year Established	No. of Members	No. of Listed Companies	Market Capitalisation (Rs.in million)
Bombay	1875	504	1295	102,190
Calcutta	1908	660	1862	53,920
Madras	1937	33	441	32,410
Ahmedabad	1894	299	265	32,460
Delhi	1947	105	952	49,910
Hyderabad	1943	36	120	8,470
Indore (Madhya Pradesh)	1930	34	43	4,320
Bangalore	1957	26	203	20,520
Cochin	1978	31	49	14,440
Kanpur	1982	350	436	16,270
Pune	1982	35	65	16,950
Ludhiana	1983	194	20	5,190
Gauhati	1984	N.A.	N.A.	N.A.
Mangalore (Karnataka)	1985	N.A.	N.A.	N.A.

Source: Bombay Stock Exchange

80% of total share-market capitalisation in India as of the end of 1985) and only Delhi and Calcutta have any significant liquidity of their own. The others exist largely to lay off orders in Bombay. BSE officials admit that one in four transactions on the exchange — where, on a busy day, some 500 or more brokers swarm on the concrete trading floor (which lacks even a central price-indicator board) needs to be queried. Physical delivery of shares can take two to three months. Of the 1,700 or so companies listed on the BSE, only around 47 are considered reliable enough for their shares to be traded on an "account" basis whereby brokers roll over net positions by paying a carry-over charge called "badla." Outside of this "specified list" of under 50 stocks, trading thins out rapidly and settlement is on a cash basis.

The Indian market still lacks many of the basic safeguards present in other markets. There are, for instance, no written rules or guidelines covering insider dealing, beyond a provision in general law that no officer of a company is entitled to use information known exclusively to him for his own advantage. Beyond that, company directors can deal freely in shares belonging to them or their companies. There is no stock exchange compensation fund either to cover victims of a broking default. (It must be noted, however, that not even the 1985/86 market boom brought any such defaults).

Official attitudes toward market regulation in India appear to be ambiguous. The former finance ministry official referred to above (D.R. Mehta) expressed the view at an Asian Development Bank seminar in 1986 that "the present is not the right time for the securities industry to be regulated by a body like the Securities and Exchange Commission." Mehta (who is now Secretary to the Government of Rajasthan, Department of Institutional Finance) suggested that such a regulatory commission might prove" counter-productive" to the growth of the Indian stockmarket and defeat the object of self-regulation in the marketplace. In other words, he believes in letting the market grow first and then regulating it, rather than vice-versa.

This does not mean that all arms of government adopt an entirely hands-off attitude to the market. Certainly, not the tax authorities. A series of raids by income-tax officials on the offices of several of Bombay's leading brokers in late 1986 sparked a protest in which brokers in effect went on strike. They were protesting against a ban on forward trading which led to deals being done purely on a cash, spot-delivery basis. Trading was halted completely for two days after Revenue Department officials raided the offices and homes of a score of stockbrokers and seized documents, cash and jewellery — all relating allegedly to transactions which had not been declared for tax purposes. This little assault appears to have been aimed more at India's "black economy," however, rather than at the stockmarket per se. Money flowed liberally out of other black-money havens, such as the property market and the film industry in Bombay, into the stockmarket during the 1985/86 boom.

What the Indian stockmarket needs now is bigger and better-quality stock issues to soak up the increasing amounts of domestic liquidity which are flowing into the market — and to cater for foreign investors who will be entering the Indian market (via special trusts initially). The ten largest companies quoted on the

Table 99

	The most actively traded shares, Bombay Stock Exchange, 1985	
Ranking	*Company*	*Turnover value (R million)*
1	Tata Steel	900.6
2	Associated Cement Companies	591.7
3	Reliance Industries	481.7
4	Southern Petrochemicals	255.4
5	Century Mills	248.7
6	Premier Automobiles	228.9
7	Tata Engineering and Locomotives	218.5
8	Orkay Silk Mills	190.8
9	Larsen & Toubro	172.2
10	Jk Synthetics	155.6
11	Indian Rayon	146.7
12	Gujarat Narmada Valley Fertilizers	137.2
13	Gujarat State Fertilizers	123.2
14	Tata Tea	98.9
15	Zuari Agro Chemicals	95.7
16	Hindustan Motors	87.0
17	Indian Organic	80.6
18	Hindustan Lever	76.5
19	Wimco	64.9
20	Gwalior Rayon	64.4

Source: Bombay Stock Exhcnage

Bombay Stock Exchange accounted for around 25% of total market capitalisation as at the end of 1985 and Reliance Industries (the market leader in capitalisation terms) accounted by itself for around 5% of total market value. (Though Reliance is biggest in this respect, Tata Steel tends to be the most active stock and at the height of the bull market in 1985/86 Tata's shares were among those placed on the "cash list" in order to slow speculative activity in the company's stock. At that time too, the authorities had to impose 100% margin requirements in order to stem speculation).

A great many new companies came to market in India in 1985 and 1986, but most of them were far from being in the blue-chip category. In fact, one Indian broker went so far as to describe many of them as being "too crappy to be traded." A roaring bull market in any of Asia's emerging stockmarkets can usually be guaranteed to bring its fair share of dubious new issues. But India probably had more than its fair share in the last bull market. Foreign merchant bankers in Bombay say, however, that some better-quality issues are on their way to market. In particular, they cite joint-venture projects linking foreign technology with Indian capital. Foreign technology is a big selling point in India and was a factor behind two of the most heavily over subscribed issues during 1985 — Kinetic Honda (which was 150 times oversubscribed) and Tata-Burroughs (80 times oversubscribed). Joint ventures with foreign parties have been popular since the FERA (mentioned above) was passed in 1973.

Some of these "FERA companies" were among those which rose farthest and fastest during the 1985/86 market boom. Calcutta was the springboard from which many of these companies were launched and their ties with the city have remained, something which has helped boost business for Calcutta's (Lyons Range) Stock Exchange, which is the second most important after Bombay. Some of the joint-venture companies have become takeover targets for Indian companies. One such is the Shaw Wallace conglomerate which used to be 40% owned by Malaysia's Sime Darby group. Other popular FERA stocks are Dunlop India, Indian Explosives, Metal Box, Chloride India, Britannia Industries and ICT.

Apart from the FERA companies, certain major public-sector projects could help boost the Indian stockmarket in future. As one commentator (Robert Cottrell writing in the *Far Eastern Economic Review*) remarked in March 1986: "The Indian share and bond markets have yet too feel the full weight of project finance requirements coming from sectors such as fertilisers, manufacturing and power generation. Six new fertiliser plants (costing more than US$3 billion in all) are on the government's investment agenda. So too is possible private financing of new power-generating capacity. The gap between public funding needs and private capacity has already been partly closed by ground-breaking bond issues in January from the National Thermal Power Corp and Indian Telephone Industries, with similar issues from other public-sector companies queuing up behind."

There is also the possibility of certain state enterprises being privatised in India and of at least part of their equity being listed on the stockmarket. Petrochemical ventures could be the first to be so treated. So far, however, the Indian government's thinking has concentrated on ending takeovers of "sick" industrial units, closing

Table 100

The largest listed companies, Bombay Stock Exchange, end-December 1985		
Ranking	*Company*	*Turnover value (R million)*
1	Reliance Industries	10,229
2	Tata Steel	8,496
3	Hindustan Lever	5,669
4	Larsen & Toubro	4,932
5	Gujarat Narmada Valley Fertilizers	4,781
6	Tata Engineering and Locomotives	4,199
7	IEL	2,861
8	JK Synthetics	2,651
9	Century Mills	2,392
10	Southern Petrochemicals	2,104
11	Orkay Silk Mills	1,934
12	Gujarat State Fertilizers	1,916
13	Peico Electricals	1,858
14	Gwailor Rayon	1,824
15	Bajaj Auto	1,805
16	Colgate Palmolive	1,729
17	Hindustan Motors	1,646
18	Motor Industries	1,587
19	Indian Aluminium	1,463
20	ITC	1,421

Source: Bombay Stock Exchange

down existing sick units and farming out to the private sector certain of the (many) key industrial activities which have up to now been reserved for the public sector.

The question of finding sufficient sources of capital to finance such flotations then becomes relevant. (Indian companies have traditionally financed the bulk of their needs through bank overdrafts or even through direct borrowing from the public). The size of future capital needs and the government's desire to reduce the power of the state-owned banking system (maybe by privatising banks too) suggest that alternative funding sources will be required. At the same time, the government is anxious to restrict future foreign borrowing for fear that India's overall foreign-exchange position will deteriorate.

One major source of capital is the Non-Resident-Indian (NRI) community whose members are to be found scattered all over the world, carrying on business and often acquiring large surplus funds. NRI's remittances have been a major positive item in the Indian balance of payments and more recently they have poured into the stockmarket, where these expatriates receive favourable tax treatment.

Not all NRIs are happy with their experience in the Indian stockmarket. Dr Swraj Paul, a leading Indian businessman who has made Britain his home and base of operations, had a major confrontation with the managements of two leading Indian companies, DCM and Escorts Ltd., after building up substantial (though not majority) stakes in them. He was encouraged by the 1980 ruling of (the late) Mrs Gandhi's government to the effect that NRIs, or overseas companies owned at least 60% by NRIs, could acquire stakes in Indian companies. However, both DMC and Escorts both refused to register the Swraj Paul holdings and after protracted court battles in India he sold out again.

A disillusioned Swraj Paul complained to the author after this episode that the "rules which govern the issue and transfer of shares listed on the Indian stock exchanges are antiquated and not designed to inspire confidence among investors. Anybody can buy shares but if managements do not like you they will refuse to register the transfer of shares and so cheat you of your ownership." This is an issue which the Indian government or the courts will need to resolve before foreign investors begin to appear in the Indian market.

Their entry appeared to be imminent at the time of writing toward the end of 1986. Official approval had been granted in Delhi for the launch of two Indian-managed funds to be sold internationally. The first of these was a closed-end fund promoted jointly by the Unit Trust of India (UTI) and US securities house Merrill Lynch. With an expected initial size of US$60 million, this fund will benefit from UTI's special tax-exempt status. This will save foreign investors the need to get involved with India's complex capital gains system under which the amount of tax charge varies according to the length of time the investment has been held, and whether the gains are made by individual or corporate investors.

Table 101

Growth Pattern of Listed Stock Exchanges

	1946	1961	1975	1983	1984
Stock Exchanges	5	7	8	12	13
Companies Listed *(Nos.)*	1,125	1,203	1,852	3,118	3,882
Stock Issues Listed *(Nos.)*	1,506	2,111	3,230	4,937	5,485
Of which Equity Shares	NA	1,303	2,019	3,358	4,094
Preference Shares	NA	659	1,014	1,008	850
Debentures/Bonds	NA	149	197	571	541
Total Capital Listed *(Rs. Crores)*					
Paid-up Value	270	754	2,614	6,533	8,703
Market Value	971	1,292	3,273	11,635	13,381
(Capitalisation: No. of times)	*(3.60)*	*(1.71)*	*(1.25)*	*(1.78)*	*(1.54)*
Equity Listed *(Rs. Crores)*					
Paid-up Value	NA	558	1,930	3,912	4,849
Market Value	NA	1,110	2,638	8,706	9,798
(Capitalisation: No. of times)		*(1.99)*	*(1.37)*	*(2.23)*	*(2.02)*
Preference Listed *(Rs. Crores)*					
Paid-up Value	NA	117	212	251	233
Market Value	NA	105	167	224	186
Debentures/Bonds *(Rs. Crores)*					
Paid-up Value	NA	79	472	2,370	3,621
Market Value	NA	77	469	2,705	3,397

Source: The Stock Exchange Foundation, Bombay

The units of this fund (which is similar in some respects to the Korea fund and other such Asian vehicles) will be marketed both to non-resident Indians and to foreign nationals. The proceeds will be invested in a special UTI equity fund.

The second fund is a joint venture between the industrial group Birla and British merchant bank S.G. Warburg. The new management company, 51% controlled by Birla family members — the Birlas and Tatas are two of India's biggest business dynasties — will offer a "pure" India fund, the Birla Mercury India Growth Fund, while a sister vehicle, the Birla Mercury International Growth Fund, will invest part of its assets in the India Growth Fund and the remainder in assets to be selected by Warburg's fund-management arm Mercury. The Birla Mercury funds were approved by the Indian government on the basis that they will be held at least 60%

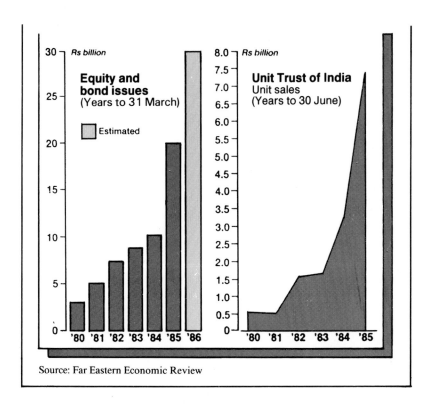

Source: Far Eastern Economic Review

by NRIs. (The strict definition of NRIs is that they are overseas Indians with particular ties to India by virtue of birth, family or citizenship, but who may be nationals of other countries). The funds will be structured as open-ended unit trusts but availability to foreigners may at times be limited by the need to maintain the 60:40 ratio between NRIs and other holders. The funds will be marketed principally in the Gulf states, Britain and possibly Hongkong. Though the Birla funds do not enjoy the same tax concessions as the India Fund, they will probably opt to hold investments for at least three years in order to minimise their tax liability. They may also invest in certain of UTI's tax-exempt funds.

Foreigners may well find Indian stocks (the market leaders at least) quite attractive on investment fundamentals. The average price/earnings ratio on 34 stocks listed on the Bombay Stock Exchange at the height of the bull market in 1985 had not risen much above 15. This is a lowly rating compared with some other Asian stockmarkets (notably Tokyo) and the average equity yield, though down to roughly half of what it was in 1982, was still above 3% at the end of 1985.

Table 102

	1984-85		1983-84	
Type of Issue	No.	Amount	No.	Amount
Initial Issue	154	5,572.8	95	1,920.9
Further Issue	165	2,413.0	110	1,273.7
Debenture Issue	193	11,132.9	104	6,093.7
Sub-Total	512	19,118.7	309	9,288.3
Bonus Issue	200	915.8	150	946.6
Total:	712	20,034.5	459	10,234.5

India's boom

Pakistan:

Pakistan's stockmarket is surprisingly large in terms of capitalisation and number of companies listed. At the end of 1985, the 353 companies listed on the country's two stock exchanges (Karachi and Lahore) had a total market value of Rs 22 billion or nearly US$1.3 billion. This put Pakistan comfortably ahead of the Philippines in capitalisation terms at the time and left it dwarfing the Indonesian market capitalisation by more than ten times. But, as in other "emerging" stockmarkets of the world, fundamentals such as this do not tell the entire story.

The Pakistan market is unloved by many Pakistanis and, is a closed book as far as foreigners are concerned. Rather than moving toward opening up its stockmarket to outsiders in the way that India is doing (on an indirect basis), the government in Islamabad seems more concerned with the gradual Islamization of the country's financial system. Though the principle of equity financing is theoretically more acceptable under Islam than is debt financing, the suspicion with which Islamic states tend to regard outside influence does not augur well for a more open attitude toward international investment in Pakistan.

The process of Islamization of Pakistan's financial system was formally completed in July 1985 and since then interest rates have been officially eliminated in line with the dictates of the Sharia or Islamic financial law. A variety of Islamic instruments have made their appearance. These include, among others, quasi equity instruments such as "Musharikas" (which involve financing based on a pre-arranged formula for profit sharing) and "Term Financing Certificates" which are in effect debentures. It remains to be seen what the impact of such instruments will be upon more conventional forms of equity financing in Pakistan.

Conventional mutual funds have in the past played an important part in the securities market. The government-sponsored National Investment Trust and the Investment Corp of Pakistan (ICP) were formed in the mid-1960s to promote such vehicles. ICP manages over a dozen closed-end mutual funds, some of which have up to 10,000 investors and a state-enterprise mutual fund with 13,500 investors. ICP, rather like Danareksa in Indonesia, was constituted as a national equity-market support mechanism and is still a major market maker. Its transactions constitute around one quarter of total trading on the Karachi Stock Exchange (KSE). (Foreign residents in Pakistan are permitted to invest in units of the National Investment Trust).

Pakistan's position as a "front-line state" bordering on Afghanistan and (as major Western powers see it) a country susceptible to Soviet influence means that in recent years it has been assured of liberal foreign-aid flows. These tend to pre-empt the need for outside commercial borrowing or equity investment from overseas. The Pakistan financial system is in any case dominated by five government-owned commercial banks and the central bank.

Nevertheless, the government has recognised the over-reliance of Pakistan companies on debt finance and is taking steps to develop the capital market. Corporate tax has been reduced for companies listed on the stock market and dividends of listed companies have been granted tax exemption. The government has also announced plans for a phased divestment of some Rs 2 billion of shares in various public-sector enterprises. This will be done via the stock-market, and could include the national air carrier, Pakistan International Airlines. There are still differences within the bureaucracy, however, over the composition of the divestment portfolio.

The government of President Zia-ul Haq is committed to encouraging and expanding the private sector in Pakistan, whose fortunes were eclipsed by a major programme of nationalisation during the 1970s. Nevertheless, the 22 most important business families in the country (who collectively owned nearly 70% of total banking assets in the late 1960s, prior to nationalisation) remain nervous about the prospect of re-nationalisation by some future government. As it is, the public sector controls key industries such as engineering, steel, automobiles and construction materials. Only in textiles is the private sector dominant.

Despite the prevelance of public enterprise in Pakistan, companies listed on the Karachi stock exchange (which was organised in 1949 and which is by far the most active of the two markets) cover a wide spectrum of activities. Cotton textiles account for some 30% of issues, engineering companies for 10% and chemicals and pharmaceuticals for a further 8%. Some 73% of the companies listed are wholly owned by private investors while 18% are jointly owned by the private and public sectors and the remaining 9% are multinationals.

According to an Asian Development Bank (ADB) survey, of the 150 shares traded regularly on the Karachi stock exchange — Lahore (founded in 1970) is a much less important market — only 30 have an active daily market. "Of these, most are blue-chip companies, among which multinationals and selected engineering enterprises figure prominently. Both the Karachi and Lahore exchanges trade only the common shares of companies registered in Pakistan. Corporate bonds are not traded but there is limited trading in government securities and (corporate) preferred stocks." But, added the ADB survey, the Pakistan stockmarket "has always been a marginal source of industrial funds. Between 1982 and 1984, only around 4.5% of private industrial investment funds were mobilised through the stockmarket."

Amin Issa Tai, president of the Karachi Stock Exchange, believes that the "fundamental weakness of the securities market in Pakistan is lack of depth, due to the limited range of securities available for trading and the low turnover value." He also believes that the "main impediment in promoting equity investment (in Pakistan) is the lack of investor confidence mainly (arising) from the siphoning off of corporate profits by controlling groups." This is hardly encouraging coming from the president of the exchange. But the KSE president believes that better auditing of company accounts and various other reforms might one day improve the situation.

Laws relating to the operation of the stock exchanges in Pakistan do not prohibit foreign investment as such, but there are restrictions which make it difficult for foreigners to buy and sell shares on the exchanges. Exchange-control regulations limit the amount of funds transferable out of the country. As foreign investors cannot repatriate their capital without permission from the State Bank of Pakistan, they do not in practice invest in the market. Another restrictive mechanism is the country's investment policy which operates against open foreign investment in Pakistan. This policy actively discourages foreign investment in the trade and services sector (including insurance companies, which are among the most profitable companies on the Karachi Stock Exchange). Pakistanis living abroad are, however, permitted to invest in the stockmarket.

Table 103

Pakistan Securities Market Data			
	1980	1984	1985
Equities			
No. of Companies Listed	314	347	353
No. of State-Owned Entities Listed	57	57	63
No. of Multinational or	21	28	32
Joint Venture Companies			
No. of private-sector companies listed	236	262	258
No. of Shares Listed (Rs million)	7,630.2	11,496.3	11,885
Market Value of Shares Listed	6,360.9	18,834.4	21,935
(Market Capitalization — Rs mn)			
Annual Turnover Volume of Shares			
(%) (million):			
In Ready Section	25.8	96.8	n.a.
In Cleared Listed Section	72.3	256.8	n.a.
Total	98.1	353.6	
Annual Turnover of Shares (in Rs mn)	25.8	115.7	33.1*
Annual Sales Value (Amount)			
General Index of Shares Prices	163.8	232.1	258.4
(Base year: 1960-70 for 75-81			
1975-76 for 82-84)			
New Issues			
Number	12	20	16
Amount Offered (Rs. in Mn)	378	297	280
Amount Subscribed (Rs. in Mn)	649	1,056	806
Rights Issues			
Number	10	16	n.a.
Value (Rs. in Mn)	103.2	540.1	n.a.
Total Corporate Funds Raised from			
Equities	443.5	841.2	n.a.
Debt Securities			
Listed Government or Public Bonds			
Number	51	46	n.a.
Face Value (Rs. in Mn)	13,345.6	24,008.6	n.a.
Listed Corporate Bonds (Debentures)			
Number	9	5	n.a.
Value (Rs. in Mn)	59.4	43.7	n.a.

Data are for Karachi Stock Exhcange. The Lahore Stock Exchange has 247 listed companies, all of which are also listed on the Karachi Exchange. Its funding activity is marginal.

* Up to May 1985.

Source: Asian Development Bank.

Table 104

Pakistan's top-10 business families			
		Net assets	
(Rs million)	1968	1974	1985
Habib	228	68.8	945.7
Dawood	210.8	767.8	800
Amin-Bashir (Crescent)	201.7	201.7	435.9
Wazir Ali	102.6	87.6	271.2
Saigol	529.8	165.3	220.4
Bawany	69.3	69.3	216
Habibullah (Gandhara)	79.9	25.8	205.0
Shaikh (Colony)	189.7	95.8	142.8
Adamjee	201.3	146.3	130
Shirazi (Atlas)	—	—	120

Note: Net assets are only those of family-controlled companies listed on the Karachi Stock Exchange. They exclude assets held through unlisted companies.
Source: Far Eastern Economic Review

Sri Lanka, Bangladesh and Nepal.

The story of Sri Lanka's securities market is one of sad decline which mirrors largely the decline of the country's plantation industry. The heyday of the Sri Lanka (then Ceylon) tea, rubber coconut and oil-palm plantations lasted for a century, between 1850 and 1950. That led to active, if informal, primary and secondary-market dealing in company stocks and left behind a legacy of 266 listed companies in the Colombo share market — an impressive number by the standards of many Asian markets.

Nationalisation, and a secular decline in the plantation industries, led to the eclipse of trading company securities by trading in government securities. To quote one Sri Lankan official: "The securities market of Sri Lanka is made up of the issue of government debt in the form of medium and long-term securities and short-term Treasury Bills. The issue of and trading in corporate stock is quite insignificant." Nowadays only around 20 companies — less than one tenth of the total listed — are traded actively.

A problem for the securities market in Sri Lanka, as in many other Asian countries that were subject to colonial influence, is that the stock exchange is a legacy of that period and, as such, is regarded with suspicion. Post-independence governments have regarded equity financing as a remnant of foreign capitalism. They have preferred to operate their financial systems through (often state-owned) banks. The extensive branch networks of such banks have acted as the principal conduit for collection of savings and the securities investment habit is hardly developed among relatively unsophisticated people. So it is in Sri Lanka where the Central Bank of Ceylon (the central bank) dominates the financial system.

The securities market, meanwhile, has been subject to a number of vicissitudes. Under the Land Reform legislation of the early 1970s, plantation stock transactions completely ceased. There were some new issues in the market after 1977, following a change of government and the adoption of somewhat more liberal economic policies. But secondary market trading in shares remained virtually dormant, reaching only Rs 33 million in 1984, or around US$1 million. The stockmarket received a further setback in 1984/85 as international recession hit Sri Lanka's tourism and hotels industry and protectionism hit the country's textile exports. Both sectors had figured prominently in the new-issue market in previous years.

Apart from adverse economic and political factors, the Sri Lanka stockmarket has suffered from lack of proper institutional arrangements. A share-brokers' association (which became known as the Colombo Brokers' Association) has existed since the beginning of this century. Until quite recently, the market was carried on informally by a number of rival associations or "trading floors," all having their own rules and procedures. Formal arrangements for stock underwriting simply did not exist.

This situation changed during 1985 when the rival trading floors agreed to give up their separate identities and merge under one trading floor known as the Colombo Securities Exchange (Guarantee) Ltd. This meant that, for the first time in the market's history, trading would be conducted at a public exchange rather than privately. The new exchange began functioning officially as from 2 December 1985. One of the most widely watched indicators since then has been the "Mercs Stock Average," computed by the Mercantile Credit Group in Colombo. This index takes the exchange's opening date as its base date. At the same time, the Sri Lanka government accepted responsibility for providing an institutional framework for the stockmarket. Legislation is being prepared to establish a Securities Council, to regulate the market and to provide investor protection. The legislation will also provide for the licensing of exchanges and brokers.

Something which promises to expand the Sri Lanka stockmarket significantly in future and move it away from its plantations bias, is the government plan to privatise certain public enterprises. Budgetary constraints and what L.E.N. Fernando, chairman of the Bank of Ceylon, terms a "continuing commitment to the market discipline in allocating resources" are the chief force behind the privatisation drive. A decision in principle has been reached to hand back to private enterprise such state companies as the State Distilleries Corp and the Telecommunication Department. "It is envisaged that there will be public participation in the issued capital of such ventures," according to Fernando.

The government has also granted various tax and other concessions to listed companies as well as to those who invest in the stockmarket. But as the Asian Development Bank pointed out in its report on selected regional capital markets, "market growth remains sluggish. The five-year restriction on the transfer of shares has slowed trading and the continuing 20% withholding tax on dividends has acted as a disincentive to investors." Despite such problems, Colombo stockmarket officials seem eager to promote their market. They have a dialogue with markets such as Malaysia's with a view to expanding and slowly liberalising their own market. For foreigners, the Sri Lanka market is closed for the present but one to watch for the future.

Bangladesh's securities market is, in the words of Mustafizur Rahman (Secretary, Finance Division) at the Ministry of Finance in Bangladesh, "small" and its secondary market is "poorly developed." Statistics bear this out. There are 72 listed companies, which is three times the number listed in Indonesia but their total market capitalisation comes to only around US$112 million. This is only marginally ahead of Indonesia and way behind all other exchanges (with the exception of Nepal).

Annual turnover as a percentage of market capitalisation is a minute 1% — which amounts to almost zero activity relative to other markets. The average price/earnings ratio for Bangladesh stocks is a very low 3.7 and the average dividend yield a handsome 13.4%. Both indicators support the picture of an inactive and neglected stockmarket.

Another measure of the under-developed state of the stockmarket is the fact that, in fiscal 1984/85, the total amount of funds raised by public issue in the stockmarket was only US$3.5 million. This in turn is consistent with the domination of the Bangladesh financial system by government banks — private commercial banks have only recently come into being — and the provision of liberal quantities of subsidised credit from the state.

The political (and therefore economic and financial) trauma which accompanied the founding of Bangladesh (formerly East Pakistan) in 1971 also has much to do with the under development of the country's stockmarket. The Dhaka Stock Exchange itself was founded considerably earlier — in 1954 — but, to quote Khurshid Alam, former chairman of the exchange, it "virtually ceased to operate" after the new state was founded. This was because most major industrial and financial concerns were nationalised at this time — a situation which continued up to 1975.

In 1976 the government shifted its policy somewhat and

assigned a restricted sphere of operations to the private sector. At
that time the Dhaka Stock Exchange began functioning again, albeit
with only nine listed companies whose total paid-up capital was
under US$5 million. After the government returned the (previously
nationalised) jute and textile mills, plus two banks, to their
previous shareholders in 1982, as well as selling other enterprises to
the private sector, the stockmarket began to grow more rapidly.
Between 1982 and 1985, the number of companies listed rose from
26 to 72 and total paid-up capital increased from US$17 million
equivalent to US$66 million. The market may gain from further
privatisation. The government has announced a policy of phased

Table 105

Sri Lanka Securities Market Data			
Share Market		1983	December 1984
Number of listed companies		254	266
Number of transactions		1,811	2,778
Number of shares sold ('000)		1,375	3,135
Value of shares sold (Rs '000)		19,939	32,876
			1984
Sectoral Distribution of Listed Companies and Their Trading Activity	1983	1984	No. of Shares Traded ('000)	Shares Traded Value (Rs Mn)
Tea Companies	49	48	131.2	1.15
Tea-cum-Rubber Companies	19	19	28.4	0.30
Rubber Companies	28	28	14.6	0.20
Coconut Companies	1	1	—	—
Oil Palm Companies	5	5	0.3	0.02
Beverages Food & Tobacco	14	15	405.1	3.32
Eng'g. Motors & Industries	55	56	1,281.4	9.69
Finance & Land	17	20	617.3	8.76
Stores & Suppliers	7	7	187.3	1.40
Hotels & Travels	34	37	88.4	0.76
Miscellaneous	26	27	320.7	6.69
Investment Trusts	3	3	60.7	0.58
TOTAL	258	266	3,135.4	32.87

Source: Asian Development Bank

divestment of 49% of the shares in certain public enterprises, including the nationalised commercial banks. Mustafizur Rachman readily admits, however, that many of Bangladesh's public-sector enterprises are "not doing well" and "have very little [by way of] commercial prospects."

The Investment Corporation of Bangladesh, a state-owned agency, has the role of market maker on the Dhaka Stock Exchange. This corporation has also been given the job of forming consortia of institutional investors (including insurance companies, banks and development-finance institutes) to invest in the stockmarket. The government is experimenting too, with promotion measures, such as exempting stock dividends (up to a prescribed limit) from tax and also exempting capital gains in the stockmarket from tax (provided the gains are reinvested). In addition, companies which list their shares on the stock exchange are entitled to a 5% tax reduction.

Nevertheless, the Dhaka Stock Exchange remains one that is probably over regulated as well as under developed at present. It is governed by the Security and Exchange Ordinance of 1969 and by the Security and Exchange Control rules of 1971 which, among other things, effectively prohibit foreign investment in Bangladesh stocks. The pace of expansion and opening up in the future is likely to be slow.

There is little to be said about **Nepal's** stockmarket except that, like the landlocked and mountainous kingdom in which it is situated, it is little. But the fact that it exists at all says something for the initiative and imagination of the government in a country where per-capita income is only US$145 per head, one of the lowest in Asia. The stock exchange, in the capital Kathmandu, opened in 1976, for trading of government bonds initially. But at the end of 1984, equity shares were introduced onto the exchange's lists in an effort to mobilise capital and to create opportunities for private investment in industry.

The Securities Exchange Centre, as it is known, boasts 13 stocks, whose prices are marked up on a blackboard in the dilapidated two-storey building where the exchange is housed. Appropriately, the listed stocks include the Hotel Yak and Yeti, though the exchange also has more conventional-sounding concerns such as the Nepal Bank and the National Insurance Corp on its lists. It even has one multinational corporation listed, or at least a subsidiary of one —

Nepal Battery which is associated with Union Carbide of India. Activity on the exchange is not exactly on a par with Wall Street or Tokyo. During the final five months of 1985, for instance, there were some 90 transactions in all, worth around US$100,000. Some weeks the exchange is relatively active and some weeks it is virtually dead. But at least it is a start.

Bombay Stock Exchange

Selected Bibliography

General:
"Capital Market Development in Selected Developing Countries of the Asian Development Bank," ADB, 1986

"The GT Guide to World Equity Markets," edited by Charles Hildeburn, published by Euromoney Publications, 1986

"Asia Yearbook," published by the *Far Eastern Economic Review,* Hongkong (annually)

"Financial Institutions and Markets in the Far East," edited by Michael T. Skully, published by the MacMillan Press Ltd., 1982

"The World Economy and Financial Markets in 1995 — Japan's Role and Challenges," published by Nomura Research Institute, 1986

"Emerging Securities Markets," by Antoine W. von Agtmael, published by Euromoney Publications, 1984

Japan
"Fact Book," published by Tokyo Stock Exchange (annually)

"The Saitori System of the Tokyo Stock Exchange," published by Tokyo Stock Exchange, October 1984

"Investment Trusts in Japan," published by the Investment Trust Association, Tokyo, 1986

"Monthly Digest of Statistics," published by Yamaichi Research Institute, September 1986

"Securities Market in Japan 1986," published by Japan Securities Research Institute

"Listing Regulations of the Tokyo Stock Exchange," published by Tokyo Stock Exchange, 1984

"The Present View of the Japanese Capital Market," paper by Keisaku Mitsumatsu, Director, The Industrial Bank of Japan, January 1985

"Tokyo's Managed Market," by James Bartholomew, *Far Eastern Economic Review,* 19th March, 1982

South Korea

"Fact Book 1986," published by the Korea Stock Exchange

"Fear of Letting Go," by Anthony Rowley and Paul Ensor, *Far Eastern Economic Review,* 21st August, 1986

"Stock Market in Korea," address by Tai Ho Lee, Chairman of Daewoo Securities Company, 1985

"The Securities Market in Korea," published by Securities and Exchange Commission, June 1986

Taiwan

"The Taipei Fund," Prospectus issued by Prudential-Bache Securities International, May 1986

"Securities Investment Journal," published by the Taiwan Stock Exchange, March 1986

"Financial Reform Recommended by the Economic Reform Committee, Republic of China," paper by Kuo-shu Liang, Chairman, Chang Hwa Commercial Bank in Florica, November 1985

"International Investment Trust Committee, Monthly Review," December 1985 published by IIT, Taipei

"Taiwan Investment Service — The Leading Listed Companies," published by Vickers da Costa, July 1983

"An Introduction to the Taiwan Stock Exchange," published by Taiwan Stock Exchange — Periodically

"Taiwan Stock Market — A Review of its 20-year Performance," Taiwan Stock Exchange

"SEC Annual Report," published by Securities and Exchange Commission Taiwan, annually

Hongkong
"Commerative Book on Opening of the Stock Exchange of Hongkong," published by the Stock Exchange of Hongkong, April 1986

"The Securities Bulletin, No. 1," published by the Stock Exchange of Hongkong, May 1986

"The Experience of Market Regulation in Hongkong," paper given by Robert Fell, former Commissioner for Securities to the International Conference on Securities Regulation, Singapore, August 1984

"Recent Developments in the Regulation of Securities," paper by Derek Murphy, Deputy Commissioner for Securities, March 1986

"Guangdong Publishers Regulations on Securities," *China Daily,* 11th October, 1986

Singapore/Malaysia
"Fact Book," published by the Stock Exchange of Singapore (annually)

"After Pan-E1, Division of Markets Likely," Anthony Rowley, *Far Eastern Economic Review,* 6th February, 1986

"Investing in Singapore and Malaysia," published by Vickers da Costa, October 1986

"Discussion Paper on Recent Capital Market Development in Malaysia," Dato Malek Marican, Managing Director, Arab-Malaysian Merchant Bank Berhad, January 1986

"Securities Industry in Malaysia — Perspectives Vol. II," by S. K. Lam, published by SSS Snd, Bhd., Ipoh, Malaysia 1986

"Divided they rise," (article on the History and Development of the Singapore and Malaysia Stock Exchange, by Lincoln Kaye, *Far Economic Review,* 12th April 1984

Thailand/Philippines/Indonesia

"Investing in Thailand — a Guide to Investment Procedures," published by Vickers da Costa, September 1986

"An Overview of Government Bond Market Development," paper by David Gill, International Finance Corporation Capital Markets Department, April 1985

"Paper on Development of Thai Capital Market," by Manas Leevirapahan, Ministry of Finance, January 1986

"Investing in the Philippines — a Guide to Investment Procedures," published by Vickers da Costa, June 1986

"Paper on Philippines Capital Market Regulation," by Manuel G. Abello, Chairman of the Securities and Exchange Commission, Philippines, January 1986

"The Case for Investment in the Philippines," published by the Thornton Group 1986

"Tunnel Without Light," by Jose Galang, *Far Eastern Economic Review,* 9th May, 1985

"Capital Market Development in Indonesia," paper by J. A. Sereh, President Director of P. T. Danareksa, Jakarta

"External Systems for Capital Market Development in Indonesia," paper by Barli Halim, Chairman of Bapepam, January 1986

India and other sub-continental markets
"Recent Capital Market Developments in India," paper by D. R. Mehta, Secretary to the Government of Rajasthan, Department of Institutional Finance, January 1986

"Stock Exchange Listing," published by the Bombay Stock Exchange, 1985

"Unit Trust of India, 21st Annual Report 84/85," published by UTI

"Present Position of the Stockmarket in India," published by the Stock Exchange Foundation Bombay 1985

"Capital Market Development in Pakistan," paper by Amin Issa Tai, President of the Karachi Stock Exchange, 1985

"Paper on the Bangladesh Capital Market," by Mustaf Izur Rahman, Secretary, Finance Division, Ministry of Finance, Dhaka 1985

"Paper on Sri Lanka Capital Market," by M. Casiechetty, Deputy Director of Economic Affairs, Ministry of Finance and Planning, Colombo, January 1986

Index

List of Displays